Published in 2020 by Hardie Grant Travel,
a division of Hardie Grant Publishing

Hardie Grant Travel (Melbourne)
Building 1, 658 Church Street
Richmond, Victoria 3121

Hardie Grant Travel (Sydney)
Level 7, 45 Jones Street
Ultimo, NSW 2007

www.hardiegrant.com/au/travel

A catalogue record for this
book is available from the
NATIONAL LIBRARY OF AUSTRALIA — National Library of Australia

Hardie Grant acknowledges the Traditional Owners of the country
on which we work, the Wurundjeri people of the Kulin nation and the
Gadigal people of the Eora nation, and recognises their continuing
connection to the land, waters and culture. We pay our respects
to their Elders past and present.

Loving Country: A Guide to Sacred Australia
ISBN 9781741176483

10 9 8 7 6 5 4 3 2 1

Publisher Melissa Kayser
Project editors Alexandra Payne and Marg Bowman
Design Pfisterer + Freeman
Typesetting Megan Ellis
Index Max McMaster
Research support for travel listings Lee Atkinson, Ben Willey
Colour reproduction Megan Ellis and Splitting Image Colour Studio

Printed and bound in China by LEO Paper Products LTD.

LOVING
COUNTRY

A guide to sacred Australia

Bruce Pascoe
Vicky Shukuroglou

Hardie Grant
TRAVEL

VING
NTRY

Contents

Introduction

Bruce Pascoe

The invasion of Australia more than 250 years ago attacked the core of Aboriginal and Torres Strait Islander spirituality, not just the life blood of the people. The prolonged and continuing assault has wreaked incalculable damage; but that damage is not permanent because resilience built over 120,000 years is hard to break.

The age of Aboriginal and Torres Strait Islander people's occupation of this country will be a surprise to most Australians, but recent archaeological digs are revealing ages of that kind, and some in process may offer even older ages. Instead of recoiling from this science as if it is fake news, we should embrace it as part of this great country's history. Archaeology of the Aboriginal past in Australia is intensifying and the next few decades will reveal a wonderful story.

The injury of invasion was not just to Aboriginal and Torres Strait Islander people but to the land itself. Blue-green algal blooms, salination, deforestation, exotic crops and weeds, soil erosion and ocean poisoning are just some of those damages.

But Mother Earth is a determined woman, she is determined to survive and we had no better example of that than the summer of 2019–2020. The conflagration caused by poor forest management was catastrophic, but within a week many forests had begun a recovery. The forest will never be the same but within most there was a massive will to live. Not every tree survived, some massive old trees important to Aboriginal people were deliberately cut down after the fires because they were 'Killer Trees'. Now their logs are being collected quietly by the forestry industry. Nothing to see here!

When Rio Tinto exploded one of the oldest art galleries on earth, this country almost shrugged its shoulders. When Al-Qaeda destroyed Christian statues one-twenty-fifth as old, when Notre-Dame burnt, our press couldn't wring their hands enough. Money poured in for the resurrections. In Australia we continued to mine, business as usual.

Despite our continued blindness to our country and its history, Mother Earth pulsed sap into the forest to give us one more chance to consider our land management.

There is a lot to be said about how Australians have treated this country in the past, but the only things we can control in the present are our relationships with the land and each other, Aboriginal and non-Aboriginal Australians.

This book hopes to introduce Australian travellers – as well as those of you who are visitors to our shores – to parts of this country you may not have visited. But its primary aim is to introduce you to the people, history and culture of those places because we believe that the better angels of Australia want a more inclusive, thoughtful and loving country. That lovingness may decide on a treaty between all Australians. Every other colonial country has done so. We mustn't let that decision be made for us during our silence by narks and naysayers. Australia has a history of refusing wowserism, why change now?

In the progress to full knowledge of this country, you will have many questions for Aboriginal communities, but do remember that Aboriginal and Torres Strait Islander people are just three per cent of the population and it is exhausting to answer all the questions from the other ninety-seven per cent. Be patient: not every phone call can be returned, not every Aboriginal person you meet will be able to answer every question. In some cases the lore will restrict the response.

Aboriginal organisations were drastically defunded by the Australian government a decade ago and the staffing of offices was drastically reduced. As we Australians walk together to learn the full story of our country, we will need patience in improving our ability to build a bridge across the last 250 years of neglect. This is not an impediment to the journey, but an opportunity to find a path towards generous and peaceful collaboration.

The pandemic virus meant that we, Vicky in particular, worked under great hardship, and if some places of interest have not been covered or only mentioned briefly it is because travel was curtailed during the last phase of our work.

Enjoy the book, embrace this country and learn, really learn about Aboriginal Australia. Help us make this the start of genuine conciliation.

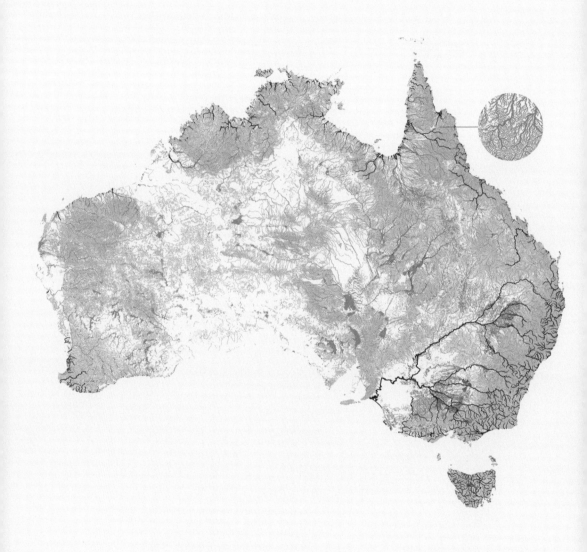

Permanent waterways

Ephemeral waterways

Introduction

Vicky Shukuroglou

The many challenges slipped out of mind as we all walked together down the dusty road and Johnny pointed to the ground saying, 'There, look, that's your little foot.' Jokes were shared among the group as we concentrated on finding a rock I had moved from the path of tyre tracks and placed behind a tree. The road was strewn with rocks, and trees were fairly dense. I'd walked there three days prior, and the Elders and rangers wanted to see that rock. We hadn't known each other long, but days were full and lives were intersecting in ways we all cherished.

Rich conversations, long walks, humour and vulnerability shaped this book. Through every community, people embraced discussion and appreciated being heard. They want their stories to be told, for country to be better understood and loved. Details of the stories in this book are small parts of an intricate web, gatherings of many voices, understandings developed through repetition, often from different angles. Each person carries their own story. For these reasons and more, individuals' names are rarely included.

Elders ask that no matter where we come from, we seek to deepen our connection to each other and the country that nourishes us. Through the following stories you will understand some of their anguish, and also learn of their love. As we open our windows, envision a cherished view, travel through unknown country or continue to explore places we know intimately, we see a reflection of our humanity. Here, we are warmly invited to embrace knowledge accrued by thousands of generations and to contemplate relationships. We are privileged, for this knowledge gives life to dynamic stories spanning the country and can inform our ways of being.

It's a joy to be immersed in the biodiversity nurtured by this country's Indigenous people – its decline within the last 250 years creates a stark contrast. Through the photos, I hope to reveal the grandeur in the details of its character. In contemplating the many thousands of years Indigenous groups have inhabited distinct areas,

I would be limiting myself if I focused simply on age, size or other such measures. The ethos and practices of a civilisation that maintained such abundant and extraordinary life captivate my deep consideration. We hope this book provides connected paths along which you can travel.

This land, its waterways and creatures they sustain are spectacular. More than eighty-five per cent of its mammals and plants are endemic, meaning they evolved here, nowhere else. Equally impressive are its reptiles and amphibians with more than ninety per cent endemicity. Each is highly specialised and plays important roles within ecosystems. How many of us know Australia's southern coasts support more than 1150 species of red and brown algae? Let's understand, celebrate and protect these realities. Countless generations ago, people here watched carefully. They did so alongside grandmothers and aunties, uncles and sons. They observed not just for their own survival, but because they also had curious and inventive minds, laughed and loved and revelled in the delights of watching animals at play, parades of courtship, and births from eggs, cocoons and pouches. Their loving observations shaped them as individuals and as societies, as is reflected in dances and songs, complex stories and the vitality of the country itself. Across the land, groups expressed their ethos in unique ways. This was bound to occur given the inextricable bonds of people and country, where natural variability defines so much. Consider Australian annual rainfall averages: from 270 to 4000 millimetres.

Since invasion of Indigenous homelands, agricultural attitudes and therefore methods underwent dramatic change. Native species continue to feel the effects of the mouths and hard hooves of introduced animals. The scale is startling when examined. In 2019, average numbers of these animals slaughtered every week exceeded 415,000 lambs, 178,000 sheep and 163,000 cattle. Annually, that's more than 39 million mouths and 157 million hooves. This does not include pressures applied by calves, goats, pigs, horses, donkeys, buffalo, and others such as soft-footed hungry camels and rabbits. Then add invasive plants. The map on the previous pages shows ephemeral waterways. These only flow seasonally and can remain dry for many years or decades. If you were to compare this to a map showing only permanent waterways, you might think the printer ran out of ink. The differences are staggering and give us some insight into this country's complex life. Its waters provide habitat for innumerable, largely unknown creatures, including more than 5000 species of freshwater and saltwater fish, and 9000 types of crustaceans. The combinations of pressures have proven to be too great and many species have been driven to extinction.

We can all learn more, observe carefully, understand local seasons that rarely match spring, summer, autumn and winter, and act on ancient knowledge. In these ways, we can address severe shrinkage of populations and changes in distribution. Seeds of native plants lie waiting for suitable conditions, and if we ease the pressures of our current practices, we can better ensure they germinate and survive. If honouring the earth were to once again become our top priority, there would be hope for what remains of our biodiversity. Importantly, we still have choices.

Soil and waterways around the world have had human blood seep into them as a result of horrific brutality. Nations continue to suffer invasion, with similar procedures of violence and oppression. Impacts manifest in various ways long after the act and invaders do not walk untouched. Like many families here, mine carries stories of dispossession, and I am of the lucky generation that narrowly escaped firsthand terror. All Australians have an opportunity – unavailable to many peoples – because here, we have what it takes to cultivate new ways. People we meet in our travels can add great depth to our lives and shape what we treasure. We must be cautious of assumptions, of making demands without knowing the full story, and of alienating each other. Listen to the quiet voices, take time to observe and learn.

During difficult times working on this book, I thought of the oldies and their yearning for people to be compassionate, united in caring for country and respecting proven ways, and I felt their arms embrace me. None said we must stop and turn back the clock, but all said we can do much better in our care for what we have today. Incredible knowledge and new technologies are available to us, but how we make use of these and honour what people have achieved here across thousands of years are two of our greatest challenges. I hope your explorations of this great land, its ancient stories and its diverse people will enrich your conversations with yourself, your loved ones and those you are yet to meet, all strongly held by this loving country.

Considerations for readers & travellers

We are pleased you have chosen to engage with the beauty and complexity of this country, a great living legacy of its Indigenous people. We are grateful for your interest in diverse stories, listening carefully and allowing them to guide your journey. Enjoy the opportunity – and conversations with your family, friends and others as you share your experiences.

Please remember that not every Aboriginal person you meet will necessarily have all the information you might be seeking, and for many, English is not their first language. Every individual you encounter along your journey presents an opportunity for deepening your understanding of this country's layered history, much of which is out of view.

Moving carefully through country is important for the preservation of culture and the earth, and the more you learn, the more you will be immersed in their interconnection. While many distinct features in the land are of particular significance and hold wonderful stories from long ago, the same applies to areas that might appear to you as unremarkable by comparison. Some elements of those stories may be reserved for the cultural growth of local people, but most have meanings that can be shared. The stories you hear have come from sustained thought and care for our earth over thousands of generations. For many readers, this will be your country too; but no matter where you come from, please be gentle in your treatment of her.

You will probably see Aboriginal artefacts during your journey. Enjoy the presence of Australia's ancient past and discover the ways it is retained today, but please always leave these objects where you see them. They carry protection under various Australian national heritage acts, and more importantly, it is up to every one of us to ensure they remain on country. If you can, take the opportunity to see this country's diverse art sites. They are incredible and irreplaceable treasures. Many communities have an art centre where their art is available for sale, and this is a great way to support local economies.

As always, ask before photographing an individual or group and respect their wishes. Please be aware that you may be requested not to photograph certain areas and images. It is also advisable to show respect for protocols regarding men's and women's areas – some of which strictly apply to locals, others more widely.

As you venture away from home, be sure to take care of yourself, your vehicle and your companions. Carry plenty of water, spare tyres, blankets, a first-aid kit and communication back up. Travel or roadside insurance is worthwhile. Many camping sites have very basic amenities, so travel with your own requirements well covered. Look after your campsite so that the next visitor can enjoy it too. Bird books, plant books and other natural history texts are very good company in this great country.

Please consider that not all places you visit will be easy to access if you are in a wheelchair or have other special needs – but many are. Let people know where you are travelling to, and how much time you expect to spend on that section of your trip. Many information centres and ranger stations have logbooks for such purposes. Include vehicle registrations, phone contacts and the number and age of travellers.

Make use of those centres as well as road departments, local councils and tourist organisations. All provide useful information to make your travels more enjoyable.

Be aware that weather conditions can change quickly and dramatically, often severely affecting roads. Always check with local authorities, who will also be able to inform you of any local restrictions placed on alcohol or fuel, and requirements of a permit for entry. Permits are essential to pass through some communities, and it is wise to prepare early. We urge you to be sensitive to communities' needs, which vary widely across the country and according to current situations. For example, during the Covid-19 pandemic that is occurring as we write, some communities have asked that no one visit, even after other borders open.

On your journey, remember that the writing of Aboriginal and Torres Strait languages is a relatively recent undertaking, and the complexity of recording the unique sounds of these diverse languages is evident in the great variations in spelling you will likely encounter – even for people's names and places. There are many worthwhile language resources – enjoy investigating!

GULA BIAM

Bruce Pascoe

GA &
NGA

Far south coast of New South Wales in the area between
Pambula and Narooma,specifically centred on Tilba Tilba
and Bega.Eight hours' drive south of Sydney on the Princes Highway.

The Yuin (you-in)

Language group

As you travel along the coast towards Tilba Tilba, you find yourself among the green hills of the country rising off the coastal plain. Eruptions of granite boulders are common, looming out of the landscape, drawing your eye, threatening story.

Two of those mountains, Gulaga (The Mother) and Biamanga, have special meaning for Yuin people. The mountains are the centre of Yuin lore. Gulaga, formerly known as Mount Dromedary, its European name, is a place for both men and women, but the top third of the mountain is for the exclusive use of women, and part of the lower mountain holds significance for birthing rituals.

Climbing Gulaga is a sacred act and climbers are asked to ascend respectfully, wearing a red wristband in deference to its sacredness, in bare feet if possible, and preferably in silence.

Biamanga (also known as Mumbulla Mountain) has both men's and women's lore sites. From these mountains the lore is taught and disseminated. While different groups from country have different stories, all agree that this is an area central to the people for whom Yumburra, the black duck, is crucial to the country's wellbeing.

Lore sites are places where Elders introduce the tenets of the lore – the spiritual rules of knowledge and behaviour – to young men and women. While not all contemporary Yuin people undertake the lore, many do and ceremony for the support and protection of country is conducted frequently and attended by as many as a hundred people at a time. The lore is still strong. Not all ceremonies take place on the mountains but their spirit originates there.

A recent ceremony for the protection of the headwaters of the Murrumbidgee River where feral horses have destroyed the sphagnum moss beds of its origin was conducted by over one hundred people. Some have done this from as far as the Coorong in South Australia where Uncle Moogy has been conducting water protection ceremonies for decades.

Recently a healing ceremony for the Murray–Darling basin was attended by thousands of Aboriginal and non-Aboriginal people. It rained within three days!

In the country between Tilba and Braidwood there are a number of bora rings. These are circles where men, women and children danced their ceremonies. In most cases the circles interlock, a little like the Olympic rings, and this is an indication that while men's and women's lore are different, and largely hidden from the other, there was a confluence of philosophy and a cultural inclusion of the children. The participation of the whole community in particular ceremonies was a vibrant and reassuring glue for the people.

Despite surviving as visible imprints on land stolen over 230 years ago, it is clear that these incredible cultural sites are vulnerable both to vandalism and ignorance about their importance to our cultural fabric.

Protection of the sites is important because their ceremonies are being revived and strengthened for all purposes to do with cultural observance. In 2019 a large ceremony was conducted over three days to heal a massacre site on the Brodribb River. Many Yuin men and women brought their lore from Gulaga to remember the dead. The families of the perpetrators, survivors and fallen took part together in the ceremony.

History is preserved by continuing cultural practice and the ancient stories still being told by Yuin people. Men's and women's groups frequently perform dance and story rituals for the general public, but some are restricted to lore holders and initiates.

On Gulaga one of the main stories surrounds the fate of a mother and her two sons, Baranguba and Najanuka. The older son, Baranguba, wants to go out to sea and explore the world, so he ventures out into the ocean, and remains there today as the island named by Europeans as Montague. The younger child, Najanuka, wants to go too but his mother refuses and keeps him close to her. He is the smaller mount, Najanuka (Little Dromedary), resting at the foot of his mother.

The island of Baranguba has a fabulous heritage of history and lore. Aboriginal people visited the island in their canoes but story tells us that on one journey a sudden storm enveloped the fleet and many lives were lost. It is a tranquil passage on some days, but don't be deceived: the strait has moods of dangerous tempest.

The island is a haven for many ocean birds and to sleep on it is to be surrounded by these oceanic travellers. The following is an excerpt from the story 'Sea Wolves' in my book *Salt*. It's an evocation I wrote of that magnificently wild place, a place of legend where a man and his son and brothers woke one cool autumn morning:

Short-tailed shearwaters blundered through the heath, colliding with the men who, locked in darkness, had no idea what spirits were assailing them. And they

Right: Gulaga Mountain path.

Below: Bilima the turtle, another important cultural figure of Yuin, is represented in the shape of this headland at Bermagui as she makes her way out to sea. From the same parkland you can look north and west towards the expanse of mountains and valleys so central to Yuin lore.

Part of the spiritual journey on Gulaga Mountain. Yuin people are made up of thirteen language groups from Botany Bay to south of the Victorian border, including the eastern slopes of the Great Dividing Range.

were spirits – spirits of *gadu*, the ocean. Their voices began at four a.m., at first as tentative contact calls: *way coo, way coo; I am here, so am I, me too, way coo, way coo.* Then they projected their voices in long wails, an ancient ululation exactly like the howl of a wolf, a sound preparing the birds for their day coursing the crests of waves in hunt for small fish skipping and darting on the surface of *gadu*. But first they had to gain momentum before launching themselves into the darkness, and collision with crouching Yuin men was the least of their concerns; they were seeking the wind's clear air and the cushion it provided between them and the ocean's surface. They glided and curved against that cushion, and when they leave these shores they will ride it for months.

There is something mythic about islands but in Australia they are also steeped in legends of whales and sharks and their instructions for the correct behaviour of humans. Contemplate this on Barunguba and then turn back to the west and observe Gulaga and her message. As I wrote in the story in *Salt*:

> Any Australian can climb Gulaga Mountain and visit the seven chapters of Yuin lore. Women can walk to the summit if they wish, but men can go no higher than the gallery of granite tors. It is on the walk through those tors that the gentleness of Aboriginal culture is most apparent.

The emphasis is on the role of women in our society, the need to respect women because that is where we all originate. At one point the guide will ask you to observe a stone child on the back of a stone woman:

> Look at that child's eyes and, if you are a parent, allow yourself to be engulfed by the memory of your own children's births.
>
> But where are the swords and war machines, where are the gilded halls of selfish men, where are the severed heads of people who disagreed with the king? On Gulaga Mountain you are invited to rub the belly of a pregnant woman.
>
> I never fail to be moved by the gentleness of my culture and never fail to wish that the directionless among the men of our people could muster the energy to climb the mountain barefoot to absorb the profound respect our old people had for women.

Some of the
expressive
granite tors of
Gulaga Mountain.

This is not just a lesson for Aboriginal men but for men across the planet. Do not climb the mountain if you want to revisit a quaint and forgotten culture – but if you want to contemplate a world without war, that sees women as the centre of civilisation, this is the place to go. You can be guided to it by Yuin men and women who share the lineage of those who insisted that this was the destiny of humans and saw that story writ in stone. It will cost you much less than a speeding fine.

That gentleness extends beyond women to the land itself, and surely now we can see that respect and care for our soil and waters is in our own selfish interests.

We can keep our computers, and for at least another twenty years we can keep our cars, but we can also contemplate the Murray River and the outlandish idea that it is within our capacity to make sure there is water in it. We can contemplate the Biamanga granite spire and the petroglyphic 'bible' at Burrup Peninsula and realise we can enjoy a rich standard of living and keep these representations of the human spirit at its profound and elegant best.

You don't have to be Aboriginal to understand Burrup art or listen to the sea wolf shearwaters, but it would serve you well to understand Aboriginal philosophy if you wanted to save them and the land on which they exist. We cannot leave such momentous decisions to the craven and vindictive legion of red and blue politicians fascinated by the prospect of their own survival. We are Australians; it is we who have the power. And the philosophy.

The post-contact history of Tilba is typical of much of Australia. The rich soils and wonderful climate soon attracted European settlers from the new town of Sydney. It is easy to say that Francis Hunt held the first 'run' there in 1839 but how did he do that when Wandandian people of the Yuin nation were in residence? Hunt was one of the first Europeans to take possession of land in the district but was quickly followed by many others including the Bate, Corkhill and Berry families. No regard was given to the culture or land responsibilities of the Wandandian people, as it was assumed they would simply fade away in the presence of the superior European.

Australia likes to cloak these facts in obfuscation and use words like 'settlers' for the invader and 'clearances' for the murders and massacres they committed. War and smallpox decimated Aboriginal clans all around Australia, making occupation of the land possible for Europeans. While warfare, murder and massacres accounted

Murnong, pink heath, kangaroo grass and fringe lily are some of the many plants that were essential to human survival. These can still be found in the few remaining healthy grasslands, where native hoverflies, bees and other insects pollinate as they feed.

for thousands of Aboriginal people, disease also took an incredible toll. Smallpox (variola) sometimes killed up to eighty per cent of any given population. It has been claimed that the pox was introduced by spreading the virus on blankets that were then handed out to Aborigines. Major Robert Ross came to Sydney at the same time as the contagion began to spread and he had been involved in the same procedure in America before coming to Australia. For more on this part of our history, read books by Judith Campbell and Chris Warren. Although it is hard to make unequivocal claims, the history of the deliberate introduction of smallpox in other colonial frontiers makes its release highly suspicious.

British law aided and abetted the theft of land by excluding Aboriginal people from its processes. Aborigines could not give evidence in British courts of law conducted in Australia so had no way of expressing grievance for loss of land or life. The legal furphy of terra nullius (empty land or no one's land) is largely debunked by most Australians today, but in colonial times it was seen as the underpinning legal precedent for dispossession of Indigenous people.

By 1869 many settlers had flooded into the rich lands the Wandandian people had been managing for thousands of years. Their burning, cultivation and husbandry had produced a land ideal for grazing but the light soils of Australia and low rainfall could not cope with the European farm animals. The compaction of soils by hard-hoofed animals, felling of vegetation along watercourses, overstocking and a failure to understand Australian soils led to erosion and fertility depletion, which we are still dealing with today. Professor Michael Archer believes sheep and cattle have had a major impact on Australia fertility and soil depletion. He describes the process in his book *Going Native: Living in the Australian Environment*, written with Bob Beale. If you are interested in finding out more, it is worth a read.

It is common these days to see the roots and butts of trees standing metres clear of the surrounding land, a clear sign of massive erosion. How can Australia continue to tolerate the loss of our topsoil? Some regions have lost as much as thirteen metres of soil as a result of inappropriate farming and forestry techniques.

European-style agriculture was undertaken here despite the huge differences in the soil and climate of Australia and Europe. In accordance with colonial arrogance, all Aboriginal food crops, grown here for thousands of years, were completely ignored.

Left: Erosion, as seen here, can be readily minimised by retaining and replanting diverse indigenous vegetation and adjusting agricultural systems to meet the needs of country.

Above: Looking across cleared land with patches of bush towards Najanuka, Little Brother.

The effects of these introduced practices have caused the catastrophic destruction of soil. Along the highways in the region you will see those aforementioned tree stumps with metres of exposed roots and kilometres of deeply eroded creeks, an indication of the detrimental effects of European ploughing and deforestation.

Excessive water use, expended to support thirsty northern hemisphere crops, has led to enormous reductions in river health, and the widespread fish kills of the summer of 2019 tell us of the country's stress.

But history is never clear-cut. The settlers in the Tilba region south of Narooma included the Bate family, who recorded Aboriginal culture and treated the people better than most, although they still took over the land. The family produced politicians, academics and local officials who prospered from the south coast lands but some in the family were relatively kind to local people and recorded language and cultural matters. Some of these records by the Bates and other families are crucial cultural archives. The photos taken by the Corkhill family are widely used in the publication *Biamanga and Gulaga* by Brian Egloff and others, which records the history and families of local Aboriginal people. You can also see some of these photos online in the National Library's digital version of *Taken at Tilba: Photographs from the William Corkhill Collection*.

The Walkers, Imlays and Mannings were instrumental in taking acreages on the south coast. An example of how quickly Europeans supplanted the local culture is the cricket ground, Lords View, on the old Kameruka Estate. Australia played England there in 1837. Before that it was part of the sacred cultural landscape of the Yuin.

The estate was a model English dairying village with a church, chemist, butchery, manor houses and workers' cottages. Many of these can still be seen there today. It is a privately owned estate and tours are not encouraged, so if you want to see it you'd better learn to play cricket, preferably for Mallacoota. Kameruka has its own team, the Kameruka Black Cockatoos, but they're not much chop.

I play at the ground once or twice every year and take all new cricketers to look at the scoreboard featuring the record of that game in 1837. Within just a few years of European entry into the district, a game of cricket was being played in a farm village modelled on the lords' estates of England. The kids are usually just keen to get on with the game, but I can't pass up the opportunity to give them a chance to reflect on their country's history.

Today, you, the traveller can accept an invitation to join local Yuin in appreciating that culture. The lore belongs to Yuin people, so you can accept it as part of the ancient testament of Aboriginal philosophy and spirituality. We can share much of this knowledge of country but only if we accept the fact that it existed. You cannot accept history as an interesting gift, you have to accept it as part of this country's heritage.

Seventy-two years ago a young Yuin man was asked to climb Biamanga mountain and find the 'two scar tree'. He looked and he looked but couldn't find the two scar trees. Twice he came back to his Elders admitting defeat and eventually they said to him, did you listen to us? We were asking you to find a two-scar tree not two scar trees.

The young man went back and walked straight to the tree he'd seen on his first visit and saw that it had two scars. It was a good lesson: listen carefully to what you are told and make no assumptions. That same man issued me an instruction to find a five-ring tree on a nearby mountain. Having seen ring trees before, I was looking into the upper trunk and branches, and missed the tree entirely because the rings were carved into the tree's base. That tree has important cultural resonance so it was incredibly disappointing that during the New Year's Eve fires of 2019 the tree was cut down. Not burnt down, but cut down in some random attempt to slow the fire. Authorities had been told of the tree's cultural importance but that held no weight with authorities.

There is no point in berating the people who did it, for they were just doing what they were told, but surely we can expect more sensitive treatment of such crucial cultural history in the future. These sites tell stories that go to the heart of Australian history.

The two-scar tree of Biamanga is warning that there are two ceremonial sites in the vicinity. Lyrebird, Ngaran Ngaran, plays a pivotal role in Yuin cultural life. The bird is always seen or heard at Biamanga and Gulaga. The lyrebird is important to those mountains and it is almost impossible to visit the area and not see or hear the bird. It mimics other birds so if you hear a black cockatoo, crimson rosella, whipbird or grey shrike thrush but don't actually see those birds, listen carefully – it may be the lyrebird. Stand still, don't try to hide; the lyrebird may continue his repertoire as long as he can see where you are.

On Biamanga, lyrebirds contribute to cultural ceremonies. The sound of the clapsticks is identical to the lyrebird's contact call as it strides about the forest floor. On Gulaga, ceremonial visitors notify the ancestors of their arrival by clapping two sticks together – one clap for each person. The lyrebird has been known to repeat exactly the number of claps sounded, and recently a bird repeated the count of thirty-one claps. It is interesting to wonder if Aboriginal people produced clapsticks to replicate the call of the bird or whether the lyrebird, one of the world's greatest mimics, chose as its default call the clap of our sticks.

It is a shame that the massive granite tor on Biamanga was dynamited in the 1970s to make way for a communications hut made of asbestos. The spire-shaped rock could be seen from all parts of Bega Valley, a cultural beacon for the entire district, but now it lies in pieces like a slain giant. Modern technology has made the hut redundant; perhaps technology could restore the granite needle as the eye of Bega, a way of the two communities coming together and appreciating the entire history of the great valley.

Perhaps here is a symbolic opportunity to bring understanding and some concili-ation. Typical of Australia today there is often prejudice and racism directed against the Aboriginal community and in turn, many Aboriginal people feel they do not belong to the wider mainstream community. Many Aboriginal people do not believe we have to reconcile as we were not the transgressor, so conciliation remains the more potent need.

Traditionally young initiates at Biamanga descended the mountain and bathed away the ochre and the signs of their initiation into Yuin lore. Both men and women have the advantage of learning their lore from people initiated by the decedent of a lone survivor of a massacre at the very beginning of the invasion. Those ceremonies continue today so visitors are asked to show respect towards the pool where those ceremonies conclude each year in unbroken succession since before colonisation.

If you do climb Gulaga, remember it is a sacred act and perhaps choose to climb with an Indigenous guide. On the mountain's girdle you will be acquainted with the principles of Yuin lore. You might be asked to think of those who are unwell, those on the brink of being born, those who have already left mortal life, but you will never be asked to think of yourself.

You will be introduced through story and geography to Nyaardi and Tunku, the first woman and man. You will notice that Nyaardi is much larger than Tunku, you will see the birth of the child, the raising of the child, the lessons for the child and you will be asked to consider your place in the universe, but you will not see a weapon of any kind. This lore is about women and children, not about war and

Looking towards Wallaga Lake from Gulaga.

death. In most instances Aboriginal lore concerns itself with the correct behaviour of people in relation to Mother Earth.

Soon after you begin the ascent of Gulaga there are a few points where you can look back down to the coast and there you will see Wallaga Lake, a township of huge importance to local Aboriginal people. In the middle of the lake there is an elongated island, which we say is in the shape of Yumburra, the black duck, the major totem of southern Yuin people. This island is also called Merriman Island and it is where King Merriman, senior lore man at the time of dispossession, took the women and children as a last refuge during an attack on his people. Merriman was an important and dignified local man who held to his lore despite all the change occurring around him. Many local families are direct descendants of this great man.

It is important to note that Merriman Island was the first Aboriginal place to be gazetted in New South Wales.

You can also look out to the offshore island, Barunguba. You will be told of the invisible umbilical cord that tied the elder son to his mother. This is represented by a crystal reef that extends from Gulaga to the island and expresses itself as a fresh-water spring on the island.

Opposite and above: Wallaga Lake and Merriman Island.

Right (top): Spotted gums are one of the iconic species of the area, renowned for their tendency to morph and form grafts. Some trees were purposely altered to provide information such as boundaries and directions.

Right (bottom): Mangroves are a vital part of incredibly complex systems that provide habitat for innumerable species above and below the changing waterline.

Yumburra (Pacific black duck) taking off, revealing emerald feathers. Yumburra live in waterways across Australia except for the most arid regions. Populations are at risk of cross-breeding with the introduced mallard.

Recently roadworks severed that cord even though local Elders had begged for this important spiritual link to be respected. The government and road company ignored the request and the damage was done, but, after pleas from Elders, the wound was sealed and you can see that perfunctory repair today as you drive the highway near Tilba Tilba. Patches of concrete have been used to stop the wound, a constant reminder of European contempt for Aboriginal culture.

One of the stories tour guides on Gulaga will tell you is of how Aboriginal people saw Captain Cook sailing past them on his way north in 1770. They lit signal fires on every headland to advise clans of Cook's progress, a warning to be aware.

When the people first saw Cook's sails they thought of them as the wings of a giant pelican. They observed the ship from their vantage points on Gulaga and Biamanga. It is interesting that the Yuin name for Montague Island, Baranguba, is very similar to the word for pelican, Garanguba. (We thank Warren Foster snr for this information.)

Within the parks and forests of the district you might notice trees that have been altered by Aboriginal people in the process of pursuing their culture. The ring trees, scar trees and altered trees are often quite discreet but are found all over Australia and always indicate cultural practice. Often the altered trees are in the shape of rings or ovals and indicate to travellers that they are entering sacred cultural precincts. Today these trees are often unnoticed or misunderstood, but they represent an important part of the country's cultural heritage and should be respected for their part in our national life.

There are hundreds of sites in this district – rich and ongoing stories – and Biamanga and Gulaga and the continuing cultural practice of the Yuin are central to them all.

Some of these stories have been included in Bangarra Dance Theatre's *Dark Emu*, to which many Yuin people contributed with story and song. This dance was inspired by my book *Dark Emu*, which explains the agricultural economy of Australian Aboriginal and Torres Strait Islander people.

During the dance performance, the audience was entranced by a song sung by Uncle Guboo Ted Thomas, a descendant of the local clan. Such an ancient legacy – and one that could be embraced by all Australians. If we choose.

Gulaga & Biamanga

Indigenous cultural experiences, tours and relevant organisations

Ngaran Ngaran Cultural Awareness

Workshops, cultural performances and multi-day tours, including overnight hiking and glamping trips.

0408 272 121
ngaranaboriginalculture.com

Max Harrison

Discover the stories passed down the generations by Uncle Max Dulumunmun Harrison on a guided cultural awareness tour in and around Narooma.

islandchartersnarooma.com.au/charter-tours/bus-charters-tours/guided-aboriginal-tour

Umbarra Aboriginal Cultural Centre

Check with the Narooma Visitor Centre before you go as this centre at Wallaga Lake isn't always open – it reopened in 2019 after being closed for 10 years and future plans were still up in the air at the time of going to print – but when it is, there is art on display, workshops, regular performances and storytelling.

FMB Wallaga Lake, via Narooma
02 4473 7232
aumuseums.com/nsw/umbarra-aboriginal-cultural-centre-and-tours

Jigamy Farm, Eden

The Bundian Way – as it is now called – is a long-distance path from Mt Kosciuszko to Twofold Bay, and part of extensive routes established by various local Indigenous groups. The routes were used for many purposes, at times with a focus on the bogong moth of the mountains and the whales of the sea. Sections have been, and continue to be, rehabilitated and prepared for today's walkers.

4381 Princes Hwy,
Broadwater
02 6495 7177
bundianway.com.au

Minga Cultural Experiences

Walking tours, art, bush foods, fire making and overnight culture camps in local national parks.

Bergalia
0407 076 511
mingaaboriginalculturalservices.com.au

Bingi Dreaming Track

Allow four to six hours to hike this 14km trail between Congo and Tuross Head in Eurobodalla National Park that links traditional campgrounds, ceremonial sites and sources of food as it traces ancient songlines.

nationalparks.nsw.gov.au/things-to-do/walking-tracks/bingi-dreaming-track

Other things to see and do

Murramarang National Park and Cullendulla Creek Nature Reserve

These two areas protect a diversity of sites, including a midden on the South Coast so large that it holds the remnants of thousands of shared meals, generation upon generation.

Scar tree

Look closely at the large forest red gum on the corner of George Bass Drive and Broulee Road, and you'll see the scar left when bark was removed to make a canoe.

Tilba Talks Heritage Walks

Join a three-hour walking tour through the historic village of Central Tilba.

0433 114 374

Region X tours

Explore the backwaters and national park trails on a guided cycling or sea kayaking tour.

1300 001 060
regionx.com.au

Narooma Visitor Centre

80 Princes Hwy, Narooma
02 4476 2881
narooma.org.au/visitor-centre

Narooma National Parks and Wildlife Office

9 Burrawang St, Narooma
02 4476 0800

Narooma tours

Whale watching, snorkelling with seals, evening penguin watching, historic lighthouse and tours of Baranguba (Montague Island). Ask at the Narooma Visitor Centre for details of tours.

02 4476 2881
narooma.org.au

Narooma Oyster Festival

Savour the flavours of what the locals say are the world's best oysters at the annual Narooma Oyster Festival held in late April through early May.

naroomaoysterfestival.com

Further reading

A collection of stories and essays I've written over the years: *Salt: Selected Stories and Essays*, Black Inc, Melbourne, 2019.

For more on the history of the area, track down a copy of Brian Egloff's *Biamanga and Gulaga: Aboriginal Cultural Association with the Biamanga and Gulaga National Parks*, Office of the Registrar, Aboriginal Land Rights Acts 1983, Surry Hills, 2005.

See the photos from William Corkhill's *Taken at Tilba: Photographs from the William Henry Corkhill Tilba Tilba Collection* at the National Library of Australia website.

Above: An old story tells of the birth of a baby on Gulaga Mountain.

NAMA

Bruce Pascoe

ADGI

Namadgi National Park, at the
northern end of the Australian Alps
and about forty-five minutes' drive
from Canberra

Ngunnawal

Language group

Your country wants to talk to you.
It needs to talk to you.
In this valley you are only an hour from your
country's federal parliament. But the political
decisions here began 120,000 years ago.
Evidence of the culture is all about you
as you walk through this national park –
rock art, scar trees, stone arrangements,
tools. It is so tempting to take a souvenir
but please stay your hand. Those specimens
have yet to be fully studied and we need
them to explain and defend our culture.
We need our cultural objects in situ, not on
your mantelpiece only to be turfed out by
your grandkids when you die.

Walk here and wonder. It is a beautiful, wild landscape, immerse yourself in its story. That story will be found at every corner.

A dingo observes those ascending a rocky mount. It watches, ears jigged forward, wondering. The people keep climbing and he sits on a boulder to watch. He has a reason.

As soon as he is seen he bounds from the boulder but his curiosity and need cause him to pause. The visitors see him and wonder at his rich golden pelt, his intelligent eye, his need for conversation. He sniffs, he plays, he suggests, he proffers a wounded foot.

There is an exchange of intimacy between two entirely different creatures. A strange, beautiful and puzzling conversation with Australia.

And on the flat land below the mount, a beast is seen lounging on an emerald sward. Alone.

What is this creature that looks most of all like a casual camel? It is an earless kangaroo. Some years ago dingoes hatched a plan to bring down the roo but his vicious kicks had gained him a reprieve while the dingoes withdrew to catch their breath. The roo lost an ear.

The dingoes returned, grabbing his other ear, hauling him to the ground, but once again the roo fights back, this time, losing the other ear. But survives. Camel headed. So this valorous, earless roo becomes known as Vincent and his presence is a constant reminder of that tender balance between hunger, bravery, energy and hope.

Just above the elbow flat of the river where Vincent reclines, almost always alone, a rising ridge line displays a peculiar wall of stone. Built by humans. But which ones?

The complex history of Namadgi and surrounding areas lies among the valleys and slopes, evident in tangles of heritage-listed wire, rocks in various formations, and trees showing signs of human interaction.

Moss and lichen grow slowly, inching over centuries, creeping over aeons, so their passage across the intersections of stones speaks of centuries. Black centuries. You can measure the time it takes for lichen to grow across the interstices of two touching stones. Beginning as a stylish rosette it can grow into a tablecloth centimetre by centimetre, measurable. So, if human hands put those boulders next to each other, the lichen betrays how long ago it began to form. This wall is ancient, much older than the era of energetic Scottish shepherds. But we know that because of the wall's style and its placement; it's useless as a guide or barrier for sheep.

This was used for something else – directing the travel of kangaroos. There is evidence of such structures in other ranges close by, but the question is: when will we start to test its worth? When we've replicated every peg and rib in James Cook's *Endeavour*? Or when we've had one last good look at the pyramids in Egypt, because they need another survey like Macbeth needs another review.

Elsewhere in this incredible valley, your valley, hardly visited, stone arrangements wait as puzzles do. A grandmother tree sprawls protective, not spectacular in height, but stupendous in her embrace of the valley floor.

Ready Cut Hut at Gudgenby was brought here by pastoralists so they could mind their sheep and she is a beautiful building in her modest simplicity, but all about her are the tools of the world's most modest civilisation.

Not modest in the sense of innocence and inability but modest in demand upon the earth, modest in the refusal to abuse, the fervent desire to care and protect, that kind of hopelessly unpopular conservatism.

In the clefts of the huge rocks at the art site of Yankee Hat there are handprint stencils and other figures left by the Ngunnawal people. You will see images of animals, humans and abstract figures and be awed at the enormous rock overhang that provided shelter for thousands of years. Careful, this is world art, hugely important for understanding this ancient land. Be proud, treasure it, protect it.

Bogong moths used to cluster in these crevices and all the way up to the tip of the alps during their aestivation over summer, a slow torpor in deep caves, and the focus of the moth festivals that brought the confederacy of Aboriginal nations together each year for a massive feast and ceremony. People from all the surrounding clans gathered here for social and cultural celebrations, and those times are saved in the memories handed down to both Aboriginal and non-Aboriginal people in the district.

Those ceremonial times are remembered by all the associated clans of the moth, but haven't been practised since the killing times in these mountains when men like Angus McMillan and Fred Taylor abused, subjugated and murdered the people. The war waged for possession of this soil commenced in the late 1840s and, within a few short years of escalating violence, ended as early as 1850 with the poverty of the dispossessed.

This page: Living shelters are found on mountain slopes among the granite tors.

Opposite: Namadgi is one of few refuges for dingoes – listed as vulnerable to extinction. They play an important role as an apex predator in the ecosystem, which includes a significant population of kangaroos.

Fortunately there are energetic moves to hold that confederacy together. Aboriginal people of the region are trying to negotiate cultural rights with state and federal governments so that these practices can be maintained. Unfortunately, though, the moths are rapidly dwindling due to the use of pesticides in the agricultural lands to the north in New South Wales and Queensland where the moths feed in order to fatten for the trip south to the alps.

There are songs and recipes for the moth harvest and European reports of Aborigines glowing with health as they descended the mountains after the ceremony. Nineteenth-century anthropologist Alfred William Howitt and others wrote in amazement as they witnessed people returning from the festival, their skin radiant after the nutritious feasts of moth.

The world is experiencing a massive reduction in insect numbers and diversity. Some scientists predict that our failure to save bees and other pollinators from destruction by agricultural chemicals will be the single most important factor in deciding the ability of humans to live on the planet. No bees, no pollination, no flowers, no fruit, no grass – no people.

Part of that unfolding story is being told at Namadgi. While Australia is contributing to the dangerous absence of insects, we still have national parks and reserves where, if our policies are rigorous, there is little or no use of agricultural poisons.

Two years ago we witnessed a cultural burn here. The local Aboriginal work crew were wanting to burn and the Rural Fire Service were going to collaborate; however, when light rain fell they could not proceed with their contribution. But the young Aboriginal men and women lit cool controlled burns in the caves where there is still great art to be found.

This was a really useful intercession because in previous wildfires the caves burnt so hot the stone ceilings and walls delaminated in the intense heat and priceless art was lost. This burn under these conditions got rid of a dangerous fuel load with hardly a degree in increased temperature. Watching the work made you proud to be Australian.

Driving through the countryside beyond the national park, however, makes you wonder about the intensity of modern agriculture. Thousands of sheep straggle across barren paddocks raising dust, hammering the earth with their sharp hooves, nibbling tenaciously at every prick of green that is foolish enough to show itself.

Cool burns in progress in Namadgi and Canberra district.

It is hard to imagine how this type of land use can be sustained. We need sheep to eat but how many do we need and at what cost to our soil? Smaller, more appropriately grazed flocks are being proposed for this industry and a man of this district, Charles Massy, has written a wonderful book, *Call of the Reed Warbler*, on this very issue. It is highly recommended along with *The Biggest Estate on Earth* written by Bill Gammage, another man of the district. Both offer new ways of looking at an old country, re-examining our history with curiosity rather than cringe. We are lucky to have Namadgi to speak for country. And the country wants to talk to you. And she is.

Listen for the frog near the Ready Cut Hut's drain, watch the kangaroo puzzling over the dewdrop from the shed roof, watch the swallows and hawks coursing across the marsh, become mesmerised by the trickling water searching for a course between the rocks, the wood ducks serene on the handrail of the bridge. And if you walk along the road searching for internet access, look away from the glow of your device for a moment, down at your feet, because here is a real feat: the tools of a people who managed this land for 120,000 years, as current research at Moyjil in Victoria indicates, an aeon without thistles, foxes, sheep or barbed wire.

Look to where the sun lets her blood seep and drench, where a woman of stone seems to recline. Is she dying or living? Is she from the ground or on the ground?

Australians, this is your Namadgi, she is a mystery, a relic, a vibrant pulse in the earth. Within the frosty dawn, jewels of frozen dew on the barbed wire might be the pearls on the breast of a most beautiful woman, the breast of your country.

Your country.

This is your invitation to enter this sacred valley, allow your breath to slow, allow your mind repose, rest in the verdure of the valley and embrace these secrets. It's your country after all. She is your responsibility.

Indigenous cultural experiences, tours and relevant organisations

Tidbinbilla Nature Reserve

Forty minutes south of Canberra, Tidbinbilla is on the edge of Namadgi National Park and also has important Aboriginal sites. Go for a bushwalk, spot some wildlife or enjoy a barbecue. The visitor centre has information on the area's Indigenous culture and history.

Tidbinbilla Reserve Rd, Paddys River (off Paddys River Rd via Cotter Rd or Tidbinbilla Rd via Point Hut Crossing/Tharwa).

02 6207 7921
tidbinbilla.act.gov.au

Murumbung Yurung Murra Cultural Tours

Explore the Gudgenby Valley in Namadgi with an Aboriginal ranger to learn more about the rock art of the area and the culture of the Ngunnawal people.

02 6207 0078
environment.act.gov.au/
parks-conservation/parks-
and-reserves/recreational_
activities/murumbung-
yurung-murra-cultural-tours

Dhawura Tours

As well as various tours around Canberra, Dhawura offers a Namadgi National Park tour.

0407 517 844
thunderstone.net.au/services

Traditional Owners Aboriginal Corporation

0413 908 408
traditional-owners.com.au

Note: At the time of writing the Namadgi National Park Visitor Centre and much of the park, as well as Murumbung Yurung Murra Cultural Tours, were not open as the result of the Ororral Valley bushfire that occurred in early 2020. Be sure to check the current status before you visit.

Other things to see and do

In Canberra you can wander through the Australian National Botanic Gardens or go to the many cultural institutions found in the capital. In the country surrounding Canberra you can visit a solar farm at Royalla, the Christmas Barn at Bredbo (an hour south of Canberra), the famous bakery at Nimmitabel (two hours south of Canberra) and the pub at Nimmitabel (now there's an experience). There are the snowfields in winter and the wildflowers on the same fields in summer. This is rich, rich country.

Namadgi National Park Visitor Centre

Just south of Tharwa, this centre has guides to Namadgi's 160km of marked walking tracks, including the Yankee Hat Rock Art Walking Track, and information on the camping and hut accommodation available in the park.

Naas Rd, Tharwa
02 6237 5307
environment.act.gov.au/
parks-conservation/parks-
and-reserves/find-a-park/
namadgi-national-park/
namadgi-national-park

Further reading

Charles Massy, *Call of the Reed Warbler: A New Agriculture, A New Earth*, UQP, Brisbane, 2017

Bill Gammage, *The Biggest Estate on Earth: How Aborigines Made Australia*, Allen & Unwin, Sydney, 2012

RRINA

Bruce Pascoe

On the banks of the Barwon River in
north-west New South Wales

Ngemba, Murrawarri,
Yuwaalaraay, Wayilwan

Language groups

The Brewarrina fish traps, or Baiame's Ngunnhu, are arguably the oldest human construction on earth, thought to be at least 40,000 years old. These magnificent traps, built to provide sustainable food for the local community, stretch along the Barwon River for around half a kilometre, but similar constructions are found in most other Australian river systems and estuaries. It is amazing that such significant engines of economy have received so little attention.

Previous pages: Baiame's
Ngunnhu was damaged
for the construction of the
weir. Water is now held
back up the river for over
30 kilometres, altering the
ecosystem both upstream
and downstream.

Left: Detailed layers of the
shell of a freshwater mussel,
once abundant in the
river system.

Consisting of rock weirs, pens and pools, the traps have ecological and egalitarian functions embedded into their operation. The building of these complex structures is intriguing enough, but when the cultural and social ethics under which they were constructed are considered, their importance to the world is enormous. Unfortunately Australia seems to have insufficient interest in this momentous moment in the history of the human species, preferring instead to forensically examine old convict ruins or erect a hall of fame to the shearers of sheep.

It is not just the age of these structures that ought to hold our attention. Baiame's Ngunnhu presents a story that enriches our country. The traps show a way of living that involved cooperation and relationship within families and with neighbours, with the river itself and with all other life forms. The structure is like a net of rock laid across the breadth of the river. It was designed to support an ongoing diversity of life, including fish, shrimp and crayfish, while enabling the builders and carers of the traps to catch and share a good meal.

Baiame, the creator Spirit Emu, is central in the old creation stories of the rivers, flood plains and rocky outcrops, the fish traps and their people. His travels through this country give guidance to the keepers of the stories, and through their retelling, knowledge is maintained. The stories reflect seasonal change, which can be seen in the way the traps work with the natural changes in river flow. By observing the traps, you can see that the shapes differ according to their function as pens or passages, all in careful alignment with one another.

Baiame's Ngunnhu, today also known as the Brewarrina fish traps, with the recently constructed weir disrupting the river's natural flow.

There was thought to be very little local stone in this district so the builders of this system had to employ skilful and economic methods. The skill required was noticed by Europeans, with William C. Mayne, the Commissioner of Crown Lands, saying in 1848:

> To form these must have been a work of no trifling labour, and no slight degree of ingenuity and skill must be exercised in their construction, as I was informed by men who had passed several years in the vicinity, that not even the heaviest floods displace the stones forming the enclosures.

There are legends to explain the origin of the stones and the creators of the first fish traps. It is hard, though, to validate the claims about the age of this site because so little archaeological effort has been expended on it. It is not the failure of the archaeologists – it is more complex than that – but it's worth questioning how funding is assigned for research projects. The oldest human structure on earth ... nah, let's have another look at the foundations of the Windsor Hotel in Melbourne – we're sure to find pennies and fascinating boot buckles, maybe even an ancient tobacco tin!

So little study has been made of the area that the only book dedicated to the traps was written in the 1970s and is only about 60 pages long, with a cheap black and white cover. It is almost as if the country could be deliberately hiding the antiquity of its history from itself and the world.

Left: The channels, small weirs and pens of Baiame's Ngunnhu, as seen here, enabled the catching of fish while also allowing natural cycles to continue.

Below: Detail of the fish ladder recently constructed to try to address the weir's disruption to fish movement. Hundreds of locals voiced opposition and signed petitions expressing their objections on cultural, environmental and historical grounds. Concerns about the predicted ineffectiveness of the fish ladder were also heard by government ministers.

The distinctively designed Brewarrina Aboriginal Cultural Museum runs tours of the traps and river. Yet this area of such importance in world history is not teeming with visitors. Those who do come are often just passing through on their way to the Shearers' Hall of Fame at Hay or the Tree of Knowledge at Barcaldine, which marks one of Australia's biggest industrial disputes. Both those sites are important to the recent history of Australia, but pale in comparison to the international value of the Brewarrina fish traps. Visit the museum, which overlooks the traps, and enjoy a guided tour. Sit by the river and wonder at such an incredible achievement as this.

Approximately sixty kilometres south-west of Brewarrina is another important site for the Ngemba people, a site that describes and connects the water sources across the country. Travel here, a place now known as the Byrock Rock Holes, and you will see the marks left by Baiame's presence, the stone tools he laid down and the areas where he sharpened them. The story of this place teaches its people important skills, including the collection and grinding of seed for bread and the sharing of resources among family members and beyond. The grooves and depressions in the

Opposite (left): Brewarrina Aboriginal Cultural Museum.

Opposite (right): Brad Steadman, designer of Brewarrina Aboriginal Cultural Museum's floor, describes how the old people say not only does the ancestral being Wahwae live in the river but he also lives in the Milky Way. In this design, Wahwae is also the metaphor for the river. He creates the mist and fog of the river with his body heat. The circles of black, red and grey represent the people, their blood, and ashes from their fires that they left for us to follow. Semicircles show colours of the land, with green representing leaves of our native trees.

Right (top): Interior of Brewarrina's Aboriginal Cultural Museum, showing a canoe tree, a map of the area with language groups, and various tools beneath a goondi (shelter).

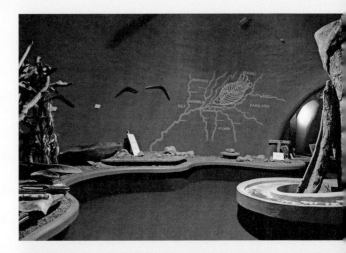

Right (bottom): Some of the tools shown in a goondi are:
beirr: come-back 'boomerang', pronounced a bit like beerr with a strong 'r'
boompil: emu caller, pronounced with 'oo' a bit like book
gunay: digging stick, pronounced a bit like 'gann-ai'
marrga: thick shield, pronounced with a kind of rolling 'r'
gudjul: wooden dish, pronounced a bit like 'katchl'
yaway: grinding stone, pronounced a bit like 'ya.way'

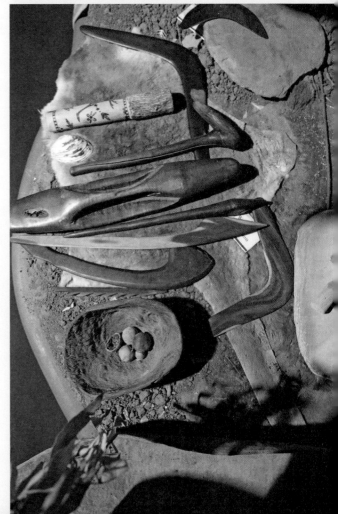

Left (top): Baiame's actions of shaping and sharpening the first waggarr (stone axe) are evident at Waggarrbugarnea (today also known as Byrock). The stone tools he laid down, and areas where he worked them, relate to the name of the place.

Left (bottom): When Baiame hunted a kangaroo and dragged it to where he would cook, channels were formed that today guide water to the rockhole. He made and used the first waggarr to dig the hole in the rock. This deeper hole is close to the shallower one where he sharpened his waggarr. In much the same way that Baiame showed the people how to build the Ngunnhu at Brewarrina, he showed the people how to make, use and care for waggarr.

Opposite: Changing colour with the afternoon sun.

Right: The area of Waggarrbugarnea is less than a hundred kilometres south-west of Baiame's Ngunnhu and connects water and stories across the country. This waterhole was significantly altered in the last hundred years – and more recently with machinery that caused further damage – to provide water for livestock.

expansive rocky outcrop speak of the movement and retention of water. It is easy to imagine the laughter and yarns shared on this country, the admiration of the rock's colour with its dramatic change according to the position of the sun, and the everyday learning essential for healthy country and healthy people.

In the era of the Australian bush poets of the early twentieth century the mystery and remoteness of the area had Australians calling it the Back of Bourke, a romantic and wistful phrase yearning for the old Australia, a land of hardship and loneliness. But when Thomas Mitchell rode through this country in 1831 he passed through Aboriginal towns and always envied the comfort of the homes and the tastefulness of their design. He admired the people for the aesthetics of the town planning and the serenity and prosperity of their lives. In his 1839 book *Three Expeditions into the Interior of Australia*, he wrote:

> In crossing one hollow we passed among the huts of a native tribe. They were tastefully distributed amongst drooping acacias and casuarinae; some resembled bowers under yellow fragrant mimosae; some were isolated under the deeper shades of casuarinae; while others were placed more socially, three or four together, fronting to one and the same hearth. Each hut was semicircular,

Left: Bottle trees standing among the skeletons of other trees.

Opposite (left): Ploughing, exposing the soil to erosion.

Opposite (right): Permanent scarring of the land caused by extensive mining operations reveals part of mining's impact.

or circular, the roof conical, and from one side a flat roof stood forward like a portico, supported by two sticks. Most of them were close to the trunk of a tree, and they were covered, not as in many parts, by sheets of bark, but with a variety of materials, such as reeds, grass and boughs. The interior of each looked clean, and to us passing in the rain, gave some idea, not only of shelter, but even of comfort and happiness. They afforded a favourable specimen of the taste of the gins, whose business it is to construct the huts.

Mitchell said that most of the towns could accommodate as many as a thousand people. He passed different villages every day for several days and recorded that one building could accommodate forty people.

Despite such frequent and positive reports, our history books have failed to refer to these towns. Is this because they are inconvenient reminders of the illegitimate 'settlement' of the country? How can we allow our academic system to distort the history of the land, and to render the prior occupiers as undeserving of the land, barely human nomads?

Walking around these sites with local people, we are taken to cotton fields – ploughed land where north and west winds carry the topsoil away as farmers wait to plant the boom crop. Cotton farming is an industry that relies on the massive damming of Queensland and New South Wales rivers so that downstream farms are starved of water. Each year Australia bemoans the annual fish kill as the stagnant streams of the Darling and its tributaries dry up and the water temperature climbs. In 1835 Mitchell camped along the Darling River, writing of it in his journal: 'The water being beautifully transparent, the bottom was visible at great depths, showing large fishes in shoals, floating like birds in mid-air.' Now when the fish die, we act as if it is a confounding mystery and we blame drought and bad luck instead of facing the reality that we cannot take every drop of water from the rivers without experiencing a catastrophe. This is not just the effect of global warming; it is the effect of greed and negligent land use.

The lands where the wind carries the soil away used to be home to grasses that, as Mitchell reported, were higher than his horses' saddles, an incredibly prolific crop and much favoured by grazing animals. Those perennial grasses protected the soil and their massive root systems also sequestered carbon. A partial return to these grasses alone would more than help Australia meet its carbon-emission reduction targets.

These grasses also benefited human health by providing food. The flour produced from the grain was flavoursome, nutritious and gluten free. An Aboriginal grinding stone from the region around Cuddie Springs, about eighty kilometres south-east

of Brewarrina, was found to be 35,000 years old. Even at that age it shows that Ngemba women were making bread from seed 18,000 years before the Egyptians. Some scholars have argued against this theory but then have been largely silent since a seed-grinding stone dated as being used 65,000 years ago was found in Madjedbebe in Arnhem Land.

This incredible contribution to world diet, culture and development happened in this country, Australia. Visit the area because its history is so much more than the Henry Lawson trope of valiant battler against a hostile land. There are stories here that help explain the ascent of the human species.

And, naturally, where such organised labour and food production took place the necessary social organisation meant that people collected together in the towns that Mitchell studied with such surprise.

As climate changed in Australia some locations lost their streams and suffered desertification, but new archaeology in these areas shows that communities were able to adapt their social and commercial activities when the drier conditions arrived. These may well be the world's oldest villages. So, not only did this country perhaps invent bread, it may also have invented society and democracy. There is much work and research needed to test these theories but, as geologist Jim Bowler has proven, there is already a mountain of evidence to allow us to form an opinion. And that opinion will be informed further over the next five years as studies awaiting peer review add exciting new evidence.

Understanding lore stories and songs is an intriguing way to anticipate future science. It often offends Aboriginal and Torres Strait Islander people that their own recital of history and science is never believed until validated by a university but, as the two truths converge, it is possible a more respectful communication may evolve.

Today is a new day and more adventurous archaeologists are working with Aboriginal communities to study and reflect on the claim, 'We have always been here.' This discussion is covered in more detail in the Moyjil (Point Ritchie) chapter later in this book. By visiting Baiame's Ngunnhu, the Brewarrina fish traps, you take an important step towards understanding this incredible and little celebrated history.

Indigenous cultural experiences, tours and relevant organisations

Brewarrina Aboriginal Cultural Museum

Book a tour of the museum and fish traps area. New projects include a nursery and garden of native plants important to human health.

18 Bathurst St (cnr Darling St)
02 6839 2421
brewarrinafishtraps.com.au

Through our Eyes film series

A series of short films presenting ecological knowledge of Elders and communities.

2cuzFM

Indigenous community radio station. Brewarrina and Bourke 106.5.

2cuzfm.com

Brewarrina Aboriginal Mission

Established in 1886 and located 14km upstream of the township. The community maintains the original cemetery. To visit, contact the Brewarrina Local Aboriginal Land Council.

02 6839 2273

Bourke Aboriginal Cultural Tours

Run by Jason and Joseph Dixon, their one-and-a-half-hour walking tours start and finish at the Back O' Bourke Information and Exhibition Centre.

Kidman Way, Bourke
0436 368 185
bourkeaboriginalcultural
tours.com

Bourke Cultural Walks

Easy walking tour around Bourke with George Orcher. Book through the Bourke Visitor Information Centre.

02 6872 1321

Other things to see and do

Brewarrina Visitor Centre

50 Bathurst St
02 6830 5152
brewarrina.nsw.gov.au/
tourism/visitor-information.
aspx

Bourke General and Historic Cemetery

Graves reflect the diversity of people who came to live in the area. A tiny tin mosque was used by cameleers of the late 1800s, predominantly of Afghan descent, whose connections to Indigenous communities and early industry is worthy of investigation.

Cobar Rd (Kidman Way), Bourke

Waggarrbugarnea (Byrock)

Take your time at this significant site as you contemplate its ancient stories and enjoy the birds.

Nearly 80km south-east of Bourke, just off Mitchell Hwy

Gundabooka National Park

The Gunderbooka Range is an important place for the Ngemba and Paakantji peoples. Check road conditions at the Bourke Visitor Information Centre.

49km south of Bourke
02 6830 0200
nationalparks.nsw.gov.
au/visit-a-park/parks/
gundabooka-national-park

Further reading

Download a PDF of *Aboriginal Women's Heritage: Bourke*.

environment.nsw.gov.au/
research-and-publications/
publications-search/
aboriginal-womens-heritage-
bourke

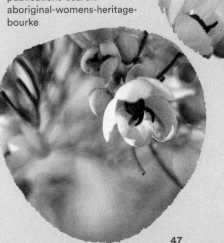

The memorial to the Hospital Creek massacre.

Note: The Hospital Creek massacre site and memorial is not readily accessible to the public, but you can see it from the road.

Further reading

https://c21ch.newcastle.edu.au/colonialmassacres/introduction.php

Hospital Creek Massacre Site

Vicky Shukuroglou

A contorted strangling of wire may have once protected an area now barely noticeable to a passer-by. It is situated sixteen kilometres from Brewarrina along Goodooga Road, in a vast expanse of barren land so severely abused an occasional fly or vehicle are the only interruptions to the unnerving quiet sitting heavily on the country. Within the tangle of lines is a broken-down memorial – boomerang-shaped cracked concrete with three rocks standing in its middle. Nearby, a sign informs us that the vague depression equally marred by recent abuse is Hospital Creek.

If we know our history, we know that oral records describe this as the site that bore witness to one of the region's worst massacres, with the slaughter of now unknown numbers of men, women and children. Exactly what happened is contested and details of all those killed seems impossible to know. This is unsurprising given the immense confusion and dispersal of families, with the keeping of full official records not a priority, often for unjust reasons. We know such events were excessively common, but perpetrators were rarely held to account.

Several years prior saw the trial of some of the eleven or so men who carried out what is known as the Myall Creek Massacre. In one foul attack, at least twenty-eight Wirrayaraay people were killed. Again, specifics are now unclear even though it was one of the most comprehensively documented massacres. This was the first time perpetrators were sought out, tried and punished, with seven executed for their crimes. This outcome caused a great deal of conjecture and argument, along with fury at the possibility that colonists could be hung for killing Indigenous people. Massacres continued and the guilty roamed unchecked, while the Governor recognised that his decisions to pursue justice posed great risks to his position.

If we witness this site and our hearts do not break, we are in greater trouble than we realise. A memorial should remind us of what we can learn from the past. Here, a subtle construction merging with the land would be an honourable approach, but what we see is, perhaps, the ultimate Australian memorial for all it encapsulates today.

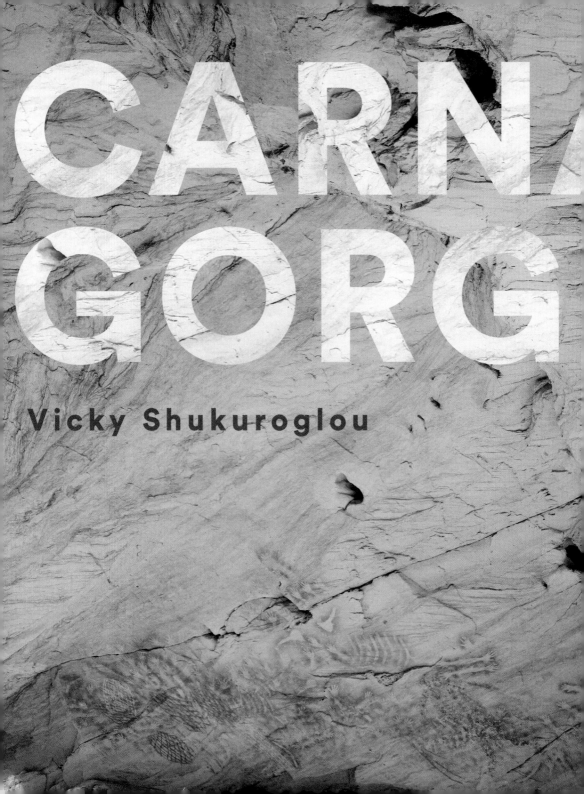

CARNA
GORG

Vicky Shukuroglou

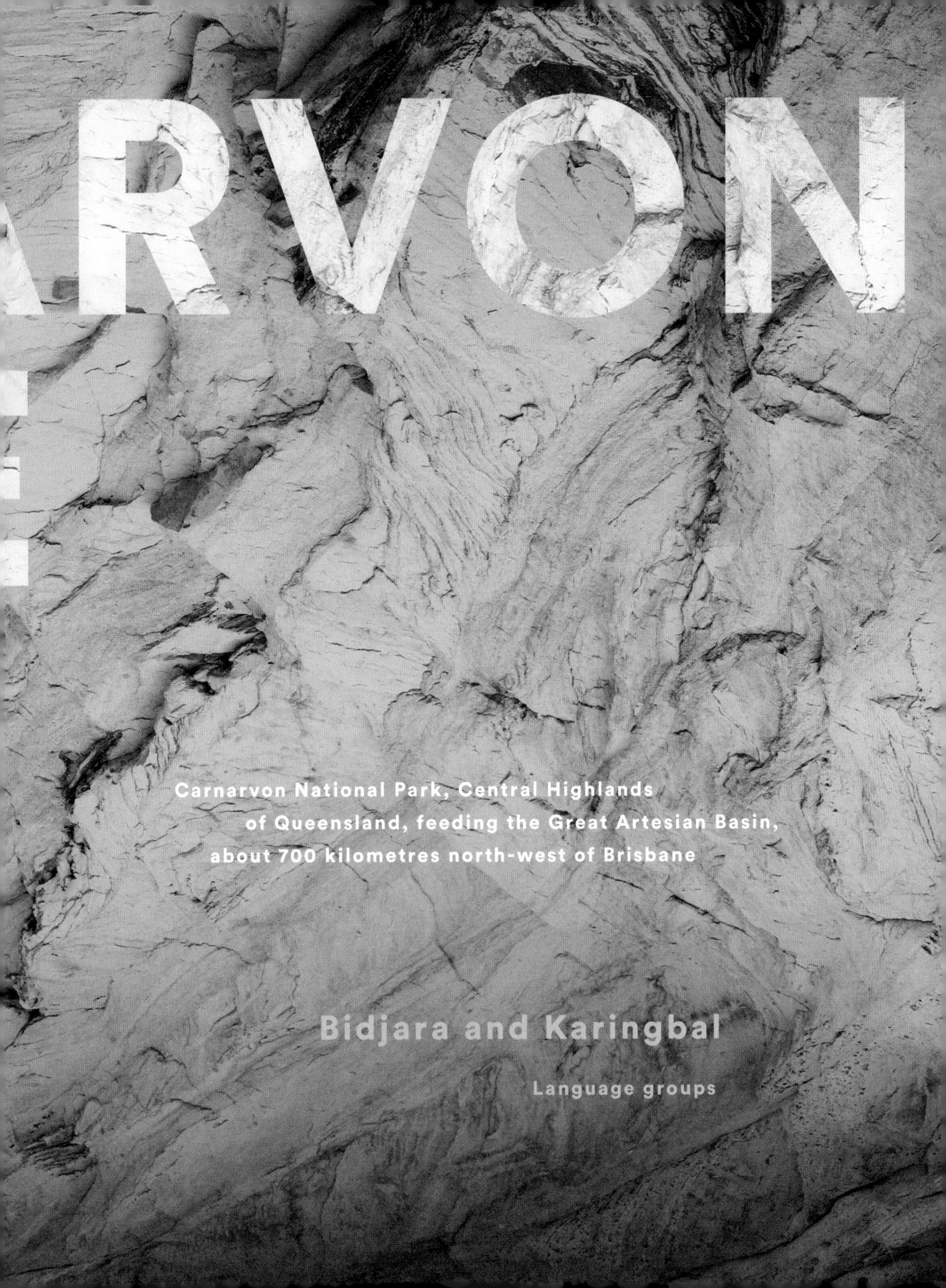

ARVON

Carnarvon National Park, Central Highlands
of Queensland, feeding the Great Artesian Basin,
about 700 kilometres north-west of Brisbane

Bidjara and Karingbal

Language groups

A flash of movement is followed by a red streak. Both disappear by the time our eyes find focus. Finer vegetation gives clues to where this pair of red-backed fairy wrens dance about. Their curiosity is almost as strong as ours. We peer through the tangle, quietly hoping to coax them out of their shyness. Our breathing slows as we marvel at their legs and the brilliance of his racing feathers. Given what we know about these wrens, we wonder if this is a nesting bond or a quick reproductive fling.

Our knowledge falls short of understanding what their high-pitched song is saying. We wonder just how long ago Bidjara and Karingbal women and men first marvelled at these tiny creatures, and how observations developed into language.

Recent studies suggest when a male fairy wren perceives a threat posed by the presence of another, the most effective response is singing a duet with the female rather than duelling with his rival. Careful now, for romance is a different thing for birds. Flowing water among boulders accompanies the song, but as the two birds soon depart we decide to skip across.

If you make your way to Carnarvon Creek you may be tempted to go too quickly. Side tracks are numerous and achievable in a day, but this is a place for softening your breath, calming your stride. Search for stories in the creeks, in curves of well-trodden paths, and the lean of giant ferns. You'll find one in a large, partly submerged rock, close to the beginning of the walking track not far from the visitor centre. Its shape tells a story of the human body, seated, with water flowing on either side, tools being sharpened in smoothed forms reminiscent of the broad cups above a human collarbone. Much of this stone is worn – a lot of tools have been sharpened. As you continue along the path and contemplate those who have walked here before, keep a look out higher in the trees for oozing cuts made by squirrel gliders that land with a slap softened by their fur and impressive flexibility. These cuts release sap – important food for these marsupials and their close relatives such as the much larger yellow-bellied glider. While looking, the Bidjara Elder recalls his younger eyes scanning trees for the dark red marks as he walked with his father and heard stories of these remarkable creatures.

Left and opposite:
Perspectives of
Carnarvon Gorge.

It takes an extremely well-trained ear to identify more than 200 distinct bird calls, and this region provides an excellent tuning ground. Among them is the dramatically swelling night-call of the bush stone curlew. Old stories for this bird tell us something of its character, and of course differ across the country. Many of these stories are said to be related to death, but only through their fullness do we better understand their significance, emphasising transformation and life.

If you haven't heard this curlew call, be prepared for a surprise. Less likely than hearing them is seeing them. Long, slender legs and patterned body, entrancing yellow eyes highlighted by short pale lashes encircled by black somehow make brilliant camouflage in many situations. Before cats and foxes appeared, during hundreds of years of change and adaptation, the curlew's primary worry was raptors, given their eyesight from above easily detects movement. Stillness is invaluable. They compress to the ground, like a snapshot of a stalking kelpie. At times, the curlew walks away with an air of grace and a stealthy gaze. Are they persuading themselves they haven't been seen, or convincing the observer to pretend they haven't noticed?

Yellows punctuate forest greens. Ageing leaves and fruiting bodies catch the sun and glow. Closer to the ground, unblemished growth bursts among blackened stumps and fire-trimmed blades, revealing survivors of the blaze that passed not so long ago. Frond ends, like relaxed fingers of a resting palm, hang gently and play in the breeze, accentuating the wonderfully rounded tops of thirty-metre-straight trunks. This is a luscious forest, a feast for our senses – vibrant, diverse, contrasting.

Left and opposite:
Life of Carnarvon Creek
including a blue-winged
kookaburra – which lives
in northern Australia
and differs to the
laughing kookaburra.

Over 1500 species of flora and fauna live in the area now called Carnarvon National Park. Each species holds equally wonderful quirks of character and roles within ecosystems. Immersion enables every human to better understand. What might you contemplate of stories that can emerge, particularly when people live alongside plants and animals, observe, respect and relate to them in considered ways, generation upon generation? In your contemplation, add oral traditions carrying stories made memorable, personal and relevant, told in languages that are born of, and reflect, this infinite complexity, all held here, on earth, and in relation with stars, moon and sun.

Ethics are embedded in languages, and their formation, interpretation and use reveal much about the heart and mind. *Progress* was born from the Latin marriage of *forward* and *to walk* and is connected to making an advance. On the whole, one way or another, humans walk, have forward movement. Our walk is our choice, whether observant, respectful and responsive, an advance in love, or invasive with a steady march.

The old Bidjara and Karingbal people made decisions about the way of their walk and its imprint on country. You can see those decisions in the rich biodiversity and in sites for gathering, honouring and acknowledging transformative stages of every human, including birth and death. Perhaps for similar reasons, since colonisation, people saw that wealth in this forest was greatest when left standing.

Varying in tread from fine gravel and sand to welcoming stepping stones across water, the main path gently undulates. It branches off several times, leading to areas that, while remaining connected, hold distinct purpose. You can observe how the forest changes, at times it's dramatic, other times barely perceptible, all relative to earth's structure. Grass trees spread and gather in suitable conditions, offering a seasonal feast as flower-covered spikes push skyward. Tall trees take to an area, the canopy thickens, blocking light, changing the environment below. Dark, soft soil, nourished by springs from porous sandstone, meets expanses of hard, flat rock and protruding forms. Bold shapes of cycads' sturdy leaves crisscross with those of fan palms creating their particular sound, dropping shadows that wrap, evocative of giant nets. The creek, whose flow and power over time has sculpted the steep-walled gorge, provides for platypus, turtles, fish, frogs, insects and more.

The forest gives welcome shade along most paths, where you will probably meet people of all age and character, also imbibing the completeness of the forest. If you are in luck, among them will be people who have walked longest on this earth, and you can admire their spirit as they determinedly walk with sticks and linked elbows for support. Right here is a celebration of our shared humanity, a reverence for our earth, a feeling of gratitude for people who have loved this place from the earliest

Below: Treasures of the forest including palm fibre; flowers of a black bootlace orchid, which is endemic to eastern Australia; and flowers of a broad leaved bottletree, also endemic to eastern Australia.

days of their consciousness. In conversation with Bidjara Elders, much like Elders across the nation, we hear and cherish their welcoming words, their desire to share this place and for all of us to feel a deep sense of belonging. They invite you to see, look and listen. In the language of this country, naga yimba.

You'll probably receive suggestions to walk as far as you intend to go and visit side paths on your return, ensuring most ground is covered when the sun is low and your energy is high. Heat can make distances a challenge, so be well prepared with ample water. Remember an early start increases your chance of seeing more animals.

A different approach is at times taken by Elders, based on their observations and learning from their Elders, in turn to be passed on to young ones. They speak of challenges in re-assembling knowledge fractured by forced dislocation of their ancestors from country. This took hold in the 1840s when reports of the area's potential, seen in verdant growth and permanent water, triggered the incursion of pastoralists. At the time, progress meant mounting pressure and widespread violence. Bidjara, Karingbal and surrounding groups upheld fights of resistance, often suffering fatal pursuit. Limited access to their known foods, introduction of diseases, and complexities associated with the importation of opium and alcohol further interrupted and dislodged known ways.

Records reveal attitudes of the day – some express great concern for people's wellbeing and a determination to improve on extremely complicated situations, while others convey perceived superiority and possibilities for exerting control over once-free lives. In their recollections, some Elders around the country ask that we are careful if we speak of the missions as they describe the good old days and genuine care they experienced. Others are still battling with impacts of much harsher experiences.

Line after line, brief words and recently given names in government documents, such as Queensland Aboriginal Removals 1912–1939, provide a window into the past, informing today (we have deleted names for the privacy of individuals and families):

6 Aboriginals from Roma to Taroom
4 children from Fossilbrook to Cape Bedford
N, further re half-caste and her child being taken away by Police
B, immorality with a white man, from Kanuna to a reserve

3 destitute children, from Augustus Downs to Cape Bedford

J, bush lawyer, an educated blackfellow and inveterate schemer and loafer

6 boys from Coen to Taroom

N, Barambah. Asking to go home to his wife and boy

M, will not work, indulges in opium, to Barambah

T, and child, L, to Taroom

Toowoomba, recommend removal of natives from Moonie to Taroom, wandering about

Chillagoe Natives. Local residents consider proposed removal to Mission Station too drastic and quite unnecessary.

Missions and reserves were scattered across the state – from Birdsville in the south-west, north to Mount Isa and Doomadgee, all the way to northern Torres Strait Islands such as Erub, which is closer to Papua New Guinea than the Australian mainland, and southward along the east coast through Laura, Bloomfield River Mission (today's Wujal Wujal community, and not far from Yarrabah), all the way south – including islands such as Stradbroke and Bribie – and beyond Brisbane, with others inland such as Woorabinda and Whitula Station. The scale of the system is startling.

On your walk, an initial visit to the Moss Garden offers a living balm, a sanctuary for the past and preparation for days ahead. As you venture down the path and feel the temperature drop, you'll be welcomed by the hum and sparkle of life thriving on little sun and constant moisture seeping from sandstone. Secluded among rock walls, ferns shimmer and moss sponges spread, slowing drips that hang as though teasing gravity's draw. Water has left its mark over thousands of years of passage, seen in rocks' varying colour and ongoing shaping. As you inhale deeply, water murmurs its journey month after month.

Once you return to the main track and continue deeper into the gorge, listen for a shallow path of water fed by nearby springs. If you choose to gently cup your hands in it, cast your eye across the playful surface and travel to places of meeting, where water hugs around a twig, flow ripples with the curved edge of a leaf, a small stone gently and slowly abrades. Touch your lips, your brow, the back of your neck and, as you feel the cool, think of the hands that have cupped before.

Left and opposite:
Weathered rock faces
with painted and
carved overhangs.

Falling naturally into stride with each other means we share stories more easily and soon hear how a father showed his son sugarbag. Prized across the nation, sugarbag encompasses all things to do with native stingless bees, including their larvae, wax, honey and pollen. These bees live in groups, usually in trees or gaps in rock. Childhood recollections bubble up as we admire the flight of a tiny bee, just one of 2000 or so different bee species belonging to this country. Some are two millimetres long, others more than ten times longer. Some sleep within a gumnut or flower that closes overnight, while certain plants rely on native bees as their primary pollinator. Vibration at a particular frequency causes pollen capsules to burst in many plants, making native bees a vital link in ecosystems. Colours vary from bright yellow to black, white spots and blue bands, made visible as light interacts with the finest of patterned hairs.

Find the tiniest pool of water and you might observe at least one kind of native bee coming in for refreshment. Our eyes try to follow the small, dark body, its wings an impossible blur. Its presence animates the story of father and son seeking sugarbag. Carefully avoiding harm to a bee, they would dust it white, making it easier

Expanses of ancient stories at Cathedral Cave and the Art Gallery.

to follow back to its nest. Once found, a finger or stick might twirl in the entrance. Sometimes a small tree or branch is cut, sometimes the hole where bees come and go is enlarged. Taking sugarbag is a disruption, nests are damaged, and so caution and respect instilled long ago ensure ongoing cycles.

One thousand kilometres north-west, in meandering conversation, a senior knowledge holder wants to share an ancient story. With typical flair and sing-song voice, he describes epic travels of a man and son. Across vast country they left their formative mark, bringing life and knowledge connected to distant places. In their travels, they too sought out little bees. This story speaks of precious white clay and its qualities as a very fine powder, and sugarbag as important nourishment for people and country. The story gives guidance for vitality and preservation, for humility and conservative interaction. In its sharing, it reveals the magic of the storyteller, bound to countless generations of performative traditions for retention, adaptation, use and transmission.

Striking carvings declare the presence of young women. Spanning countless generations, the forms speak of a wealth of human consciousness, fertility and learning, cautioning men in their approach. An elliptical depression is embraced and accentuated by a ridge that expands around the central shape, rising from engraving. There is a beautiful flowing interplay here.

You will have entered through a passage of rock surrounded by forest with rich understorey, along the curve of a hill. This leads to the massive wall, variably leaning, its inclination protecting the memories it holds. The scene resonates with the forest's complexity; textures mingle and shadows play with layered colours, forms endlessly touching and crossing. Infinite relationships and timeframes are bold in their presence but beyond our full comprehension. Sprayed outlines of splayed hands, here known as murra, dance across metres of pale rock, dispersing higher and further than we can see. Some end at the wrist, others include part of the forearm, and a few are two forearms seamlessly joined at the base and extending outward to murra with fingertips spread, like the wingspan of a high-soaring eagle.

Information along the boardwalk tells us that this image, when intersecting at right angles with a similar one, signifies neighbouring tribes from north, south, east and west. The expanse of murra, knowing hands of young and old, predominantly in shades of red ochre with occasions of golden yellow and white, are interlaced with images including various wangal, burrgu, barroo and lil lil (boomerang, shield, stone axe and wooden club). Nets are also depicted here, giving some clues to their prominence in a complex society. The Bidjara and Karingbal people, known for their strong nets many metres long, used them in the hunt for large animals. Nets were also part of complex processes associated with death and burial. Some are painted as solid forms created with a brush that's long decomposed, while others are made using the same technique as the murra, where objects are held to the rock and over-sprayed, coming to life in the space they delineate.

An engraved line curves along metres of rock, affirming the significance of Mundagurra, one of the great beings responsible for shaping the area when earth was still soft. Recurring animal feet – predominantly emu – are portrayed in pigment and engraving, at times clearly in pairs. As often seen in other places hundreds of kilometres from here, eggs of this important animal are gatherings of circular forms. Search among these, the hands, tools and carved ellipses, and you'll find an occasional human foot, a goanna and other images. They are deftly made, giving impressive clarity. The porosity and protection of the rock wall, and the bonding of pigment when prepared to ancient recipes, mean they remain vibrant over thousands of years. Across the country, ochres held diverse significance and use, and as pigments for painting on rock were variably mixed with water, fat, saliva, honey, plant extracts and blood.

Temptation to approach and peer at each richly coloured grain may be strong, but boardwalks are there for good reason. Damage is easily done, often without realising, as the finest of dust particles kicked up by the most careful feet can affect paintings. If you have the opportunity to visit this area now known as the Art Gallery, you will see sections of rock have been made smooth by repetitive human touch – when people sought to connect with what they saw and in doing so caused its deterioration. You too will likely feel bewildered and outraged when you see marks recently scratched into the wall, many cutting through vibrant colour – typical signs alerting us that we all have a long way to go.

The track continuing along the river is more lightly trodden and recommended for another full day. You will have walked around five kilometres by the time you arrive at the Art Gallery, along the way seeing signs for the Amphitheatre and Ward's Canyon. Depending on the day and the walkers, it is possible to visit these on the way back if

Stone tools and grinding dish.

your time here is limited. Ward's Canyon is now named after brothers who used the area in the early 1900s in their hunt for animal furs. Possums, kangaroos and koalas were the main victims of the international trade and many of their fresh skins were stored here, as the cool environment provided ideal conditions. In stark contrast, many years prior, this narrow gorge was known for its significance as a birthing place for innumerable generations. As you make your way up the hill and revel in the gentle water and luscious growth, the intensity of algae, moss and liverworts in gleaming greens and reds, perhaps contemplate the pregnant women who also walked here, preparing themselves and their babies. Giant ferns also rely on this water to feed their growth, with impressive fronds growing up to nine metres long.

Soon after you return to the main track and continue towards the visitor centre, you'll see a path to the Amphitheatre. As described by some Elders, this too is a place of great ceremony, specifically for the preparation of those who have died and their appropriate interment. Some speak of its dramatic formation, which initially appears to be a slit in the rock, as a portal to the spirit world. They say it is also a particularly significant site for men.

If you do follow the track beyond the Art Gallery, winding through forests and across water, you'll find another breathtaking gathering now commonly known as

Above: Striking sandstone shows stories of travel across vast distances with the repeated stencils of che-ka-ra.

Right: Series of wangal (boomerang) among other tools and murra (hands).

Cathedral Cave. This is approximately nine kilometres from the visitor centre, four kilometres further than the Art Gallery. Here, among diverse images comparable to the Art Gallery, exists a different emphasis and expansion of cultural stories. Earth holds remains of human activity going back thousands of years, and here this includes discarded parts of macrozamia nuts, quite possibly from the very plants you walked past. This cycad provides excellent nutrition with correct preparation, without which it is lethal. The creek you have walked along has leached toxins from many kernels, providing excellent nutrition for groups that gathered here.

Evidence of trade networks across the country are seen with repeatedly stencilled che-ka-ra. Images of these oval baler-shell pendants are so carefully made that some show the hole at one end through which a length of string was looped, while others show a short section of this string as a small tail at the end of the oval shape. These che-ka-ra arrived here via routes maintained by, among many other actions, dancing, singing and negotiating in multiple languages. These routes were preservations of cultural identity involving exchanges of innumerable valuables, both tangible and intangible, transforming as cultures continually adapt to change.

It is said that these che-ka-ra originated from coastal Cape York, around Ngulun, or the area around the west side of the Cape. Early written records mention the involvement of many groups including the Karundi/Kotanda, Mitakoodi, Wunumara and Yirandali. That's over 1000 kilometres as the crow flies, and no readily available evidence suggests birds were used in such ways. So, consider navigating the terrain across this expanse of country, with its plains, hills and escarpments, and the powerful capacities required. Some such shells may have continued along the paths, increasing in value with use, with a similar ethos to the treasured pearl shells imbued with rich custom and similarly traded from many communities of the northern coast to southern groups.

We learn that pulsing series of wangal (boomerang) are part of revitalisation or increase rituals, where replenishment of energy in various forms is nurtured. We also see the figure of an unwelcome spirit locally known as Yakajah.

The beauty and clarity leave us wondering about the details of how they were made. Images surround narrow openings in the rock wall, similar to those you may notice in surrounding cliffs. Earlier in conversation, around the time of the oozing trees, the Elder wanted to convey the particular significance of these rock hollows in rituals associated with death. He explained how this region holds many such crevices and gaps, how loved ones were honoured. Bones and objects were, in the past, stolen for various collections, research and profit, and today across the country many are being respectfully returned to where they belong. Communities are now receiving or preparing to receive their ancestors and are continually developing ways to contend with this new reality. Signs at Cathedral Cave explain further:

> In our culture when a person passes away their spirit must be returned back to country. Complex rituals prepared a person for burial. In certain situations an elaborately made burial cylinder would be crafted from the bark of the budgeroo tree. Important items such as a necklace, plant material or a net were placed inside. The cylinder would be bound with marsupial skins and fastened with string made from plant fibre. Often the cylinder was decorated with ochre designs. After a time the burial cylinder was placed within the caves and tunnels that naturally occur in these ancient sandstone walls.

In this great complexity, we could miss the image of a firearm high on the wall. It is unclear how and when it was acquired by the people who used it as a stencil. It may have been through trade or direct violence that was relatively commonplace during the years Bidjara and Karingbal homes were invaded. Across Australia invasions by new arrivals were usually with weapons against which the locals had very little defence. The stresses on the people are unfathomable for most of us in this country who have not personally lived through war on our homeland. During these desperate times, attacks on the recent arrivals also took place in concerted attempts to drive them away. Suspicion and fear gripped many. While some negotiated friendly relations, offered food and various tools or objects as they understood the loss of plants and animals, and put their own welfare at risk by standing against the discrimination they saw, various acts of violence, including the abduction and rape of women, the poisoning of families, and the deprivation of people's nourishment and basic freedoms, were horrific realities.

Punishment – often corporal, at times including death – is part of maintaining social structures strictly established by Indigenous groups over countless generations and is discussed by Elders across the country. A great deal of cultural complexity describes how, when warranted, the offenders are not the only ones to bear the consequences, as certain familial obligations dictate. Strict rules, supported by elaborate protocols for entry, lessened invasions into another group's area or the inappropriate taking of resources. These protocols included welcoming ceremonies, where a key focus was carefully understanding and honouring how people related to one another, which delineated responsibilities and behaviours. Incursions by the new arrivals had no bounds, and consequences included immense distrust and long-running acts of retribution by all.

It is said that in establishing a new pastoral lease 10,000 sheep were brought to Gayiri country, just a little further north of here. It was the early 1860s and such activity applied greater pressure on already tense situations. The sheep were accompanied by a small number of families employed by the pastoralist, whose demeanour established relations with the Indigenous people they met. All seemed to be going well, but the new arrivals were perhaps unaware of various previous brutalities and associated responses. Tragically, the dominant story says that this led to the massacre of nineteen of the people travelling to establish new lives. This was the biggest massacre of colonists and, typically, led to the massacre of Indigenous people. The numbers of those killed are unknown but through records it is estimated to be in the hundreds. A sign was installed in memory of the pastoralists stating:

This is the site of the massacre of 19 people by a local aboriginal tribe on 17 October 1861. The people killed were in a party led by Horatio Wills and were resting in the early afternoon when the tribe moved into the camp and killed the ten men, two women and seven children.

We know there is more to this story.

Many fans of cricket and Australian football would be familiar with the name Tom Wills, as he was instrumental in the creation of the latter sport. Evidence points to a game played by Indigenous groups of western Victoria – and likely others – as the primary influence. During the late 1800s, James Dawson recorded the game being played by two teams. The ball was made of possum skin and filled with pounded charcoal, making it solid but light. Hand passes and kicks were used to maintain possession of the ball. Similar records describe games played by Indigenous groups across the country, often demanding physical and mental prowess, involving stalking, acute observations, deft hand movements, performance, manufacture of balanced objects and more.

As a child, Tom grew up with the Djab Wurrung people of western Victoria, played their games, spoke the language, understood their humour and experienced how that country was regarded by its people in their every day. His demeanour and relationships also enabled him to coach a successful cricket team whose players were Indigenous men from western Victoria – reportedly from Jardwadjali, Gunditjmara and Wotjobaluk groups. Among many other events, they played a Boxing Day game in 1866 and in 1868 toured England, though twists and turns of events meant that Tom was unable to join them. They were the first Australian team to make such a trip. This story and all its connections develop greater depth when we understand that this happened just a few years after Tom's father, Horatio Wills, was killed in that massacre not far from here. At the time, Tom did not participate in the retributive excess.

As you walk through the gorge and think of the Elders who speak of their desire for everyone to feel a deep sense of belonging, remember that they also say no matter where you come from or who you are, you are connected to this country. As we contemplate stories of lives lived long ago, whose presence is dynamic today, how do we feel in our belonging? The origin of the word belonging is said to come from *properly relating to, being suited to*.

A black and white photo shows a truck well loaded. Bulges form from ropes pressing the mound, tied down for transit, giving clues to the fabric of the goods. A dog stands on top, two men lean on the side. These are the skins of koalas. In the late 1920s the hunting season was once again opened by the Queensland government, citing the need for jobs as a primary concern. In that time 600,000 koalas were killed and skinned for coats, hats and gloves. The activity was brutal and descriptions are horrific – animals suffered extensively, young were orphaned and, reputedly, some were skinned alive.

How do we reconcile these stories held here, within this country so long contemplated by Bidjara, Karingbal and other people, in one small area of our earth? What can our travels tell us of our belonging, and connections to similar stories seen in handprints of people living thousands of years ago in today's Egypt, Argentina and beyond, so strikingly similar to those we see here among the sacred crevices of the ancient gorge?

Top: Vegetation well adapted to crevices and impressive rises.

Bottom: Detail of rock surface and paintings at Cathedral Cave.

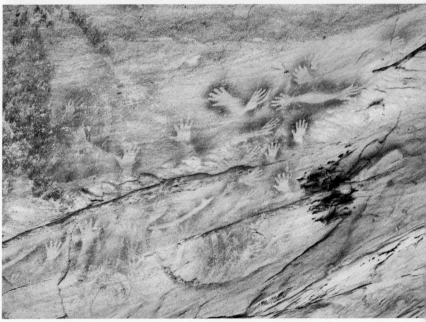

Carnarvon Gorge

Important information

Love where you walk. Please stay on the designated tracks, respect signs asking you not to enter, and remain behind barriers installed for good reason. You are asked not to swim anywhere except for the Rock Pool, accessed before the main carpark. If you decide to swim here, remember whatever you apply to your skin will end up in the water where many creatures live.

Water from creeks needs to be properly treated for drinking. As with anywhere you go, be sure you carry more water than you think you will need and wear appropriate clothing to protect yourself from the elements.

Always walk within your capacity, which only you can know. It's wise to carry a torch, just in case. Many areas here do not have phone reception.

Keep a look out for snakes, and please let them be.

Be sure you have enough fuel if you are driving and enough supplies, as services are limited.

Indigenous cultural experiences, tours and relevant organisations

South West Queensland Indigenous Cultural Trail

If you approach Carnarvon National Park from the south or south-west, take your time to explore the South West Queensland Indigenous Cultural Trail, a journey through seven communities. You can begin from Dirranbandi in the south, heading north through St George and Surat to Roma, then west to Mitchell and Charleville, and south to Cunnamulla, before heading back to St George. You will learn about scar trees, old Aboriginal camps and reserves, language and tools, birthing trees and more. Visit the website for more about the communities and the trail, as well as a trail map.

swqict.com

Other things to see and do

Carnarvon National Park Visitor Centre

The visitor centre is excellent. Before you go walking, check the board here as important details are changed daily. Rangers are sometimes available but are often elsewhere, on country. If you're lucky enough to cross paths with a ranger, take the opportunity to have a conversation, for they are knowledgeable and willing, and some are Bidjara and Karingbal people. For more information about Carnarvon Gorge, Carnarvon National Park and options for accommodation, search the Queensland National Parks website. The same site also provides information, maps, updates and more, for all parts of Carnarvon National Park, Ka Ka Mundi, Nuga Nuga, Mount Moffatt and Salvator Rosa.

parks.des.qld.gov.au/parks/carnarvon-gorge

Boolimba Bluff track

A short distance off the main track from the visitor centre, this walk takes you through diverse ecosystems. Slopes patterned with cycads lead to towering angles of sandstone cliffs. Lichen-covered rocks hugged by figs and clasped by giant eucalypts accompany your path, which becomes a steep series of ladders and 300 steps, with open, grassy forests high above the creek. Signs tell of the shaping of the earth and waters that once were here, evident as ripples in the rock. A different appreciation of the country is gained here, and has surely been useful over thousands of years.

Cathedral Cave, Boowinda Gorge and Big Bend tracks

If you would like a longer walk, choose these tracks. Around 20km, they offer spectacular colours, changes of vegetation, peace and tranquillity. You are asked to remember that this is sacred country.

Baloon Cave

This is a significant site that closed to the public due to devastating fire in late 2018, involving controversial boardwalk structures. It is being cared for, although damage is too extensive for restoration. Please check Queensland National Parks' website for the latest information.

Mickey Creek Gorge

You can reach this gorge from a carpark close to the Rock Pool. A marked track dwindles, leaving you to your own devices. Be conscious of where you are, and respect that some places need their peace.

Carnarvon Great Walk

Nearly 90km, this epic walk requires solid preparation and links the Carnarvon Gorge and Mount Moffatt sections of the national park.

parks.des.qld.gov.au/parks/carnarvon-great-walk/about

MARR

Bruce Pascoe

At the junction of the Oodnadatta
and Birdsville tracks in the
north-eastern South Australian outback

Antikarinya, Arabunna,
Dieri and Pitjantjatjara

Language groups

Marree is not sleepy but it is quiet. After two days you might forget to look right, look left and look right again. Traffic is not one of Marree's problems. It is a beautiful town, with wide streets, old timber buildings, a big sky and galahs and corellas to shriek across it. It has the sound of small outback towns; the dogs are individuals, the birds argumentative.

But like Roeburne near the Burrup Peninsula in Western Australia, the quietness of humans is deceptive. In Roebourne every building is given over to art, and in Marree history broods under every awning. The quiet tick tack of a keyboard at the Arabunna Centre is potent with intent. Slow down, listen, take time to look at the photos, the stories, this is Australia trying to talk to you.

To Marree's north the lake that Australians decided to name Eyre after the lost explorer is in difficult terrain. Difficult, but not impossible. It is dry, flat country between Oodnadatta, to its north, and Marree. Charles Sturt in an earlier exploration than Eyre's was met just to the east by 400 Aboriginal people who fed him roast duck and cake and loaned him a new house in their town. It wasn't desert or the Dead Heart for them, they were prospering.

Sturt was surprised by their lifestyle and full of a grudging admiration. I wonder if it was a confusing moment for Sturt knowing that his brother, only a few days behind, was pegging out the land of his 'discovery'. Here is the passage from Sturt's 1849 *Narrative of an Expedition into Central Australia* where he describes his surprise:

Several of them brought us large troughs of water, and when we had taken a little, held them up for our horses to drink; an instance of nerve that is very remarkable, for I am quite sure that no white man (having never seen or heard of a horse before, and with the natural apprehension the first sight of such an animal would create) would deliberately have walked up to what must have appeared to them most formidable brutes, and placing the troughs they carried against their breast allowed the horses to drink, with their noses almost touching them. They likewise offered us some roasted ducks and some cake.

The reference to roast duck and cake in what Australians see as harsh country is striking, as is Sturt's later revelation that the cakes were the lightest and sweetest he had ever tasted. But think, also, about the relationship between horses and Aboriginals. The horse recognised the black man as a man from whom it could receive kind help; black people recognised the horse as a fellow being who needed help. Such a pity that so many Europeans didn't have the sagacity of the horse, a recognition of human to human.

Most important is the knowledge that high-quality produce was being harvested in an area we now write off as desert. There is much to learn about our country's productive capacity when working in sympathy with the land.

It would be fascinating to know what was going through Christian minds at that point of revelation. So much of history has speculation and assumption as part of the scholarship. Looking at the two-storey facades of the structures built by the First Nation Canadian people, it is a shock to read the word 'savages' applied to them by the British Christians.

How could you stand before these wonderful structures with the whole spiritual cosmology carved into the columns and call these people barbarians? Because they didn't know a man called Christ who was born a mere 2000 years ago?

Sturt, in the face of a more discreet but nevertheless successful civilisation, was in momentary awe. He was trying to cross Australia from south to north. There was a feverish belief that the Australian rivers falling westward must devolve into an inland sea, creating a cornucopia in the centre of the continent.

Instead he was halted by ridge after ridge of sand dunes. Almost blind with scurvy, and with the horses and other men in the party weakened to the point of death, he was saved by the prosperous Aborigines.

After Sturt, Edward Eyre also tried to cross the centre of Australia but ran into salty mud in the area that would later hold his name. He turned back to cross to

Albany in the west instead. That was called a triumph because no one had ever done it before. No white one.

The British gentlemen were appalled by the extreme conditions of the region but the Aboriginal inhabitants were sowing, harvesting and processing local food plants, building appropriate housing, consolidating townships and enjoying their country. Archaeological work on villages in this area indicate some houses were built sharing exterior walls with neighbours. This work is preliminary but one estimate is that at least one village had around thirty buildings attached to each other with a potential population of eighty to a hundred. Other sites appear to be smaller and with mostly unattached buildings. These are new investigations and hold great promise of extending our understanding of the society.

Eyre, however, thought the country uninhabitable, but Sturt and his brother had a more optimistic outlook. Unfortunately, in the 1840s, when Europeans first began farming the region, the country experienced one of its best series of seasons. Grass grew, sheep flourished and innocent but unreal expectations were developed. The decade of drought that followed destroyed these empires and soon lavish houses and expensive sheds and infrastructure were abandoned to the sand. Sturt's experiences are vivid in his journals and I have quoted at length from them in *Dark Emu* as his observation is crucial.

Later European incursions into this country were more realistic but still exploitative and reliant on the saltbush for animal fodder. Denudation of the soil soon followed and, as elsewhere in Australia, erosion and depletion of fertility resulted. It is shocking to drive through these regions where Sturt and others described such rich grasslands and see that they are now all gone. The hard-hoofed animals ate out the herbage but also compacted the soil, and today you wonder that such productive land is almost bare and has been removed from Aboriginal care – the local Aboriginal culture eradicated for the sake of a handful of families and a few thousand bullocks. This is not the time to point fingers and direct blame but to instead imagine the country how it once was and see if we can adjust grazing patterns to allow the ground cover to return – or farm kangaroos and emus.

Aboriginal people also had livestock in the region. European entrants after Sturt witnessed local people corralling and harvesting young pelicans. There were fish and bird traps throughout the region. The harsh country had other animals on

Echidnas' unique combination of adaptations – including being monotremes (egg-laying mammals) – enable them to survive in a wide range of habitats across Australia.

which the Arabunna, Dieri, Pitjantjatjara and Antikarinya could depend, but in general terms, like most other Australian Aboriginal people, theirs was a diet rich in vegetables and fruits.

Quandong of one type or another was found across this part of Australia. The beautiful fruit was eaten fresh but could also be rendered into a thick paste, the modern equivalent of today's fashionable fig paste or the school lunchbox standby, the fruit strap.

The people lived well but nothing in their understanding of the universe had prepared them for an invasion of people with no more respect for the land than for its short-term yield. Extraction and exploitation was the mantra of peoples who left their own countries to plunder that of others. Aboriginal lore was strictly conservative whereas the capitalistic Europeans were resource radicals and exploited the mineral wealth of Central Australia. The Broken Hill mountain of minerals 700 kilometres south-east of Marree is a legend in the annals of mining billions, and Roxby Downs uranium mine, less than 200 kilometres south-west of Marree, is not far behind.

The mining operation is built on quick returns for the company and maximum input from the government and the Australian people. The system of mining is simplistic and relies on the extraction of minerals by using massive amounts of water – free water extracted from the Great Artesian Basin, water that belongs to the country, water that makes any kind of human activity possible. The Great Artesian Basin has been reduced to such a low level that many mound springs no longer reach the surface. Even then the contaminated outfall from the mine seeps back into the Artesian Basin, spoiling it forever for all Australians.

Aboriginal life and prosperity in the area have depended for millennia on this water reaching the surface, not to mention as have the budgerigars, galahs, bustards, raptors and the almost extinct night parrot. Feral animals trample the mosses and plants of the springs further robbing the region of its prosperity.

On page 106 of Reg Dodd and Malcolm McKinnon's *Talking Sideways*, they indicate that:

The terms of the South Australian government's *Roxby Downs (Indenture Ratification) Act* (1982) give the proprietor of the Olympic Dam mine special exemptions from the provisions of various regulatory mechanisms that control and restrain similar endeavours elsewhere. This includes legal authority to overrule the South Australian *Aboriginal Heritage Act* (1988), the *Environment Protection Act* (1993), the *Natural Resources Management Act* (2004) and the *Freedom of Information Act* (1991).

All of those actions hampered the ability of Aboriginal people to intercede with the proposal.

Reg Dodd, an Arabunna Elder, is a survivor of the protests but only just. Reg was born at Finniss Springs Mission Station in 1940. By the age of thirteen he was working as a stockman on Anna Creek Station. He joined the railways in 1960 and left in 1986 before working for various government departments including the Department of Planning and Aboriginal Heritage as a field officer. When funding ran out for this position, Reg established the Marree Arabunna People's Committee and began taking visitors on tours of the region.

The journey of this employment gave Reg a distinctive experience of white bureaucracy and capitalism and its various manoeuvres of self-interest. So when the big miners entered his country he was as prepared as it was possible to be. But the mine's methods of rewarding one group over another was so effective that violence broke out and Dodd was lucky to escape it.

He now conducts his tours from the Marree Arabunna Centre. On a visit to the desert and Kati Thanda–Lake Eyre I made with Reg over a decade ago, we saw many wonders in the lakes and springs, but the most potent of them all was a tiny rock spring that the old people covered with a series of overlapping slabs of rock like the lens of a camera. The descendants of the old people still do it. The water and the reverence held by past and present people for this little jewel is an inspiration of care.

Reg's tour takes in a tour of Kati Thanda–Lake Eyre where participants sleep in swags under the stars and listen to stories of the cruel colonial past but also the resilience of local people and the determination to keep looking after country. Some of the stories talk about the hardships early Europeans endured, partly as a result of not understanding the nature of the country they had entered, and the important role Aboriginal people played in caring for and sustaining land.

This tour begins with a welcome to country but stresses that there is another kind of land use that has been wrought over the last 120,000 years. One major difference

Above: Bladder saltbush.

Right: Common names for these plants include (top) curious saltbush or hard-head bassia; (middle) sago bush, also known as shrubby bluebush; and (bottom) silver emu-bush.

between that old care and today's profligacy is water and its hugely important role on country, not as a resource for profit but as a sustainer of life – animal, plant and human. Reg talks of the boom and bust approach of European land management and its antithesis in Aboriginal care of Mother Earth.

This is a fragile place but it is still vivid with life when it can escape from the predation of mining and grazing. An old story tells of the carpet that once covered the desert – flocks of budgerigars so dense that it seemed you could walk across them. Such flocks are gone now, not because the water has entirely disappeared, although uranium tailings from the mine might be helping. No, they are dwindling because their food has gone. The grasses have disappeared. Australia needs to re-examine how we use these lands, much of it leased from the Commonwealth. Are our current methods the most efficient or ecologically sustainable? Might a more vibrant tourism industry based on the return of wildlife produce as much wealth and provide more care for our fragile land?

This is not a 'bad miners, good Aborigines' argument but rather all about sustainable land use.

You might be lucky to visit Goyder Lagoon, almost 400 kilometres north of Marree along the Birdsville Track, in a good season and see the inland dotterel among a host of other birds. A small population of yellow chats exists here and seeing them on the drier plains surrounding the lagoon thrills and disturbs at the same time. The entire system and this tiny creature are threatened by our excess exploitation of upstream water and the trampling by hard-hoofed animals, both feral and farmed.

The budgerigars described so potently in the old people's story are grain eaters and the traffic and voracious hunger of cattle, sheep, goats, camels, horses and pigs have eliminated the old grain fields that the people nurtured, while the hooves of the destroyers have compacted the soil into a hard, impervious pan. Destruction wrought by Europeans cannot be overestimated but it is not irreversible because the earth is a great engine and she wants to heal herself. All we have to do is allow it.

And we will need those grains too. Not just for the return of the magical budgerigar carpet but, in a drying continent, we need food that can grow in dry areas. How we choose to harvest that food and who we allow to harvest it creates an array of other problems but these are not insoluble. All are within our ken; sharing and care, it is not rocket science. Perhaps this conflict of interests also opens up an opportunity to imagine the world that Sturt, Mitchell and Ashwin saw but one re-established under more gentle and profitable management.

The genuine enthusiasm many Australians have for Aboriginal history and culture must be harnessed into something greater than a bubble of warm, cosy air. Many things need to be addressed. Let's start with the number of people on the planet. There are too many of us. We cannot all survive here with a western standard of living. Either we allow a world where only some can eat, get healthcare and receive an education or we look at an entirely different model of utilising resources. The current model should be anathema to all world religions and governments but both have revealed that they are satisfied with this imbalance.

Do not think this is an argument for communism – environmental destruction in the displacement of Indigenous peoples is as common to the communist world as any other social system. No, this is a call to take care of the only globe we have.

Despite the enthusiasm mentioned above, contempt and apathy for Aboriginal culture are a modern part of Australian life. At some stage someone thought it was a good idea to grade a giant sculpture of a clichéd Aboriginal man into the land close to Marree. It became part of district folklore and tourism operators conducted scenic flights to admire this figure that had nothing to do with Arabunna culture. In 2016 tourism operators, alarmed at the gradual disappearance of the shape, had it re-inscribed on the landscape but neither then, nor on the original occasion, were the Arabunna and Dieri properly and sincerely consulted. Just one of many occasions where little or no respect is paid to the Aboriginal custodians or their culture.

Things need to change or we will never see carpets of budgerigars again – they will go the way of the other beasts we have slaughtered, not by our sword but by our greed. The auk, dodo and thylacine have gone this way in the past and the polar bear, panda and bilby are likely to go the same way in the near future. But we can act to avert this fate if we choose. Tourism isn't necessarily a holiday; the best tourism is tourism that is undertaken with responsibility.

Indigenous cultural experiences, tours and relevant organisations

Marree Arabunna Centre

Home to Marree Arabunna Peoples Committee, it also features a small Aboriginal Heritage Museum.

Railway Tce
08 8675 8351

Arabunna Tours

Take a tour with Elder Reg Dodd to explore and learn about local Aboriginal culture, tradition, sacred sites and rock arts.

arabunnatours.com.au

Wabma Kadarbu Mound Springs

Two natural artesian springs – Thirrka (Blanch Cup) and Pirdali-nha (The Bubbler) – have created a wetland in the middle of the desert, attracting great flocks of both birds and tourists. Nearby Wabma Kadarbu (or Mt Hamilton) is an extinct spring central to an Arabunna creation story.

On the Oodnadatta Track, 125km west of Marree
08 8648 5328.

Other things to see and do

Marree Visitor Information

marree.com.au

Kati Thanda–Lake Eyre National Park

See the stunning Lake Eyre, the country's largest salt lake. It is dry most of the time, having filled to capacity only three times in the past 160 years. If you see it after rain or flood waters have arrived, you'll find an incredible range of birdlife.

parks.sa.gov.au/find-a-park/
Browse_by_region/flinders-
ranges-outback/kati-thanda-
lake-eyre-national-park

Further reading

For more on the destruction caused by mining in the area and the divisive protests that so distressed the communities, read Reg Dodd and Malcolm McKinnon's *Talking Sideways: Stories and Conversations from Finniss Springs*, UQP, Brisbane, 2019.

Marree

Below: Hawk moth caterpillar and Burton's legless lizard, whose colours are remarkably variable.

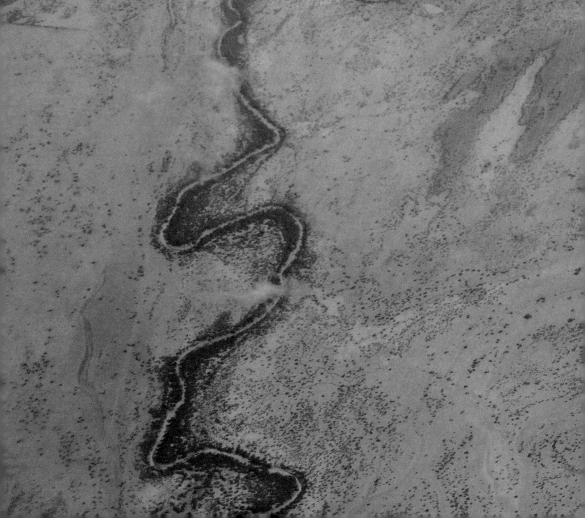

MPAR

Vicky Shukuroglou

NTWE
(ALICE SPRINGS)

In the heart of Australia, roughly
1500 kilometres south of Darwin

Arrernte

Language group

We can feel the flow of a river, even when its bed is dry. Broad and sandy and patterned with trees. The town's gullet. Life force. Since the beginning, its coarse sides pressed up against giant caterpillars. Now, in parts, a highway lies between them. The caterpillars journeyed from afar, creating and naming as they went. They danced and camped, metamorphosed and laid their eggs. Here in the glowing heart of this ancient continent their great forms burst above the surrounding country, their spines often stretching out as though pointing to the rising and setting sun.

The Arrernte people have long cared for this land of subtlety and dynamic scale, where the smallest of creatures is held in the highest regard and remains firmly connected to the vast skies and far-reaching ridges.

As you enter Mparntwe, or Alice Springs, from any direction, you will be welcomed by the meandering limbs of river red gums. If you travel along the Stuart Highway from the south you will pass through Ntaripe, now also known as Heavitree Gap. Arrernte people have always said this is a place of great significance, and a men's site. The women understand those stories, the protocols and their purpose; in the same way, the men honour the women's sites. Today, for the sake of the country and all of us, the Elders have worked hard in response to significant changes and with grace and forgiveness have shifted certain cultural expectations. And so we travel through, but how many of us know? This reshaping of cultural life has been necessary as the town's infrastructure creeps ever outwards, often without fair agreement, and the land, its people, and their intergenerational stories feel the pressure. Is it coincidence that this town was established in an area of such concentrated cultural significance?

The river is Lhere Mparntwe (also known as the Todd River). Follow alongside and your eyes will feast on the patterned bark of old trees and striking shapes of limbs entwined. If you can, walk. Go slowly, look closely, and you'll see the homes and hatcheries of various insects as they bulge and burst through the cells of leaves or clasp to the surface of a great trunk. Soft testaments to the wonders of evolution. Galahs gather and trundle about feeding on seeds and other morsels, the sun

gleaming an orange hue into the pink of their breast and underwings. The many other birds of the area, from tiny wrens and finches to bowerbirds and great raptors, can also be seen if you watch a while. Keep a look out for ayepe (tar vine). You might be fortunate to find the ayepe-arenye caterpillar, as this tar vine is the primary food for the white-lined hawk moth during this stage of its development.

The Ayepe-arenye, the caterpillar that belongs to the tar vine, is one of the most significant caterpillars in Arrernte 'epics', which embed the knowledge necessary to care for this country and each other. As with many places, plants, animals (including humans) and particular concepts, their close ties and individual characteristics are acknowledged in their naming. These indicate complex and layered understandings of biological systems coupled with spiritual awareness, and the impossibility of separating the two. Today it is increasingly hard to find this colourful and brilliantly patterned caterpillar, as its habitat has dramatically altered in recent years. As well as the encroachment of buildings and roads, bright lights and invasive weeds, fire regimes no longer in keeping with ancient knowledge compound the issue. Additionally, young caterpillars prefer the soft tips of new leaves, and these are the first to be grazed by much larger mouths. This is a signifier of many issues, which call on all of us to resolve.

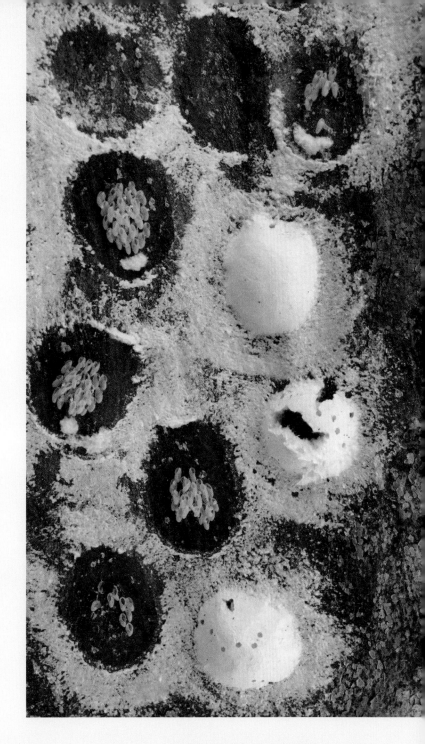

Opposite: View from a track that follows the river, south of the old Telegraph Station.

Right: Soft testaments to the wonders of evolution.

Opposite (left): Looking toward Ntaripe (Heavitree Gap) from Untyeyetwelye (Anzac Hill).

Right and opposite (right): Part of the caterpillar story along Barrett Drive.

Arrernte people's knowledge of country relates to the movements and interactions of Ayepe-arenye, Ntyarlkarle Tyaneme, Utnerrengatye and Irkngeltye, the main caterpillars of the area, which created the sites throughout this region and set out protocols for a harmonious life. These caterpillars travelled from afar, fought great battles with other beings, including Irlperenye (green beetle), and converged here. The kangaroo, emu and dog are among other prominent story holders.

If you proceed along the east side of the river, you will see buildings and infrastructure in stark contrast to those old trees and the life they support. Grand hotels, a golf course and a casino are surrounded by iridescent lawns and partly shaded by palms and other exotic species. Just beyond this cluster, you will come across a pale-coloured rocky rise that quietly stretches to the east, indicating a traverse of the river. Ntyarlkarle Tyaneme's long ago journey was severely affected by the comparatively recent construction of Barrett Drive. The signage near the roadway, where the end of the formation was blasted, gives some indication to its significance and connection to the caterpillar. Another sign along its back warns of fair and heavy penalties should one venture beyond. Barrett Drive was constructed around Christmas Day in 1983, against the wishes of the people who regard the care of the land as their greatest responsibility. Astonishingly, as described by the Aboriginal Areas Protection Authority:

when the Northern Territory achieved self-government in 1978, one of the first pieces of legislation to be introduced into the new Legislative Assembly was the

Aboriginal Sacred Sites (NT) Bill 1978. This became law in November 1978 and led to the establishment of a permanent Aboriginal Sacred Sites Authority a year later ... With the new law it became an offence to enter, remain, carry out works on or desecrate a sacred site anywhere in the Northern Territory.

Justice is yet to be served for the local community, and they face similar challenges on an ongoing basis. Such sites retain cultural strength but now carry the scars of indifference, at best, and speak of divergent perceptions of value. The small street that runs parallel to this ancient being has been named Caterpillar Court. What are the intentions behind such a name?

In this country, what may appear to some as mere mounds of rubbly rock are in fact embodiments of a powerful tradition in caring for a place that will define who you are.

Sitting discreetly to the west is Akngwelye Thirrewe. Perhaps he is waiting for better times, to once again hear familiar songs and feel the rhythm of attentive feet. Surrounded by chains, concrete and the usual bustle of a town's parking lot, he survives imbued with spirit. Not so long ago, people gathered around him and danced, sang and honoured. Knowledge was passed on and community bonds were maintained. Today this old rock may fool many a passer-by – if he is even noticed. This is the brave local dog of an ancient and vital story, the dog whose battles with an intruder remain in the landscape. This dog lived with his family and they too remain in the land. Many of the puppies lie at the base of a nearby hill, Untyeyetwelye (also known as Anzac Hill), with the ever-present threat of being overlooked – or worse. The information obtained from an initial search on the Alice Springs Town Council website was threadbare. It read that 'Tourism' is the 'Location type', and provided an address and relevant map. Other than that, it stated, 'Pets: No dogs permitted'. The irony cannot be missed.

Alhekulyele (also known as Mount Gillen), the distant peak rising steeply to the west, speaks of the intruding dog's presence, his interactions with the male and female locals, and his fatal end. Many choose to walk up Untyeyetwelye for a clear view of Alhekulyele, of lower plains and ridges and the lines they take, and the important spaces between them. This rise, Untyeyetwelye, is another women's sacred site. It has been overlaid by a war memorial and lookout called Anzac Hill, with plaques that encircle an upright obelisk. Here we can read about the various

The prominent obelisk on Untyeyetwelye (Anzac Hill).

wars Australian soldiers fought on land across the seas, with the imperative 'Lest We Forget' prominently shining in the centre. There is little mention of the involvement of Australia's Indigenous population at the time, who also represented their country. Importantly, there are glaring omissions of the battles fought on the soil beneath one's feet. Perhaps in time to come the information will acknowledge the hundreds of lives brutally taken during multiple massacres in the region. If we are to remember and honour lives lost, all of which are equal, surely it is for the purpose of redefining our path in order to better care for each other?

Many simple gestures can go a long way, and we can see how a concerted effort spanning more than three decades has finally come to fruition. Before 2018 only the Australian and Northern Territory flags flew atop this sacred rise. In 2018 a motion was passed in Alice Springs Town Council that allowed for the Aboriginal flag to be raised alongside them, but only for special occasions such as the duration of NAIDOC Week, National Sorry Day and National Reconciliation Week. Once these brief days were over, the flag was removed. In 2019 a significant decision was made when the town council voted for the Aboriginal flag to fly as a permanent symbol of recognition. In the same year, the High Court deliberated on the case of *Northern Territory of Australia v Griffiths and Jones* where compensation was sought for the Northern Territory's extinguishment of Native Title rights of the Ngaliwurru and Nungali people, in relation to the township of Timber Creek, situated more than a thousand kilometres from Mparntwe towards the coast. The court made the decision for payment of $2.5 million, setting a significant precedent, and, although no amount of compensation can rectify the harm done, this may set the tone for all future governance and decision making.

According to the Aboriginal Areas Protection Authority, there are 137 registered Sacred Sites in the township of Alice, with many more recorded but not yet registered. Wandering around the town we can contemplate the stories embedded in every detail. We can deepen our understanding of the infinite layers and interconnections, the generations they carry and the knowledge they continue to transfer. It is the simple request of the Arrernte people that we all take notice and give due respect. So as we play on sports fields that were constructed by tackling and breaking ancient eggs and walk along contested boardwalks laid at the base of sacred hills, we can ask ourselves, what alternative decisions could have been taken here, and how can we each shape a fairer shared future?

As inland rivers and creeks overflow following heavy rain, the country transforms. Precious waters gather, forming important swamps, evident by the change in vegetation. Ankerre Ankerre (Coolibah Swamp) is part of this great density of known sites and was an important gathering and ceremonial ground for its people, as it was for the caterpillars. An old sign marks the area and speaks of the various threats to the survival of the Coolibah Swamp, which used to extend beyond its current boundary. Here the soil is slow to drain and, as with all plants, the seeds of the two species of coolibah (*Eucalyptus coolabah* subsp. *arida* and *Eucalyptus intertexta*) have evolved within their local niche. Their seeds require inundation to germinate, but recent changes affecting the presence and quality of water are putting this community at risk. As described on the information sign, the common impacts of urbanisation are evident, such as:

The construction of open drains, altered water tables, lack of flooding, weed invasion, filling and uncontrolled access. A major impact on the natural community has been the lack of flooding. This has increased soil salinity and allowed the domination of the understory by old man saltbush (*Atriplex nummularia*) usually only found on the fringes of coolibah swamps.

Aged flower of native caper
bush and distinct patterns of
'minni ritchi' bark, common to a
few acacias and eucalypts.

Today you can walk through and see the trees that persist among the telling signs of disruption seen in the prevalence of saltbush and tyre tracks. These trees still dance as their ancestors once did, and the spirit of the land remains strong. In its own way, it asks for our concentration and care.

Approximately ten kilometres upstream lies an area known as Junction Waterhole. Rocky hills glow in the low-angled light, yet conceal the soft fur of rock wallabies. There are multiple connected sites – of great importance to both men and women – whose stories travel to the furthest reaches north and south. Their far-ranging significance cannot be understated, yet the risk of desecration for the building of dams or levies has been felt and fought in recent years. The Australian Heritage Database states that:

> The Dreaming stories associated with these sites travel through the countries of many Aboriginal groups and provide a narrative basis for positive social and cultural links between distant people. This is so for the cycles of both the Two Women and the Uncircumcised Boys, who are said to originate close to Port Augusta on the South Australian coast and to travel via this part of the Todd River on their journeys traversing the continent to the North Australian coast.

As we stand at the edges of these rivers and waterholes, and respect the presence of caves and carvings, knapped stone and paintings, we can fill our hearts with the vitality of this country's powerful heritage. These ancient formations and the diversity of life they have sustained since the beginning of time all need our greater sensitivity and understanding. The stories they hold and the care with which they have been nurtured give us important clues to the wisdom that could guide our every day.

Venturing further away from Central Arrernte country the stories abound with equal power. They too offer insights that science is only now discovering. Some beautiful examples of knowledge long-held through Indigenous traditions of communication are those of rising sea levels and celestial events. The Inteyere, Twenge, Ipmengkere, Murtikutjara, Aniltika and Nthareye groups are Native Title holders of the area now known for the Henbury meteorite craters. Situated 140 kilometres south-west of Alice Springs and close to the banks of the Finke River, the craters are estimated to have been created around 5000 years ago. At 350–400 million years old, the Finke may be the oldest river in the world. The stories associated with its life are no doubt complex and revealing.

To the west of Alice Springs lies Tnorala (Gosse Bluff). The Western Arrernte people speak of and honour its story of celestial origin, which is also reflected in contemporary science.

We can see in these and other stories that each is imbued with morals that couple with insights into the biology and geomorphology of our great world. These tell us of our shared human story and its connection to a complex system far beyond our view, but within the realms of our wondering and spiritual understanding.

Indigenous cultural experiences, tours and relevant organisations

Alice Springs Visitor Information Centre

For the latest Indigenous tour information within the Alice Springs area and further afield, ask at the visitor centre. Currently there is a walking tour that departs from the visitor centre in the mornings (for two or more people). You must book ahead at the visitor centre.

Todd Mall, cnr of Parsons St
08 8952 5800
discovercentralaustralia.
com/alice-springs-visitor-
information-centre

Karrke Aboriginal Cultural Experience and Tours

Tours include walks focusing on bush foods and bush medicines along with talks about the art and artefacts of the area.

South-east edge of Watarrka National Park, approximately five and a half hours south-west of Alice Springs
08 8956 7620
karrke.com.au

Akeyulerre Inc

This important Arrernte-run organisation is a 'service developed by Aboriginal people to acknowledge and promote Indigenous knowledge, practice and expertise recognised as being integral to the wellbeing of the community'. You can read more on their website, and find the wonderful women who sell some of the products at the Todd Mall Sunday Markets.

08 8952 2339
akeyulerre.org.au

Red Kangaroo Books

Pop into this independent bookshop that sells a range of excellent publications, many of which are by local and Indigenous authors. You can also search their catalogue online.

79 Todd Mall
08 8953 2137

Tinkerbee Sandpainting Workshop

Learn about traditional symbols and create your own piece of art.

0457 132 153
tinkerbee.com.au

Mparntwe (Alice Springs)

Other things to see and do

Here are other places that are worth knowing about in and around Mparntwe (and you don't need a four-wheel drive to visit them).

Olive Pink Botanic Garden

On the eastern bank of the Todd River, these gardens focus on the flora of the arid zone.

27 Tuncks Rd
08 8952 2154
opbg.com.au

Anthwerrke (Emily Gap)

Of incredible significance to the Arrernte people, associated with the caterpillars.

Ross Hwy (10km east of Alice Springs)

Tyethe (Jessie Gap)

A significant place for the Arrernte people, associated with the emu.

Ross Hwy (10km east of Alice Springs)

Napwerte/Ewaninga Rock Carvings Conservation Reserve

The Arrernte custodians ask that Arrernte women do not enter this site. Consider your decision to visit or not accordingly.

Old South Rd (35km south of Alice Springs)

Tjoritja–West MacDonnell Ranges

Including Urlatherrke (Mount Zeil), the Chewings Range, Glen Helen, Simpsons Gap and Ilparpa. Here you'll find incredible and complex rock engravings – Tjoritja is thought to contain some of the most significant Central Australian rock-engravings sites – along with the Ochre Pits, an Aboriginal quarry that can be visited.

West of Alice Springs

Alice Springs Telegraph Station

Considered to be 'the birthplace' of the Alice Springs township, it's now a historic museum; you can read these articles as well for a more complete story: findandconnect.gov.au/guide/nt/YE00019 and bth.humanrights.gov.au/the-report/part-2-tracing-the-history/chapter-9-northern-territory.

Herbert Heritage Dr
08 8952 3993
alicespringstelegraphstation.com.au

Alice Springs Desert Park

A fascinating nature park (particularly if you're travelling with children) with a focus on the plants, wildlife and habitats of the desert.

Larapinta Dr, 7km west of Alice Springs
alicespringsdesertpark.com.au

Further reading

Research into the breadth and devastation of colonial frontier massacres is growing and you can read more at c21ch.newcastle.edu.au/colonialmassacres

Read more about the Australian Heritage Database here: environment.gov.au/heritage/publications/australian-heritage-database.

Discover more about the journey of anthropologists Francis James Gillen and Walter Baldwin Spencer through Aboriginal Australia based on their 19th-century collections at: spencerandgillen.net

A good resource for those interested in the bird species of Central Australia is: alicefieldnaturalists.org.au/birds.html

Left: Flower bud of native caper bush.

Above: Bower created by a male western bowerbird with various white objects he collected to attract a female.

BIRDS

Bruce Pascoe

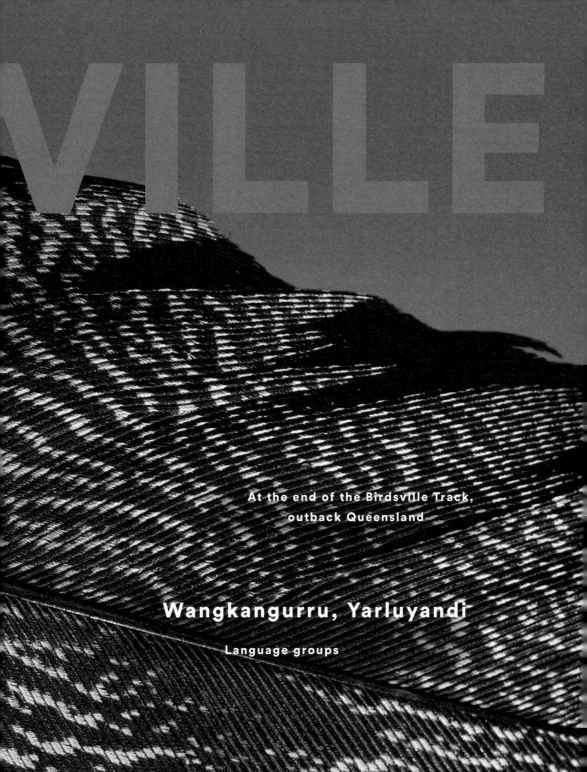

VILLE

At the end of the Birdsville Track,
outback Queensland

Wangkangurru, Yarluyandi

Language groups

Birdsville is the kind of place that Australians see as iconic: remote, hot, deserted desert. And they even have a horse race.

Every town needs the social and sporting events that bring people together with a binding focus. The Birdsville Races began like that but have now become a bucket-list option for those who want to experience the 'real' Australia.

The history Australia has invented for itself sees the outback as hot, harsh and hostile, so to drink champagne while watching bush horses get in a lather is considered to be a rite of passage. A bit of red sand on the four-wheel drive, a few insects on the windscreen and maybe a distant encounter with a snake. And then back to the office water-cooler to talk about the Red Centre.

The race began in 1882 but even in that year there was a parallel universe at Birdsville, virtually unseen and all but ignored unless a trainer with a likely horse wanted the best rider, or a grazier with unruly cattle wanted the best ringer. Then they might visit the blacks' camp or, more likely, send a messenger.

The attitude to the parallel civilisation persists to this day. Information about the town rarely acknowledges the local Aboriginal population.

But, as recent research at Moyjil has indicated, the fringe-dwelling people living by the waterhole were only the satellite to a life that had been refined for 120,000 years while climates changed and the region went from wetland to arid dunes and back again. No matter what the state of the climate, the people continued to prosper.

Westerners might wonder how you prosper in what city dwellers might call a mean existence of sand and heat. But the Wangkangurru and Yarluyandi didn't live in heat and sand; they lived by the billabong and waterhole oases, sometimes creating

Image on pages 106–7: Bustard feather.

Above and left: Pelicans squabbling over a fish, although they do also hunt in cooperative groups; and detail of their flexible scoop-like beak and delicate neck feathers.

the oasis themselves by sinking a well into the sand. These wells, mikiri, were narrow shafts often more than seven metres deep.

To reach one such well you do drive through heat and you do cross red sand and gibber plains but you will still arrive completely unprepared for the actuality of the old people's oasis. There are many of these idyllic places throughout Munga-Thirri National Park but let's talk about one that holds a memorial for the grandmother of Birdsville Elder Don Rowlands.

Today the odds are two to one that you will arrive in a Toyota, and racket and bucket along for several hours. Turn off the key, open the door, listen. What is that? A rolling warble ceases as soon as you put a foot to the ground.

You dismount from the steel chariot and the first thing you feel is the breeze through the corkwood trees. You feel as if you need to lie down immediately. The sand is soft, you are rattled from the corrugations and so you recline in the shade with your water bottle.

You drink, close your eyes and there is the sound again. Soft repetitive whistles, a churring babble, a plaintive whistle, the variety is enormous and the effect dream-like. You close your eyes and it is as if the bird is ventriloqual because, even when you open your eyes and locate the spiny-cheeked honeyeater, its voice seems to come from every corkwood, beefwood or acacia. It is the bird, with its soporific call, that compelled you to sit in the shade. It asked you to listen, to let the spirit of the country stroke the back of your neck. You shuffle yourself more comfortably into the sand and listen ...

When you wake you feel a serenity you think is unmatched by any other experience. You look about you, the shade of the trees is a balm, the light breeze a blessing, the spirit of the place a solace.

And there are people buried here too. For it is a place of rest.

At one particular oasis there are three memorials for old people who died during the mission and murder days but never made it back to their old wells. Modern descendants have brought them back. It is one of the most touching indications of the tenderness of the human spirit you will ever see.

The old people who created these wells provided for their descendants, the birds and animals too, and made sure some of the well water could flow to a pond away from the camp for the use of the animals who became assured over aeons that they could drink there in safety. They would still need to watch out for dingoes and eagles but the people would allow them to share the water.

Those animals knew that away from the oasis they would become someone's idea of a roast, but by the well they were guaranteed sanctuary. For the spirit of the place. Don't take your visit here lightly; you may never experience this peace again.

The waterholes and wells are reasonably common but many tourists choose to watch the sunset from the red ridge featured in half a dozen movies. Known to some as Big Red Sand Dune, it is certainly a remarkable sight, but don't forget the modest ponds and billabongs; they are small but vital and have much older stories to whisper.

Others come to the region to find the stands of the very rare waddi trees, some say the rarest tree on the planet. The incredibly hard, deep red timber was used by local people to make clubs but pastoralists decimated the trees for durable fence posts. Fortunately the local Aboriginal residents asked for mercy for the trees, which have intense spiritual significance.

The tourist potential of such a rare species is also helping to save them as Parks officers, many drawn from local Aboriginal groups, patrol the area. Some of the trees are very close to the town, always standing together like a well spaced family, ancient, swarthy spirits of the plain.

Birdsville is now a tourist town and so the races, the waddi trees, the giant sand dunes, the fossils all encourage visitors searching for the authentic outback experience. But do also listen for the spiny-cheeked honeyeater. Don't forget the dancing brolga or the spinifex pigeons. They are not just birds, they are the ancestors of this place and they want and deserve your attention because they are the voices and conscience of the country.

And late in the afternoon retire to the Birdsville Hotel. Yes, it is iconic too and will tell you so with bush hats, stubby coolers and ringers' shirts in Birdsville colours. And for only $75.

But it is a friendly pub. Of course there is plenty of talk about snatch straps and vehicle suspensions and mythic boggings but call on the spirit of the spiny-cheeked honeyeater to help you survive that while you enjoy a cold drink in a beautifully designed desert building. The staff might be from Argentina and Switzerland – they are on holiday to see what they have been told is the real Australia. But be patient, you

Above: Brolgas dancing.

Right: Galah feather detail.

Family of spoonbills. Opposite: Family of cockatiels.

might be lucky enough to buy a leather belt or hat from one of the lore holders of the country. He might even tell you a brolga story if you show good manners.

It's a quiet town now and the majority of its residents are Aboriginal, but a walk around its streets at dusk allows you to breathe in the desert and reflect on the subdued power of its waterholes. It might be exciting to search for gemstones, crack a whip, bet on an ill-fated horse or watch a famous filmic sunset but none of those can match the fact that you are in a landscape that has seen wetlands flourish for thousands of years followed by further thousands of aridity. This is not boom and bust; it is a story of comfort and honour. That is what the spiny-cheeked honeyeater was trying to tell you, and such stories must be whispered.

Indigenous cultural experiences, tours and relevant organisations

Wirrarri Visitor Information Centre

Cultural displays and art from local Indigenous and other Australian artists. It's also the best place for up-to-date road, track and weather information, if you're planning on heading into the desert.

29 Burt St, Birdsville
07 4564 2000

Two Boys Dreaming

Short, self-guided walking trail on the outskirts of town telling the creation story of how water wells were formed in the Simpson Desert. Check with the Wirrarri Visitor Information Centre before visiting as floods and other conditions can affect access.

Windorah Rd

Aboriginal Meeting Place

Traditional women's meeting place now has a rotunda with stone seats and a mosaic floor made by two artists, Joyce Crombie and Jean Barr. It's part of several large-scale sculptures in the Diamantina Shire made by local artists linking country, community and stories. It's also one of the stops on the Footprints in Time Indigenous arts trail around Birdsville. Maps are available at the Wirrarri Visitor Information Centre.

Munga-Thirri National Park

Among other things, you'll need a well-equipped 4WD, a satellite phone and plenty of water to explore the Simpson Desert. This park has many natural and cultural values, but is a trip for experienced four-wheel drivers only.

79km west of Birdsville
parks.des.qld.gov.au/parks/munga-thirri
07 4656 3272

Other things to see and do

Birdsville Hotel

Adelaide St
07 4656 3244
birdsvillehotel.com.au

Big Red

The highest of the Simpson's 1,100 dunes is also the closest to Birdsville, 35km from town. The view of the desert expanse from the top of the 40m-high ridge of sand is one of the outback's most impressive, particularly late in the afternoon when the colours are extraordinary.

Birdsville Billabong

Cool off with a swim, catch a fish or watch the birdlife.

Florence St, Birdsville

Waddi trees

Prized for their extremely hard wood, which made excellent waddy clubs, waddi trees are a sparsely occurring species mainly in the margins of the Simpson Desert. This stand of waddi trees is one of the few known populations, with some trees said to be many hundreds of years old.

12km from Birdsville on Bedourie Rd

Birdsville

MOU

Vicky Shukuroglou

IT ISA

& MITCHELL GRASS DOWNS REGION

Around 300 kilometres south
of the Gulf of Carpentaria and
800 kilometres west of Townsville

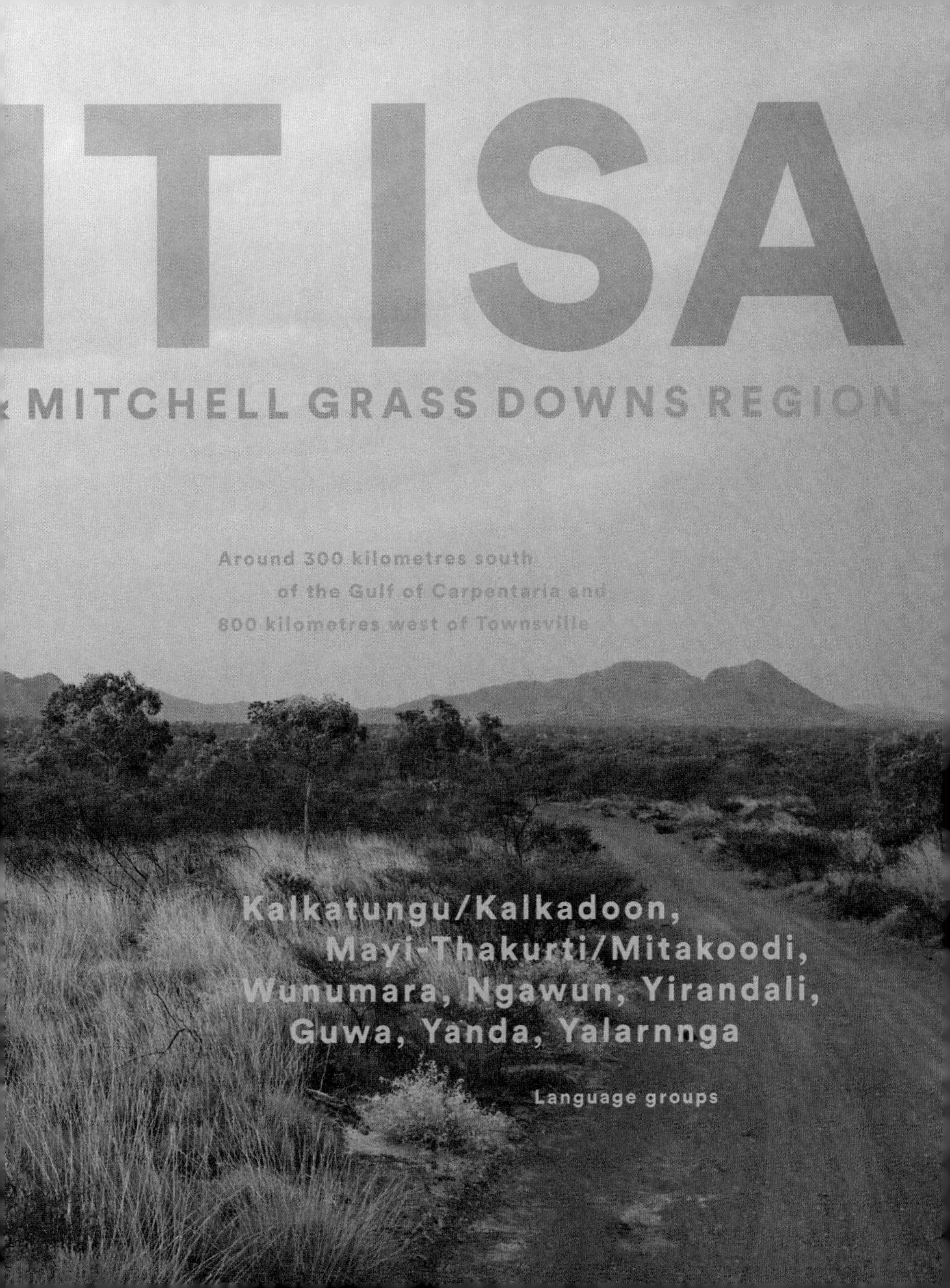

**Kalkatungu/Kalkadoon,
Mayi-Thakurti/Mitakoodi,
Wunumara, Ngawun, Yirandali,
Guwa, Yanda, Yalarnnga**

Language groups

As though to jolt the half-waking into consciousness, the rocks halted in a crooked half-crawl. Some appear to be eternally emerging muscular figures from country that maintains an unbroken horizon.

The forms are telling of dramatic processes and pulse with life born long ago. These figures have shaped the movement of people since the beginning of our presence on this land. That they are still crouching and sprawling is testament to a society that reveres these jagged rises, and embedded them in an ethos and practice of care. They stand as witnesses of the earliest human consciousness. Today the one that's a dingo pup, whose mother lies in the distance, has been excavated and turned into road gravel. The people whose ancestors cared for this pup grieve for the dingo and the far-roaming stories to which it connects and they worry for what is to come. Broken lines of ancient structures should alarm us. So, traveller, visitor, passer-by, resident, please give that pup and its relatives your attention, and yourself the time to understand more deeply.

If you arrive from the direction of sunrise, you will have travelled through part of the Mitchell Grass Downs, passing towns such as Hughenden, Richmond and Julia Creek, situated roughly 1000 kilometres south of Queensland's northern tip and 400 kilometres from the Gulf of Carpentaria. That sea shaped this expanse of cracking soil and grass country, and aquatic animals that once thrived are now imprinted in stone. It is country to which the Yirandali, Wunumara and Ngawun belong. It differs dramatically to that of the pup, closer to Cloncurry and Mitakoodi country, and each stone tells us of life and change over millions of years of watery inundation and departure. You will see the pale stones lining the streets, bordering gardens, marking points of interest, arranged according to size, strangely turned into toadstools and displayed in local museums. Some are smaller than your palm, while

others are moved off their country in the mouths of heavy dozers. Some are well-rounded, others have grown in couples, and some are wondrous conglomerations of bulges. Some split revealing the swirl of an ammonite shell or the gentle curve of a mussel. Like monstrous roughened pearls, these started life as a grain of sand or fragment of fossil, and with the right conditions of chemistry and sedimentation they were created. If you pick one up and feel its rough surface, admire its form and imagine what might be hidden within, know that you are lucky in that moment when you can decide how to honour what you hold. The park by the lake in Richmond is a worthwhile stop, with its garden describing plants of the area and their traditional uses, alongside gatherings of rocks that house the curious relics.

As told by Wunumara descendent Eden Jupurrula Roberts, in the Jukurpa time a female rainbow serpent travelled west across the plains on her way to Yalarnnga country to meet her male partner. Along her way she curled up to rest, making creeks and pushing the soil up, creating hollows that became lakes. The rounded stones across this country are sacred as they represent the eggs she laid on her return home, after making love.

Processes of planetary evolution are evident beyond these rounded rocks. In a paddock, a shrimp is found so finely transformed into stone that we can see its dainty legs, tail sections and segments of its body that would have provided flexibility in movement. What were people's responses in the earliest years of their encounters with these imprints? How did these shape perceptions of their country, systems of governance and resource management? What might have been their understanding, and did it inform decisions made in response to dramatic sea level rise and fall?

Opposite: The rocks that hold stories of ancient serpent eggs.

Left: Storm drenching the Mitchell Grass Downs.

Below: Rich colours of country.

Above: The dingo
mother and (right) the
pup, showing part of the
damage from excavation.

Opposite: Shell midden.

Across the continent, families faced challenges associated with climatic change; ecosystems altered, often decreasing available food, and water moved differently across the land. Negotiations within local groups and with neighbours would have taken place as refuges were established and communities adapted. Around Australia, Elders point to areas for which there is a story of ancient change; a bay was once a hunting ground, and the peak of an island accessible by foot. This period offers an extraordinary view into the evolution of humanity, and Australia is one of few places where Indigenous people relay such stories.

As saltwater receded, new ecosystems developed. The ancient seabed now provides a foundation for plants, animals and microorganisms that have evolved within this peculiar niche. Fissures form in the soil as moisture from seasonal rain evaporates. Water becomes scarce and life responds. The spectacular long-tailed planigale finds refuge among the cracks. Its body is shaped exactly as it needs to be, much like every animal living in its place of evolution. This is Australia's smallest known marsupial. At four to five grams and with a broad, flat head measuring three to four millimetres deep and nine millimetres wide, this planigale efficiently moves through the narrow gaps, hunting and dodging detection. Its snout tapers to suit its feeding habits – seeking out insects and larvae, small lizards and occasionally young mammals in leaf litter and soil. Reproduction can occur year-round, but their preference is for wetter seasons, when they may seek refuge on higher ground among the sparse vegetation. Females gives birth to several young, in ideal conditions up to twelve. Imagine the size of these tiny critters as they are carried for six weeks in their mother's backward-facing 'pouch', keeping them safe and clean from her diggings. These young are then tucked into a grassy nest beneath a cover of bark or plants. It is disturbing to contemplate the increased risks posed by large hooves and feral cats. The land remembers Indigenous practices evident in the relationship between ecosystem health and fire. As we travel, we can observe and wonder, what is the land communicating? Life here relies on *timely* burning. It is now more commonly known that variables within ecosystems, such as seasonal moisture, plant growth patterns, biomass and geology, dictate movements and outcomes of fires. Recent studies specific to Kalkadoon grasswrens confirm the significance of this non-linear process.

Indigenous groups across the country carefully utilised fire. Practices ensured appropriate heat, spread and containment of burns, all of which are integral to maintaining Australia's tremendous biodiversity. Animals such as the long-tailed planigale and Julia Creek dunnart depend on mosaic burns, where areas of continued habitat are available while regeneration occurs. Today Indigenous knowledge is sometimes better respected with positive outcomes achieved. As you travel, it's possible that you will encounter fires gently trickling along, triggering regeneration across the country, maintaining intrinsic elements of this nation's life.

With a great stroke of luck, you might see a Julia Creek dunnart. This bright-eyed marsupial is big enough to eat a long-tailed planigale, yet still so small that it could fit in your hand along with all its babies, up to eight. Its lengthy tail could slip between your fingers, but if the season is providing ample food the base may be too fat. If you do see one, don't try to catch it! As the name suggests, the Julia Creek dunnart is endemic to this region. Its fur is sandy brown above, pale below, with a slightly darker streak along the centre of its delicate face, framed by black-haloed eyes. An exquisite creature, wouldn't you say? A newborn dunnart is startlingly small: approximately four millimetres in length and seventeen milligrams in weight. Minuscule developing organs are visible through its almost transparent skin, and it is its *skin* that enables it to breath in its first days. That's right, a mammal that acquires the oxygen it needs through its skin. Extraordinary evolutionary refinement. This creature is at risk of being pushed to extinction.

The correlation between fracturing of ancient practices and biodiversity loss is evident. Australian ecosystems have suffered disproportionate extinction in the last 200 years, during which time the homes of Indigenous people were invaded, their livelihoods shattered, and people and their country suffered significant dislocation from each other. Of course the First People of this country left an imprint on ecosystems over tens of thousands of years. Perhaps the crucial distinction is between biodiverse complexity and abundance, and simplification and loss. An ongoing widespread commitment to caring for country through culture means that knowledge is still available to ensure the Julia Creek dunnart and other animals can remain and maintain their vital habits that recycle nutrients, provide food for other animals, disperse seed, pollinate plants, aerate soil and more. Early written records of Australia's flora and fauna were made possible with the assistance of Indigenous people who shared information and enabled collection of specimens. People such

Cockatiels and a ring-tailed dragon.

as Gerard Krefft, a scientist from the mid-1800s, described such procurement of animals, many of which are now extinct. Groups across the nation assembled their own forms of extensive records for millennia. Indigenous knowledge-holders continue to partner with researchers ensuring more complete data collection and decipherment. Krefft developed relationships with families and extended groups, and his documents describe the knowledge they instil and his awareness of impacts brought by invasions. A statement by Japanangka Lewis more recently recorded in a Central Land Council document for looking after country describes the nationwide trend succinctly: 'Janangpa (brush-tailed possum), wurlana (burrowing bettong), purdujurru (brush-tailed bettong), pakaru (golden bandicoot), yamarri (central harewallaby), mala (rufous-hare wallaby), yirdaji (pig-footed bandicoot) – Iowa! All gone! Finished!'

Once living across semi-arid to arid parts of Australia, pig-footed bandicoots were an unusual animal. Unlike other bandicoots, their front legs ended with two heavy claws somewhat like a tiny pig's hoof, and their back legs had a single heavy claw or tiny hoof with smaller remnants above, used for grooming. They were nimble and swift on slender legs, and Krefft described their eyes as very large and brilliant. Older Indigenous people from country where they once occurred are the most reliable knowledge holders and paint a clearer picture. Some names for pig-footed bandicoot from people of the central deserts include takanpa and yirratji in Warlpiri;

kalatawirri in Mangala and Walmatjari; kalatawurru, parrtiriya and takanpa in Kukatja; kanytjilpa in Kartutjarra, Manyjilyjarra, Ngaanyatjarra, Pitjantjatjara and Ngaatjatjarra; kanytjilpa, marakutju and takanpa in Pintupi; and kantjilpa and marakutju in Wangkatjungka. Pause and consider this wonderful and multifaceted speck in a wealth of knowledge across a diverse nation. Its presence was steady and honoured, its country cared for, ensuring its survival.

Despite this comprehensive long-held knowledge, highly regarded organisations continue their research into these creatures and describe their recent findings as new. They also claim that scientific knowledge arrived too late to prevent the creature's extinction. More than a hundred years earlier, Krefft predicted its demise, writing:

> The large flocks of sheep and herds of cattle occupying the country will soon disperse those individuals which are still to be found in the so-called settled districts.

This grazing, along with cats, foxes, altered fire regimes and highly invasive weeds such as prickly acacia (imported into Australia for livestock) and buffel grass (still being planted by some pastoralists), continues to have catastrophic impacts.

The spectacled hare-wallaby and grass owl no longer grace these grasslands, and although you might see vast groups of flock bronzewings they are not as numerous as they used to be. Travelling can be transformative if we are careful of our assumptions and remain open to change in our perceptions. We are lucky in this country, for the opportunities to observe and reconsider remain innumerable. As we live and travel its vast diversity, perhaps encounter oriental pratincoles, an excitable delma, a soil-crack whipsnake or a broad-palmed rocketfrog, it's worth asking ourselves what we choose to perceive. Do we have responsibilities to the old people, the country, the dunnart, and ourselves? Do we want to read yet another government paper that describes these extraordinary animals, their beauty and evolutionary sophistication, ending with the statement: 'The species is presumed extinct. No conservation management plan can offer further help.'

Habitat of such animals is often overlooked; areas like the Mitchell Grass Downs are commonly described as devoid of life, a boring chore between destinations. What could be our experience if we slow our gaze and ask more of our curiosity, travel with intention, as part of a richer story that heals the land and respects its First People?

Eden Jupurrula continues his story of this country, telling of a large forest of giant trees above which two hawks fought over a piece of firewood lit by a lightning strike. They knew it as waru (fire). The hawks battled in the skies, dropping the firestick. The forest became ablaze and burnt to a cinder. The remnants of that fire are

Termite mounds and
details of resilience
and transformation.

Above: Bottle trees near the Flinders Highway, and (right) the dingo pup behind the fence.

petrified wood, stone wood, which you can find across these plains. It reminds us of Jukurpa time and the great battle of the hawks. At a certain place as you ride across, if you look back over your shoulder just on sunset, you will see a vision of the great forest. Among others, stories of the yellowbelly fish are also told here.

This grassland, beneath which lies one of the world's greatest reserves of underground water, transforms to the more immediately spectacular country of the dingo pup and its relatives. The geology guides the flow of water northwards to the Gulf of Carpentaria, or south-westwards over hundreds of kilometres towards Kati Thanda–Lake Eyre, sparking and nourishing life.

The dark rocky rises remain important features of the area; for today's towns of Cloncurry and Mount Isa they signal the presence of minerals to be mined rather than standing as guardians of flora, fauna and great stories. With each curve of the road, another configuration is dramatically revealed.

The pup sits behind a fence as you enter town. It's unclear if the fence protects people from falling into the excavated rock, or protects the pup from further digging. Colours are rich and contrasting, the atmosphere often dry and hot. Through the day, rugged rises change tone dramatically, like a fantastic rock-colour clock. You will find the pup's mother on the south-west side of town, across a gentle flex of the Cloncurry River. She rises above a body of water known as Chinaman's Creek Dam, surrounded by vegetation typical of open spinifex woodland. In the beginning, she was still soft, and it was the actions of powerful beings that firmed up this earth. These formations were already aged when complex life began, and it is their composition that has enabled them to survive massive change over hundreds of millions of years.

While these exposed areas are immensely valuable in the ongoing refinement of our understandings, little is commonly known about the perceptions of the people who for aeons have resided alongside these rocks with a very different contemplation. It is the rocks' qualities that made them vulnerable to the exploits of humans, now using huge machines built from the rock itself.

With a distinct sensitivity, but for the same reasons of particular mineral composition, the local people utilise the stone to make effective tools. This area holds some of Australia's greatest stone-axe quarries. It's possible that you will come across a site, or a single stone, that holds this story of human creativity and tells it through

Country of the stone
axe quarries.

its shape: a curve that spans the face, delicate circles born from vibration, a smooth indentation as though formed by the pressing of an immaculate finger, ending in a fine peaked lip. Should you choose to touch one, give it your greatest reverence. You may be the first since the maker's hands, and you will be looking at what their critical eye investigated all those years ago. We know it is illegal to tamper with any tools or other objects, but, more importantly, descendants of those makers ask that we refrain.

On many walks with Elders, such finds are admired, explored with fingertips, loved, sometimes documented, and returned to their place of rest. Elders speak of their feelings on seeing a worked stone and all it holds; direct links to their old people and country from where it comes, care for its appropriate creation, respect for ancient stories bearing long-refined protocols. The stone exists in continuous time, encompassing all that has come to be, and reaching beyond today. Elders tell of highly valued axe heads travelling across hundreds of kilometres, often thousands, sometimes used and maintained along the trade routes, shrinking as they worked.

These routes saw the transfer of knowledge, ideas and objects of the everyday and the sacred. Some increased in value as they travelled, some connected to specific regeneration practices. Stones with varying purposes and other items such as ochre, pituri and shells held significance for people who would never see the cliff beneath which the ochre was dug, the sea where the shells grew or the plantations from which the pituri was harvested, but aspects of the country were familiar through relaying stories, for these were much more than objects of simple function. The presence of these astonishing networks embodies the priorities of maintaining stories that enable conservative use of resources, connect groups and individuals, and uphold profound understandings and connections to country.

While Mount Isa is well known as a busy regional centre teeming with high-vis shirts and fluoro car stripes, blinking lights and hardhats, its history of the Kalkatungu people stretches beyond the streets and highways, largely unnoticed. For some four-wheel-drive enthusiasts it's a place to be conquered and therefore innumerable steep and rugged rises near town are often extensively scarred.

For reasons similar to why the dingo pup ought not have become road gravel, and well-made tools should be left where they lie, these tracks concern many Kalkatungu people.

Right: One of the important sites today known as Three Sisters.

Opposite: The intricate engraving high on the rock wall.

Extensive waterways among these rises are mostly dry but transform quickly. They can carry thundering volumes of water and drain at impressive speed. These waters, the earth that guides their flow, and the life they sustain, are integral to Kalkatungu lore. Their stories speak of the time when the earth was still soft, and the entwinement of relationships with every thing and every action – whether eating, talking, loving, dancing, looking, making, hunting. These great stories relay vital information and transform as they stretch across country and diverse languages. They do not just speak of might and simple power. Instead, humanity is embedded within a delicate system, reflecting intimacy with place, shaping conscious decisions. For people across the country, living responsively to the earth that nourishes them often meant nomadic or semi-nomadic lives. Ensuring growth rather than depletion respected the fact that animals need their space and time to flourish. From the little witchetty grub to the bold cockatoos of striking variation, colours flashing white and yellow, black and red, pink and grey, their stories teach and so shape the land.

Stories long held a different kind of attention to what they receive today. Sites now known as Sun Rock and Painted Rock were, up until relatively recently, only visited by men and boys, and honoured as places of transformation. Visitors are unlikely to know, unless they choose to learn, and so dynamics shift. Three Sisters, also known as Three Steps, is a site more suitable for anyone to visit. A track up the slight hill leads to a lookout. The steep, angled rock shaped into several platforms by ancient and dramatic movement can be appreciated from here. A meticulous engraving on the rock face leaves us wondering about lives well lived, and hints at what else the land retains. Slightly further north the undulations and steeper rises gather together and, like the cockatoos, vary in colour from deep purple, red and radiant orange to white. In contrast, the ridges to the west hardened in a distinct north–south line. Between these formations is Lake Moondarra, fed by the Leichhardt River. This lake, constructed in the 1950s for the operations of Mount Isa Mines, is known as a place for recreation, yet is entangled in layers of loss for the Kalkatungu people. Stories indicate the significance of the surrounding range linked to witchetty grubs, black cockatoos and other animals. Certain areas are sacred country for men, so women avoid these locations. Prior to being inundated and forever altered, a permanent waterhole was honoured by women as part of ancient journeys. As you drive the sealed road, you will see rises blasted for the construction of the dam, and as you look at that dam remember ancient paintings of important figures now exist fractured, rearranged and compressed.

Islands of varying size once accessible by foot held a different presence as peaks of hills. Considering some of the country's greatest stone-axe and spearhead quarries exist in the surrounding ranges, it is disconcerting to consider how many crafted tools are covered by silt at the bottom of the lake or jammed against the dam wall. It is worth a visit to the lake; it is no doubt magnificent, birdlife is diverse and stories richly layered. The Kalkatungu ask that we approach with sensitivity and an inquiring mind, honouring what lives here even if it is beyond our understanding.

In 2008, in response to studies regarding toxic contaminants such as lead, Mount Isa Mines undertook the Leichhardt River Remediation Project, which among other actions involved relocating from the Leichhardt River approximately 160,000 tonnes of soil that contained historical mine sediment. Negotiations with mining companies is a constant distraction for the Kalkatungu, who are required to present arguments for the preservation of country. A new proposal for 'exploration' demands that they respond – sites are recorded on GPS, photographed and added to reports in language far from the language of the land.

Just as disruptive but on a different scale is a new housing area pressing upon a men's ceremonial site, reminding us of unwelcome insistence from long ago. Burke and Wills travelled through here in 1861, during the journey that was their last. Within a decade, invasion by pastoralists and miners brought devastating consequences for the Kalkatungu, despite their intense opposition. Stories told today reflect this. Attitudes of conflict are evident in innumerable early records where

Lower slopes have been dammed and inundated, creating Lake Moondarra.

unequivocal rights to land were assumed by many British invaders, and the cost to others seemed irrelevant. With the invasion came hooved animals, something the land had not previously felt. All forms of life suffered the impacts and food sources staple to the Kalkatungu diet quickly diminished.

Hunting introduced livestock was the obvious solution. By what measure would we deem it an offence ripe for extreme punishment to take something of lesser value from a plunderer if it were a matter of survival or an expression of resistance? Blood from children, women and men leached into the soil, and brutality was recorded extensively despite deliberate efforts of some of the most severe perpetrators to keep it 'undercover' while others boasted. Men in powerful positions stretched their responsibilities into illegal territory and saw themselves as saviours or cleansers of a new nation. At the same time, such action was publicly demonised, as the human conscience has always carried justice.

Diaries, newspaper articles and official records describe acts of often disproportionate retribution – even when harsh retribution was an acceptable response and despite many records having 'gone missing'. Oral records provide

Country of Battle Mountain.

a more intimate view. One Elder from country north of Julia Creek speaks of his grandmother who heard the sounds of a shooting in the Flinders River. In 1884 one of this country's many battles of resistance took place in the ranges close to Mount Isa. Kalkatungu families speak of it today, some in hushed tones, some with anger. An organised cavalry fought the Kalkatungu, who strategically located themselves within steeper slopes of their country. The area is now known as Battle Mountain, described on a memorial in nearby Kajabbi.

Aggravations in the build-up to this battle included the stealing and killing of livestock, the abduction of women and children, and the slaughter of individuals and entire families. The Native Police were led by men of rank, enabled by capable yet vulnerable Indigenous men from parts of Australia that had already suffered immense dislocation. They proved dreadfully effective in tracking and driving people out of country and enforcing punishment. The Native Police saw their role was to establish a level of control and protect the British newcomers desperate to survive after having invested everything in what was, to them, an alien and often terrifying land. Frederic Urquhart was a leading member of the Native Police and, despite ongoing concerns for his extreme actions, he was promoted several times during his career. Urquhart was a key figure in many punitive attacks along with others, such as Alexander Kennedy, whose names you'll see at prominent places in town and beyond. What happened in our nation's heart when we decided to name rivers that nourish life and streets in which we live after murderers? Despite his ruthless nature, there are also records of his concern for the horrific introduction and rapid spread of venereal disease that decimated populations across the country. Urquhart is a fine example of the twists and turns of the human being and the heavy influence of context.

A small book with a discreet cover in the style of its day, dark with gold font and an endless network of delicate flowers with hovering birds adorning its end pages, is a seemingly loving object entitled *Camp Cazonettes: Being Rhymes of the Bush and other Things*. This is one of Urquhart's books of 'humble compositions'. Among the pages that feature love and nature, and aspects of life in the late 1800s, is a poem 'Told by the Camp Fire'. Urquhart describes the murder of two women and a child, and the pursuit of those who killed them. Towards the end we read the vengeful verse:

I have heerd a lot of playin'
On piannys and organs too
But the music of them there rifles
Were the sweetest I ever knew.

The responsibility remains with us to consider the old people; theirs is a position of incredible experience, and they ask we proceed with awareness and open hearts, without division and animosity.

Accounts of these events vary – sometimes numbers of those killed will differ significantly, sometimes locations won't match precisely, sometimes there are discrepancies in the original records, the re-telling of perpetrators' names, and the

triggers for punishing actions. In recent years people have been increasingly willing to accept these truths, with research into oral histories and written records unmasking the extent of brutality. Some towns have taken steps towards acknowledging these events, but it is important to be mindful that much lies within a name and the soil.

As you travel through this land and find your way into its complexities and beauty, you will be called on in one way or another to address the pain that exists.

Flat planes of red, yellow and black surrounded by a stand-alone wall contrast with the shifting tones and turns of the country. A short gravel drive off the Barkly Highway between Cloncurry and Mount Isa leads to the memorial.

Plaques on opposites sides of the wall indicate that you are entering the ancient tribal lands of either the Kalkatungu or Mitakoodi. An invitation is made to all who pass to be brother and sister to the descendants of those dispossessed. Other plaques of prose convey tragedies of this land and its animals, and speak of invasion by an insurmountable force, as 'Spear can never conquer gun, man no more the horse outrun'.

A boomerang shape is painted on the top curve of the yellow circle. Above the elbow of the boomerang is a portrait of a man. We know it is a man because of our ability to decipher a shape even when featureless and soft of form. A striking

Opposite: Boodjamulla.

Above and right: Diversity of life
in the rivers and creeks of the
district offering refreshing oases.

Sculptured pools of Porcupine Gorge, rich with Yirendali stories.

strip of red paint roughly spans his forehead. Staring at his anonymous head and the hint of prominent brow, we can piece together a face, a character up to our own imagination, formed by our own heart. Does he hold a slightly upward gaze, telling of determination? Is his a watchful eye attending to his place? Is he one of the men who fought and then nursed all those he loved, or are his bones among those scorched by the sun, lying broken in the hills? Another anonymous person recently stood in front of this figure and judged him through a dark lens, leaving their own heart scattered as bullet holes. How do we reconcile these perforations with his graceful form? Driving along the highway you could blink and miss this story. Seek these places out and you will repeatedly confront the realities of this country, but know that you are shaping the lives of people you will never meet, healing lands that you will never see for animals you will never hold.

Important information

Always carry more water than you think you will need, plus extra in case you get stuck somewhere, and remember that water is not always readily available. If you are driving be aware that many roads are unsealed, often heavily corrugated and can be extremely dusty. Drive with great caution as trucks also utilise these roads and it can take time for the dust to settle enough for you to see. Beware of cattle and other animals on the road.

Indigenous cultural experiences, tours and relevant organisations

Kalkatungu community

The website of the Kalkadoon Native Title Aboriginal Corporation gives some information on community aims and activities.

kalkadoonpbc.com.au

Other things to see and do

Hughenden Visitor Centre

Visit the visitor centre for details about various local sites and areas to explore, from dinosaur fossil sites to graves of people with important stories.

Hughenden Visitor Centre
37 Gray St
07 4741 2970
visithughenden.com.au

Porcupine Gorge

Approximately 50km north-east of Hughenden is Porcupine Gorge, an incredible place to learn about local flora, fauna and dynamic seasonal change. Walking tracks provide wonderful opportunities but be aware that the heat is amplified in the rocky landscape and tracks demand some fitness. There are short and easy paths to a couple of lookouts.

parks.des.qld.gov.au/parks/porcupine-gorge

Tharrapatha Way Cultural Walking Trail

In Mount Isa, this easy walk alongside the Leichhardt River offers informative signs where you can learn about local flora such as various kinds of grevillea and hakea, wild orange and soap bush, and how these were used by the Kalkatungu and other groups. You will also read about local fauna – from frogs and eagles to legless lizards and birds – and their connections to Kalkatungu culture.

Urquhart St, near the junction of Kokoda Rd

Boodjamulla (Lawn Hill) National Park

Sacred to the Waanyi people, Boodjamulla lies approximately 300km north of Mount Isa. There are designated trails through this spectacular country, a sanctuary for a great diversity of fauna including the Gulf snapping turtle and purple-crowned fairy-wren. Walk carefully and you'll see signs of lives well lived, such as sheltered shell middens with incredible views over the gorge. This area is also home to the Riversleigh Australian Fossil Mammal Site, a World Heritage Area protecting fossils dating back twenty-five million years. Check road conditions before you go. Long sections are only accessible by four-wheel drive.

parks.des.qld.gov.au/parks/boodjamulla-lawn-hill

143

Vicky Shukuroglou

LAUR

COOKTOWN AND WUJAL WUJAL

Three hundred kilometres north
of Cairns, on Cape York Peninsula

A

Kuku Thaypan, Kuku Yalanji,
Kuku Warra, Kuku Mini, Olkola
and Guugu Yimithirr

Language groups

'Grab 'im! Grab 'im! Aiee! You watch. He'll go to clear water. Move that log now ... Go slow, you'll see 'im ... wait ... There now! Look! Aaw, c'mon boy, jus' get in there an' grab 'im!'

Woosh! Before another word, in dive an older pair of knowing hands holding the hat for protection from pincers. Just a few quick movements and they come out triumphantly showing us the cherabin. The Elder's lifelong practice and joyful spirit bring success. Soon after, her son finally scoops one out.

We had walked the water-sculpted rocks looking for signs of old life – engravings, tool sharpening grooves and the less likely finds in this particular spot of grinding stones and knapped blades. Chatter and laughter bubble up as reminders of a *living* place – where people continue to gather and learn, hunt and share stories. Is it ludicrous having to search for signs of cultural practices from the past when the place is cherished in similar ways today?

If someone asked you to prove that you want to keep your home, what would you say? What evidence could you give of what it means to your family? And what of your desire to keep your place healthy, especially if the most important values are intangible and perhaps hard for others to see? Speakers of Kuku Thaypan, Kuku Yalanji, Kuku Warra, Kuku Mini, Olkola and Guugu Yimithirr understand their long association with the area now known as the Laura Basin and surrounding ranges.

We had gone equipped with GPS, pens, clipboards and cameras in response to yet another proposed mining lease. Local Elders and the Laura Indigenous Land and Sea Rangers had done this before for the continuation of their ancient culture. So far, the riverbed has remained intact in this location near the Laura community, but the desire of some to disturb the land in search of gold and tin has persisted since the late 1880s. Large areas of fine-grained rock sweep and hug around gatherings of sand. In these soft depressions and gentle rises we can read stories inscribed by the feet and tails of various animals on their travels through the day and night. Near here, footprints are not able to be left on the riverbed for the riverbed no longer exists. Aerial images show lush curves and tight gullies, sharp turns and open angles.

Beaches splay on one side and the other, and when walking you can see where the water pools and giant paperbarks lean. The shapes raise questions of the travel of water – what soft spots were present and what opportunities did it find while seeking easiest flow? What tools made with breathtaking precision floated down this river and out to sea?

Amid this complexity of relationships, massive excavators and dump trucks are manoeuvred. The river transitions abruptly: honey-black tea upstream to milky coffee downstream. This signal is not subtle yet is somehow allowed. What answers would be given if questions were posed to the miners and their children, and to all of us who consume and never really pay our dues? Perhaps we would all have the same answers when asked where we would rather swim and source our food. Perhaps we would all answer in favour of the upstream water if we thought about the health of frogs and fishes, birds and turtles. What about the vibrant coral and abundant life into which these waters flow, carrying ancient stories? Elders tell of the serpent and other mighty beings, colours that glimmered and made the place now also known as the Great Barrier Reef. Stories have travelled immeasurable distances and across hundreds of generations. They have been shaped by country and, in turn, stories shape the country.

We follow the water's path, walking mainly in the dry riverbed, occasionally skirting pools. Among trees we notice a bowerbird's display and pause to admire his

Above: Roseanne George
holding the cherabin.

Opposite and right: Various
perspectives of local waterways.

Left (top): Insect egg case; kapok seed capsule (detail seen on pages 144–5) with the moon a soft speck in the background; native figs in different stages of ripening – there are more than forty native fig species in Australia, offering many benefits to both humans and animals.

Opposite, from left: Cluster of black spear grass seed with an unusual native bee structure; a dried green ant nest built from eucalypt leaves; well camouflaged insect with transparent wings.

creation, which prompts the telling of a story. The young man, the one who finally grabbed that cherabin, honours his country and his work as a ranger. He says that if you hang a necklace on a branch near the bower of this bird and you watch that bird for a long time, every day, you watch him and feel love for him, understand him a little more, then take that necklace and keep it close, good fortune in love may come your way.

Riverbed mining is banned in some countries, but not here. Overwhelmingly, we ignore evidence pointing to the immediate need to protect our rivers from this and other destructive practices. We even ignore people who have supported the rivers' health over tens of thousands of years. Instead, rivers are treated like giant plumbing systems created for our use, with no thought for the water they carry, from where it comes nor where it goes, and without appropriate maintenance. Across this vast island, its oldest people share a different ethos. They say, if you are on this country you are of this country, and because you are here you have a responsibility. That responsibility is to country. As a united family, we are part of this story. We should all speak up but it must be with the greatest respect for rivers and all the lives they sustain, the sea and reefs to which rivers flow, the hills and gullies from where water runs to feed those rivers that seek the sea. The old people have been speaking and we haven't been listening.

Even an untrained eye can see the signs of a mined riverbed; it loses complexity and mature vegetation, is often dominated by weeds and suffers significant changes in its natural structure. Fine sediments are suspended in the water at ten times natural levels. Individual grains of sand, vital for the survival of many species, can no longer settle naturally. Such significant and rapid changes are new to the creatures that have evolved in this country. Eel-tail catfish rely on their particular riverbed for a successful hatching of young, but now struggle. With his relatively broad head, a male prepares a mounded circle up to two metres in diameter. He gathers pebbles, coarse sand or twigs, leaving a central depression where the female lays eggs. With the sway of his body and tail, he keeps the area clean for seven days until the eggs hatch.

When the river's balance is disturbed, impacts flow a long way downstream, far beyond our view and usually beyond our contemplation. Along the way, pools that hold the last water for animals during the driest times are filled with sediment and shrink or disappear. Many ancient engravings telling stories of spirits, local foods and travels are now hidden from our view. The Laura rangers have been systematically documenting such sites whenever they can, but this is a big country and resources are limited.

Water seeks a path until it can go no further. A cow's hard hoof readily cuts, and so water follows. Since the mid-1800s the nation's hunger for cattle has been felt on the land we now call north Queensland, leading to cycles of degradation involving extensive erosion and widespread land-clearing in order to grow greens to feed the cattle. Here we have one of Australia's greatest national problems.

Despite what we know from observation, extensive research and, perhaps most importantly, the knowledge of the old people, the Queensland government under former premier Campbell Newman approved the clearing of more than 30,000 hectares on Olive Vale pastoral station. That's more than eight Norfolk Islands. At the same time, properties such as this receive public funds to deal with erosion and sediment flows that reach the beloved Reef. Olive Vale is just a skip from Laura township, where many of the area's traditional custodians live and gather and try to minimise harm to their home. At the ranger's station they discuss current issues, prioritise actions and prepare for trips on country. A strange dichotomy exists as tourists travel from the furthest reaches to revel in the delights of this land and yet may have little interest in understanding the Indigenous community. In the

Laura River at twilight.

late 1800s Edward Palmer, a man of wide experience in the pastoral industry and government, wrote in his book *Early Days in North Queensland* about what he saw:

> In their original state they could not have been an unhappy people; when food was plentiful, they made weapons and shaped their stone tomahawks, which of itself was a work of slow progress; they wove nets for their game, and composed or sang their wild songs, or still wilder corroborrees, or dances. Obedient to the laws and customs handed down from their ancient forefathers, and following out the rites of their marriage laws with great strictness, they lived healthy lives to a good old age, while the increase of the race was checked by the amount of food each district could supply. With the advent of the white race, the social system that held them together for thousands of years, became disturbed and broken into, and their natural food supplies were destroyed. Thus, with the introduction of new diseases, this primitive race of mankind is fast disappearing, apparently without

a thought or struggle or hope, and after a few years not a remnant of them, or any sign of their occupation of the country will remain.

While Palmer's thoughts on primitivism, disappearance and hope have proven ill-informed, there is much to consider in what he writes. Speaking with Elders who daily suffer consequences of the past and present, we can better understand their reality and solutions they imagine. Much reaches back to the immense oppression of people, and Elders articulate this clearly. What they describe follows a similar trajectory now spoken about across the country: people were forced off their land, controlled in reserves, watched by police, subjected to horrific violence and prohibited to be free and equal.

In later years, some were able to remain on or near their country by working on pastoral stations. This often meant enduring appalling conditions and labour without pay. Once the laws were changed and some notion of humanity was legislated, the reins became loose and the horse bolted. People previously strictly disallowed from places of social gathering were suddenly able to enjoy 'equal' merriment with the recent arrivals. What did the recent arrivals bring with them to foster ease and merriment? Alcohol. Add that to the dislocation and separation

Left and above: Impressive rock formations of the district.

Opposite: The more you look, the more you see in layers of paintings at the site known as Split Rock, nestled among massive overhangs and sloping walls just a few kilometres from Laura.

Diagram below indicates some of the images at the Emu Dreaming site (left and opposite top). These include a large emu with eggs and several human-like figures of various sizes, one with three-pointed hand.

Opposite (below): Powerful engraving in local river rock of figure also showing three-pointed hand.

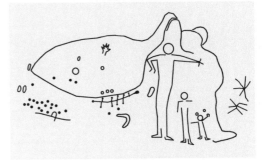

from country and vital societal structures, and what has been created? As elaborated by an Elder, we can add the confusion and disconnect that develops when one generation observes another in these conditions. If only all Australians could share a yarn with that wise man.

People across the nation are addressing these issues in their communities. Here in north Queensland, Olkola people have developed partnerships with other landholders, scientists, geologists, government bodies and not-for-profit organisations to reinvigorate more than 800,000 hectares of their country recently returned to their management. A key focus is Alwal, the golden-shouldered parrot. If you walk with Olkola people on their country you will learn of disrupted traditional burning cycles, along with impacts of the pastoral industry and various effects on the tropical savannah woodland on which this bird relies. During conversations with Elders you will likely hear that 'country is not like it used to be'. Old burning cycles are being reignited to reshape vegetation and address reductions in available foods during the wet season when Alwal can starve to death. Increased predation by cats and other animals is monitored and plans created for their control.

An important figure in Olkola culture and previously more widespread in Cape York Peninsula, Alwal relies on grass seeds for food and termites for nesting. Alwal seeks a diversity of habitats such as tall open forests, swamps, sand ridges and rocky hills, to accommodate their wet and dry season feeding, their nesting and roosting, and their feeding during breeding.

Moving through this open country you will see termite mounds of different shapes, sizes and colour, some showing severe damage caused by pigs, horses and cattle. One species of termite, *Amitermes scopulus*, creates conical-shaped mounds in which Alwal prefers to dig its small nest. One of many challenges faced by these endangered birds is that it takes these termites thirty to fifty years to construct a mound of sufficient size. The preference for the mounds of this particular termite is likely to do with greater insulation and the seasonal coincidence of parrot eggs being laid and mounds having been completed, therefore avoiding eggs getting stuck in the termites' construction. Alwal's closest relative, the paradise parrot, had similar habits and once occurred in country south of here, but is now presumed extinct. If Alwal suffers the same fate, it is most likely that the antbed parrot moth will also disappear. The scientific name of the moth, *Trisyntopa scatophaga*, tells us of its feeding habit, which provides the nest with an effective cleaning service. The relationship between the moth and bird extends beyond this and would have been observed by people of this land for countless centuries. There is much we do not know about

Rocky overhangs protect paintings and a great diversity of life including native cockroaches (of which there are more than 400 species), dazzling lizards and other vibrant surprises.

Left: Looking out over dramatic valleys, a bushfire in the distance.

Opposite (left): Formations continue to be weathered.

Opposite (right): Countless images, such as these Quinkans, are protected here.

this moth and other flora and fauna, a sad symptom of our failure to fully honour Indigenous knowledge.

Apart from its commitment to re-establishing traditional practices and survival of such species, the Olkola Aboriginal Corporation is enabling its people to return to country and strengthen cultural connections. Many who had to leave or were unable to develop a strong connection to their homeland are now making significant journeys home. There is also a strong commitment to sharing Olkola culture with interested visitors, with the hope that through common knowledge and richer understanding, culture and country will be looked after, and livelihoods that replenish can develop.

Ngulun (also known as Starcke River) curves and travels north-east to the Reef. Waters of the river support a diversity of life and at this salty end of its flow we can see dugong and turtles. Elders who know these animals and connected stories are increasingly alarmed as they observe the impacts of ignorance and greed. They talk about the need to better protect animals from numerous threats, including over-hunting that does not adhere to strict traditional protocols, and ever-present issues related to pollution. They seek new ways to proceed, bringing knowledge and resources together from diverse individuals and groups to re-establish old proven systems of care. Land and sea creatures with richly layered stories from creation times are crucial to the overall health of the marine ecosystem and their presence is an indicator of cultural awareness for everyone. Amid regular trips into town for dialysis and other similarly urgent demands, the Elders continue to carry these stories and maintain their ethos, sharing it with those who listen. They recognise that this crowd must grow if their grandchildren are to meet their totems.

In contrast, names like Hells Gate, Storm King and Emu Swamp leave one wondering what these represent and what motivates the people involved. These dams – both proposed and built – are designed to hold back the waters meant for the sacred rivers and while these rivers dry, the old people's tears flow. Most of us will not look into the eyes of the old people and see the loss that's held within, but we must all embrace the urgent need for mature conversations about a more dignified future.

As with most things, nothing is 'black and white' and there are multiple ways and countless stories. We are invited to see clearly and learn, have a yarn with open hearts and be willing to make change. In much the same way that there is a pressing need to listen and respond to knowledge of this land, there is a necessity to rethink the ways the nation nourishes itself in the stomach and spirit, and to close the gap between the two.

If we turned our gaze to the country that rises up steeply and rolls out as far as the eye can see, we might gain some clarity. Red-orange rock juts above the treeline and it's impossible to imagine the number of paintings that rest among the innumerable protected walls. Escarpments stretching through the Laura region are richly animated, reflecting the culture of those who love these places. A rock splits

Looking carefully among layers of images created over innumerable generations, we can see wonderful experimentation and technical refinement. The significance of connections to plants, animals and spirits, and among humans, are all depicted here.

away revealing giant blackboards in the greatest of schools, with enough slant to protect faces from rain and sun. We follow ancient tracks of people connected to those painted walls, the gaps and turns of shadow among them. Be wary, for it is easy to get lost here if you do not know your way, if you do not know the song that may accompany your travels. Be wary for you may be entering a space not used to the presence of a man, or a woman. Better still, go with a local.

As you observe the scale and flow of these ranges, imagine the tens of thousands of paintings and engravings that tell ancient stories of travels and relationships, significant animals and foods. Contemplate the minds of those who honoured the spirits and cautioned of certain dangers, their imagery tucked away for those who care to see. Layers of work are often so numerous and complex that we can no longer observe what came before. Imagine how many have laid their hand upon the rock or held a tool to its surface while blowing dampened ochre through their lips. Who travelled here, and how far? How bright were their eyes and how strong were their legs? Who was the great string maker, and who had a slightly bent finger? There, look, you can see it on the wall, next to another's much larger hand. And who was the one who struck a stone so deftly to create the finest of ripples along the thinnest edge, translucent against the sun? And think of the boys in that particular season who crawled through the tunnel towards their initiation, supported by their menfolk, with proud women waiting to soothe their bodies. And as you sweat, think of the cold rock platform that offered relief, and the shade provided by the informative wall. Think of their delight, knowing the small bat who lived in the hole above their heads, and how they may have concentrated on it for a while. This was a place of gathering, of learning, of growth and of burial. The walls held secrets for men and for women, and crevices cradle bark-wrapped bodies of those who passed.

Just like the engravings of Burrup Peninsula and the formation of Baiame's Ngunnhu in Brewarrina, the imprint upon the land is subtle. Many pass these sites without noticing. We do not see massive rearrangements of the earth leaving scars that grow over time. Is it worth considering what this may indicate of an ethos transferred over generations? Of course people were almost certainly prone to jealousy and anger, and desired comfort and health, but the system of what was valued and how disputes were resolved meant that the earth counted more as a healthy whole rather than fractured and transgressed. Descendants of those men and women are now scattered across the country, and you might cross each other's path, perhaps share in conversation.

Two brothers who spoke of their old people come to mind. They tell a story of early encounters with colonisers. They said, 'It's like the old people knew what was coming. They knew people would be moved away, families separated. They knew people would be killed. Those old people, they knew. They saw the future.' So those old people urgently told stories of their country. They wanted their young ones to know where they came from and for it to be firmly held even in severe and dislocating times. They believed it could keep people strong. They wanted it for their own old people, for their country and for the resilience of those young lives.

In Gundabooka, approximately 2000 kilometres south of this immense collection of knowledge, we see the same commitment to the transfer of customs. Among many images are emus and gatherings of eggs. The bird's prominence across the country is indicative of its importance. Not far from Laura is a rocky outcrop recently documented by rangers as a likely Emu Dreaming site. The rock recess in the form of a giant emu was carefully photographed and described, along with details of its numerous eggs and other figures, both painted and engraved. These sites, among many others, show us the complexity and diversity of Australia's Indigenous cultures. Perhaps less obvious are the connections across vast areas that become more apparent when we see engravings and paintings around Laura depict a similar image as seen in Gundabooka and other areas. This figure, whose arm ends in an emu foot, is powerful and part of great storylines. We can revel in robust oral traditions maintained by this land's First People as we consider 2000 kilometres of country and tens of thousands of years.

The area around Laura is also known as Quinkan country in recognition of spirits whose enigmatic forms are boldly painted on these walls. Indigenous guides involved with the Quinkan and Regional Cultural Centre can take you to selected places where these figures are seen, sometimes among animals including ibis, dingoes, flying foxes, snakes and kangaroos, or plants like the edible native yam. Often shown life-size, these beautiful images are created using vibrant ochre, mostly in shades of yellow, red, brown and white. Animals now extinct, such as the diprotodon or giant wombat, are said to be depicted here. The guides share their rich stories and, if the season is right, explain which fruit to pluck from which tree. The technique and approach

Above: Kalkajaka.

Left: Expanses of waterlilies provide refuge for birds and many other animals and were integral to the vitality of local communities.

Opposite: A view from the Mt Cook walk.

of local painters is distinct to others further afield; this is evident in the way they shape solid blocks of colour or simple lines, both fine and broad, sometimes strongly patterned. In some areas, the edges of an animal's body give shape to an image as it was held up to the rock for stencilling with ochre.

Despite the significance and irreplaceable cultural wealth of these sites, their protection is inadequate according to the Australian Rock Art Research Association. National Heritage listing in 2018 means the federal government is now also responsible for protection. Across the country, Indigenous people and landholders have developed respectful partnerships, ensuring sites are known, documented and cared for. Tragically, many others do the opposite and actively destroy these riches. In a whim of opinion and flash of time, complex works that survived thousands of years disappear. For some, it is fear fed by rumours – that 'they can take your land if there's evidence of sites'. For others, it is wilful destruction born of two centuries of a partial and surreal education. Australia has a lot to celebrate and this region presents excellent opportunities.

One hundred kilometres east of Laura, heading towards the coast, country that gradually changes is suddenly startlingly different. Black forms loom up among vibrant green as though defying every logical explanation of power and volume, not simply due to physical size. Oxidisation and algae have darkened Kalkajaka (also known as Black Mountain). The blackened boulders rest in massive gatherings, protecting the solid core that lies beneath. This is an important place for Kuku Yalanji

people. In conversation with an Elder, a comment is coupled with a question: 'Strong place that one, eh?' The response is quick and simple: 'Yuwu, we don't go there. Too strong. Some people who don't listen go. And trouble comes.' Enough individuals and groups along with their animals have vanished from Kalkajaka: logic tells us to look at the tumbled maze of boulders to explain the disappearances.

Another view is that this is one of the sacred places across the country recognised by the old people as a vital gathering of energy for replenishing the land. Some say there are places where the earth wants to be left alone, without the presence of humans. To ignore the needs of the earth to such a degree is dangerous. These boulders also provide refuge to three known endemic species: the Black Mountain skink, the Black Mountain boulderfrog and the Black Mountain gecko are not known to live elsewhere. Incredible wealth in an area of 600 hectares gives another perspective to the 30,000 on Olive Vale.

Less than thirty kilometres north of Kalkajaka along the highway that cuts its north-west edge, is Gangaarr, the Cooktown area. Situated between mouths of two rivers and cradled by coastal hills, this area holds significant history. Long honoured by the Guugu Yimithirr and surrounding groups as a haven where no human blood was to fall, Gangaarr was a place for gathering, birthing and resolving disputes. A great stroke of luck for the explorer James Cook. In June 1770 he arrived with his crew when their ship, the *Endeavour*, was in dire need of repair. They had spent arduous hours pumping water to keep her afloat at the edge of the reef they'd struck and were relieved to come across Waalumbaal Birri. This river is now commonly known as the Endeavour. The Guugu Yimithirr were not expecting such a significant intrusion into their world. In his diaries, Cook described the exchanges and interactions as amicable and often friendly, despite language and cultural differences. He wrote that 'their Voices were soft and Tunable, and they could easily repeat any word after us, but neither us nor Tupia could understand one word they said'. It's believed the first written record of an Australian Indigenous language was made during this time.

Here too Cook recorded in his diary their first-ever sighting of an Australian macropod, though there is still conjecture about which of the many species they saw. Perhaps an eastern grey kangaroo or agile wallaby, perhaps a whiptail. Guugu Yimithirr speakers confirm that today's generic term for a kangaroo originates from their language, where gangurru describes an 'old man eastern grey kangaroo'. Some people suggest gangurru means 'go away'. This is one example of many where translation across cultures can easily go awry, and the need to turn to Elders who hold knowledge is necessary.

Opposite: View from Grassy Hill of Waalumbaal Birri (Endeavour River) flowing through the hilly country.

Right: Bright orange fruit of pandanus among lush coastal vegetation and sea-swept boulders.

For Joseph Banks, the well-known naturalist aboard the ship, it was an opportunity to record plants and animals he saw and to learn with the Guugu Yimithirr people. His journals describe dingoes, flying foxes, possums and cockatoos among many other creatures so extraordinary to him. According to Banks's diary, and similarly recorded in the diary of Cook, ten Guugu Yimithirr boarded the *Endeavour* for a friendly visit and saw eight or nine turtles on deck. They returned the next day carrying an impressive number of spears. Leaving these on land with a young boy and a man, they boarded the ship communicating in a language that was understood by all. Despite the Guugu Yimithirr making it clear that they were not impressed about the unshared haul, Cook's party refused to part with the turtles. Conflict developed and a few drops of blood fell. Both parties had their say, shots were fired, spears waved, big fires lit. The Guugu Yimithirr knew that blood was not to be spilled. Despite this skirmish, things quickly resolved through common human sense-making and diplomacy, strongly enabled by the cultural governance carried by an old man. Although Cook's party could not understand the man's spoken word, they understood his approach holding a spear without a point. His lore guided him to resolve the situation and his gestures indicated this. Many people of that country say the events of those days are the first recorded reconciliation and look to it for the future of Australia. They speak with pride when talking about their ancestors who negotiated communications with Cook, and see it as a way to unite the diverse cultures of this nation. The story is played out for all to see in Cooktown's theatrical re-enactment of those days, usually held mid-year. You can visit the site, now called Reconciliation Rocks, at any time.

In describing an event that occurred just three or four days after the skirmish, both Cook and Banks give insights from their perspective. They tell how one of their men strayed off track while searching for a particular native plant for food. When he found himself in the company of four locals, he sat with them, unsure what to do, and offered them his knife as a gift. They looked at it, handing it from one to another, and returned it to him. They sat together for a while, during which time they examined his hands and other parts of his body. They soon signalled to him to leave but realising he was heading in the wrong direction corrected his path. Today descendants of those diplomats want to share and celebrate their story of reconciliation with the rest of the country. They speak of the need for the history of their country during that poignant time to be learnt and honoured. In announcing the heritage nomination of Reconciliation Rocks, the National Trust quotes Aunty Alberta Hornsby, a tireless worker for reconciliation, who says: 'We can't change the past, we all have a history. But here in Cooktown we have chosen to show a balance.'

This is just one story of contact between Indigenous people of this land and James Cook, and most do not have the same diplomatic outcome.

Cooktown was established in this area in 1873 as a supply port for the Palmer River goldfields, which brought immense bloodshed, disease and disruption to this land and its people. The industry boomed for a decade or so in which time the town reputedly had more than sixty pub licences and as many brothels to feed the lifestyles of recent arrivals. Riches of the time are still visible today, and you can explore the complex history in places like the James Cook Museum, which is working with local Elders to present a more balanced view; the Cooktown History Centre; the Milbi Wall along the foreshore; and Reconciliation Rocks. Grassy Hill and Mount Cook offer tremendous views of Guugu Yimithirr country. Hills slope and meet the sea, the river turns among them, offering another opportunity to better imagine those early days and how they can shape today.

As the sea stretches out, reefs pattern the blue and mingle with more than 900 islands. Management of the area is shaped in part by the knowledge and leadership of traditional custodians whose cultural responsibilities ensure healthy ecosystems. More than seventy distinct groups hold ongoing and diverse connection to the Reef that stretches 2000 kilometres from the Torres Strait islands. This provides incredible opportunities to honour the wealth of knowledge, as seen in the work of Indigenous rangers across the country.

One of the rivers approximately seventy kilometres south of Gaangarr is Banner Yearie, or Bloomfield. Upstream from the mouth of this river is Wujal Wujal Aboriginal Community, home to Kuku Yalanji, Kuku Nyungul and Jalunji rainforest people. Established by the government in 1886, it was predominantly run by Lutherans and known as Bloomfield River Mission. Some travellers know it as a quick stop along the Bloomfield Track, which connects Cooktown and Cape Tribulation. It is touted as one of Australia's greatest four-wheel-drive tracks, but is also highly contentious, known for significant protests against its construction in the 1980s. The logging industry, land developers and Queensland government

Above and near right: Wujal Wujal
Waterfall with Francis Walker
explaining the richness of country
and her stories.

Right (middle): The Banner Yearie
(Bloomfield River) near Wujal Wujal
provides habitat for diverse life
including enormous crocodiles.
Don't test the water here.

Far right: Spectacular tropical life
seen in this vine suspended metres
across in many directions.

strongly contested that there would be impacts on rare ecosystems of the Wet Tropics brought by increased intrusion. Vested interests moved the argument this way and that, increasing national and international attention. Despite strong government opposition, requirements for World Heritage Listing were investigated and, finally, in 1988 the Wet Tropics were inscribed onto the World Heritage List.

Those of us lucky enough to travel through these lush hills can only begin to imagine how life, and therefore the land, would be if current management more closely aligned to that of the country's First People. Priorities continue to shift between Indigenous knowledge and practices, commercial activity, biodiversity, tourism and other considerations. Many of these could complement each other if we choose to respect long-known truths.

It is said that wujal wujal means many waterfalls and the one closest to town seasonally gushes down broad rock a half-hour walk from the Aboriginal Shire Council, just beyond Bana Yirriji Arts Centre. Custodians of this significant site regularly share their culture with school groups and visitors. Why be there on your own if you can be accompanied by one of the Walker sisters, who will welcome you to their country, tell you their story and share knowledge? As is sometimes the case for bodies of water, traditional custodians ask that no one takes a dip, and not just because of the risk of becoming a crocodile snack. Around here, many waterfalls and pools are women's places, sometimes specifically for birthing. As a basic gesture

of goodwill and understanding, exercise restraint accordingly. Some may complain that such sites are not signposted with protocols and other information worthy of our attention, but the reasons are many and include protecting places that can more safely exist unnoticed. We all have a responsibility to learn and can decide to give a place its privacy by reconsidering an outing. Kija, popularly known as Roaring Meg Falls, is long honoured by men and women, but men do not venture near, despite the allure of its beauty and refreshing water.

If you choose to spend time in Wujal Wujal and share conversation with a local, you might learn about old bush camps where children would watch grandfathers making tools and oars out of local timbers, and the sadness of the old people at the overwhelming absence of majestic cedars, tragically logged out by 1877. You will see the site of the mission and old school and understand the lay of the land a little more as you imagine children walking the tracks and revelling in family time by the river. You might hear of excellent medicine made from yanga (green ants) and how flying fox helps bronchial conditions. Leaves of the important ironwood might be collected and used especially for you, and while walking you will meet some other plants and animals that nourish people – perhaps yams and pipis, eggs of scrubhens and so much more. Bulkiji (pipis) are mourned by the women as their number has dramatically diminished. The women have thoughts about why this may be and seek solutions for how to quieten the disturbance. You might learn about dulkal dulkal, whose small drooping plumes of creamy flowers tell us oysters are fat and good eating and whose big leaves were used by the old people when cooking damper. Perhaps you'll see a particular acacia whose flowering indicates it's time to look for those eggs laid by the scrub hen. The people of the rainforest maintained a relatively dense population because here the earth's great fertility sustained the ethos they chose, which they wish to share with you today.

Important information

As with all waterways in this part of Australia, be wary of crocodiles. If you cannot see them, it is safer to assume they are there, watching. Same applies to jellyfish, though they might not be watching. Always carry plenty of water and respect local laws regarding alcohol. Many communities have strict bans on entry. It is advisable to cover your skin with loose fitting clothes to help protect you from sun, mosquitoes and sandflies.

Indigenous cultural experiences, tours and relevant organisations

In or near Laura

Quinkan Regional Cultural Centre

The centre's informative display provides information regarding the local ancient culture and more recent changes. Book your tours here – be sure to ask if one of the Indigenous guides is available. The community takes the care of the incredible paintings very seriously and asks visitors to do the same. Visitor numbers need to be controlled for the long-term preservation of this place so if at any time you are told you cannot visit, take joy in the knowledge that your absence is an important part of active care for country.

2 Peninsula
Developmental Rd
07 4060 3457 or
1300 594 900
quinkancc.com.au

Rinyirru (Lakefield) National Park

This is a seasonally accessible area and is usually closed in the wet season, so please check before you go. High rainfall can make roads impassable. Ignoring road closure signs may compromise the safety of others and likely damage the roads for time to come. There are many small tracks off the main dirt road and respectful travel is necessary. There are areas where you will be asked not to enter due to cultural significance, so please respect the people and country.

2km north of Laura, on Peninsula Developmental Rd to the Rinyirru (Lakefield) turn-off

Split Rock

If for some reason you cannot meet one of the local tour guides working through the Quinkan Regional Cultural Centre for a guided tour, you can visit Split Rock on your own. The uphill walk leads you past rock-art galleries of varying complexity and story. Please always respect the signs, do not venture beyond, and enjoy pondering the ancient layers and local figures. Please be sure to carry cash and pay the very modest fee – the community appreciates it when people show good will.

12km south of Laura, on Peninsula Developmental Rd

Laura Dance Festival

This unique celebration is held on ancient ceremony grounds where many groups of the region have gathered for countless generations. Check the festival's website for the latest updates.

anggnarra.org.au/our-country/laura-dance-festival

In or near Gangaar (Cooktown)

Kuku Bulkaway Indigenous Art Gallery

You can enjoy the work of local artists whose inspiration comes from their connection to the land and sea that surrounds them. They share stories of plants, animals, bush foods and life in the Cape York region.

142 Charlotte St
07 4069 6957
kukubulkaway.com.au

Milbi Wall

This story wall is a local icon for reconciliation. You are invited to learn rich details of Aboriginal history – from the creation of ancient rivers to recent events such as the 1967 referendum. Allow time for this complex work, as images and words of local artists set in ceramic tiles deserve attention and time.

Foreshore, Charlotte St, 150m north of Hill St

Mount Cook National Park

Be ready for some steady uphills through diverse ecosystems offering expansive views of surrounding country. Keep a look out for all sorts of creatures – from beautiful green tree snakes that are not always green to birds that have travelled from New Guinea. A walk begins near a small carpark in Hannam St near Boundary St.

parks.des.qld.gov.au/parks/mount-cook/about.html

Grassy Hill

You can drive to the top of Grassy Hill for immense views and richly layered stories of the area's Indigenous people and recent changes in their country. Walking up the steep road offers some informative stops and excellent opportunities to appreciate the scale and flow of the country. The Scenic Rim walk that connects Grassy Hill to Cherry Tree Bay, the Botanic Gardens and Finch Bay can be found near the lookout.

Hope St

James Cook Museum

Exciting partnerships create interesting presentations at this museum, where a clear view of history supports a positive shared future.

Cnr Helen and Furneaux Sts
07 4069 5386
nationaltrustqld.org.au/heritage-sites/James-Cook-Museum

Cooktown History Centre and Cooktown Re-enactment Association

You will discover something new when you visit this centre, which is packed full of stories told through photographs, paintings, objects and more. The knowledgeable people who work here are committed to telling the shared story of this country.

121a Charlotte St
07 4069 6861

Cooktown Botanic Gardens

Established in 1878, the Cooktown Botanic Gardens are a wonderful place to admire and learn about local flora and fauna, with some information related to Indigenous plant use. The Botanic Gardens are part of connected bushland reserves that provide important habitat and opportunities for terrific walks such as the Scenic Rim Walking Trail.

Walker St, 1.5km from the centre of town
cooktownandcapeyork.com/do/nature/plants/botanic_gardens
cooktownandcapeyork.com/do/walks/scenic-rim-walking-trail

Mulbabidgee

Now also known as Keatings Lagoon, Mulbabidgee offers a short walk among seasonally variable expanses of water lilies and abundant birdlife, mangroves, vine forest and tropical woodland. Be sure to cover your skin with loose-fitting clothing, tight around ankles and wrists, or the mosquitoes will show their appreciation.

About 5km south of Cooktown along the Mulligan Hwy
cooktownandcapeyork.com/do/walks/keatings-lagoon-walk

In or near Wujal Wujal

Wujal Wujal Waterfall

Contact the Walker Family Tours for a richer experience when visiting this important cultural site, the closest waterfall to the Wujal Wujal community. The waterfall is less than two kilometres south of town; you can walk from town along the fairly flat road following the path of the river. The short track leading to the waterfall becomes a little steep and loose in areas. If you need to drive from town to the start of this track, there is some space to park your car nearby but be mindful of small tour buses.

cooktownandcapeyork.com/
tours/local-tours/walker-
family-tours

Bana Yirriji Art and Cultural Centre

This centre was rebuilt in 2019 after flood damage, and is a wonderful place for learning and better understanding local culture, meeting artists and purchasing their work. It is located less than one kilometre south from the centre of Wujal Wujal community, along the same road that leads to Wujal Wujal Waterfall.

736 Douglas St
07 4060 8333
wujalwujalartcentre.com.au

Wujal Wujal Aboriginal Shire Council

In the centre of town, the council office can provide information on the area.

Lot 1, Hartwig St
07 4083 9100
wujalwujalcouncil.qld.gov.au

A small sample of other places in the region

Yarrabah Arts and Cultural Precinct (YACP)

Visit here to see the impressive gallery with pottery, painting and more, and the Menmuny Museum, along with art studios and a rainforest walk. Situated in the coastal Aboriginal Shire of Yarrabah, YACP offers an excellent opportunity for connection, learning and sharing. It is said that Yarrabah is the traditional name in the language of the Gunggadji people for the freshwater creek near which the mission was built in 1892. This is another place of mixed history and turmoil, as Indigenous people from far and wide were forcibly removed from their country and relocated here.

Museum Rd off Back Beach Rd, Yarrabah
yarrabah.qld.gov.au/
artcentre

Hope Vale Art and Culture Centre

Here you will see vibrant prints, paintings, ceramics and textiles by local artists whose imagery often reflects the sea's significance and the biodiversity of the area.

1 Flierl St, Hope Vale
hopevaleart.org.au

Gab Titui Cultural Centre

If you keep heading north from Laura, you can learn about the rich cultures of Torres Strait Islanders. Gab Titui Cultural Centre is the Torres Strait's first keeping place for historical artefacts and contemporary Indigenous culture. Here, the sea and land are intimately connected physically and therefore culturally. As with Indigenous communities throughout Australia, Torres Strait Islanders hold significant celestial stories, and these provide guidance for travel, hunting, loving and more.

Cnr Victoria Pde and Blackall St, Thursday Island
07 4069 0888
gabtitui.gov.au

KATH

Vicky Shukuroglou

Near the south-western edge of the
Arnhem Land Plateau, a little over 200 kilometres
south of Van Diemen Gulf, between
the Timor and Arafura seas

ERINE
REGION

Jawoyn, Dalabon, Rembarrnga, Gunwinggu, Wardaman and Mayali

Language groups

It's said you can smell this great island hundreds of kilometres offshore as you approach by ship from crisp Antarctic waters. Complex oils of eucalypts dominate. The scent of our country. Whether lived or dreamed, we can revel in what this does for our own appreciation and imagining.

Approaching the 'top end' of Australia provides a similar effect as vegetation transitions in radiance and scent, telling us of changes in soil and movement of water. From a great distance, large areas of colour appear to seep and merge, great connected tendrils curl and open, some boundaries blur and distinctions between water, vegetation and soil become less apparent. The diversity of the Mitchell Grass Downs bioregion extends towards the north-west from the area now known as central Queensland, sweeps around the south of Mount Isa through parts of Yalarnnga, Pitta-Pitta and Wangkamanha country, continuing through Warluwarra, Bularnu, Wakaya, Wambaya and Warumungu country, dwindling around Jingili country approximately 300 kilometres south of the town of Katherine. This is the south-west edge of Jawoyn lands. Around here, the country transforms into the world's largest expanse of most intact savannah, stretching across the north of this island. The abundance of life is spectacular and diverse. Ecosystems vary dramatically and include dry open woodland, sandstone plateaus and heathlands, wet monsoon vine forests, swamps, billabongs and riverine systems – some with floodplains stretching kilometres from riverbanks. Specific tree-type forests such as paperbark, lancewood and acacia are also important elements. These complexities and the formation of the country have shaped Jawoyn language and its speakers.

Nestled among crevices and plants, encountered by all kinds of different animal feet, noses, whiskers and tongues, are some of this land's oldest stone tools and their debitage from local manufacture. A burrowing frog pressing through soil to escape the daily heat has likely felt sharp edges of stone purposely crafted by hand, and perhaps a pebble mound mouse incorporates some in the building of its home. It is worth contemplating whether a black-breasted buzzard seeking a tool to break open a hard-shelled egg would select an already honed stone. Had you been in the area a few decades ago you may have spotted a golden bandicoot who turned such tools while foraging for nutritious tubers and insects. Due to their age and environmental change, many of these implements are now buried beneath metres of earth. At times they lie in significant layers along with other signs of consistent human habitation such as remnants of hearths and plant material discarded during processing. Among the larger stones are those used by people to grind fruits, seeds and various forms of bulbs in preparations of nourishing meals. Some were used for the refinement of pigments including shades of yellow, pink, red, purple and brown, along with black and white.

Descendants of those innovators are now partnering with other researchers to investigate ancient stories embedded in these tools in the form of plant particles and marks of worked surfaces. Ongoing oral traditions describing connections to this country and ways for living through dramatic change across vast time are complemented by increasingly reliable methods for dating, analysing and piecing together information. The rich perspectives and extensive resources such collaborations generate are available for all of us to delve into; these are exciting times full of opportunities to better understand intimate details of our country and develop sensitive responses. This region has much to offer and enriches the international story.

Sandstone of the Arnhem Land Plateau rises more than 300 metres above current sea level, with some rock dated to 2500 million years. Water significantly shapes this country. Large expanses were once covered by sea, and cliffs that now rise steeply more than one hundred kilometres inland were part of the old shore. Transformation of the earth never ceases, and today the south-west outlying edge of the plateau continues to be slowly sculpted by waters that feed the river now known as Katherine. Headwaters rise deep in Jawoyn country, 150 kilometres north-east of Katherine township. These waters join the Daly River, travelling north-westwards for 350 kilometres to the Timor Sea. Old stories from and for this country tell of the magnitude of such processes and give another view to time and scale.

Jawoyn knowledge describes the earliest times when ancestor beings formed the country through their actions. Discussion of events and important figures is

Above: A little less than 300 kilometres south-west of Katherine is Timber Creek township. High Court decisions affirmed the significance of Ngaliwurru and Nungali people's connection to this country. The Nackeroo Lookout just out of town offers terrific views along with details of local history and acknowledges the Aboriginal trackers who assisted the Northern Australia Observation Unit during World War II. In the background is Victoria River.

Right: Country rich with Jawoyn stories in the Katherine region.

Far right: Katherine River.

Colourful denizens of the gorge – karrak (red-tailed black cockatoo), yey'yey (blue-faced honeyeater), purrirt (little red flying fox – must surely be a male) and one of many reptile species.

careful and at times muted. Details ought to be spoken by those who have cultural authority, and those who listen also hold responsibility. They need to be capable and ready to carry their wealth. There is much at stake. Stories recorded and shared for all of us to contemplate offer a view that opens as widely as we nurture.

Bula, a great creator, travelled vast distances from northern saltwater with his two wives, the Ngallenjilenji. As he travelled and hunted, made rope, spilled blood and carried out other essential activities, he left his imprint in multiple forms, sometimes as rocks themselves, sometimes as paintings sheltered by them. Jawoyn Elders describe the country on which we walk and plants and animals that live here as the result of these travels. Language, kinship systems, ceremony and associated protocols were handed to people by the ancestors. All kinds of details were established – from the manufacture of tools and use of fire to the structure of appropriate relations within families and with neighbours. To disregard protocols – often connected to appropriate care of country – dishonours the ancestors and brings risks to self and the broader community. These can be severe. In conversation with a local, you might hear how Bula the powerful being went underground north of Katherine and remains within. The area is known as Buladjang, or Sickness Country and it is imbued with much power. Here, water- and air-quality tests confirm high concentrations of uranium, thorium, arsenic, mercury, fluorine and radon and it is these very chemical elements that attract mining companies. Causing disturbance to the area, and therefore Bula, is perilous. Old protocols are rigorous and largely held firm today. Should you plan to visit the designated areas, you are asked to consider your approach.

Many will recall immense turmoil and political tensions over proposed mining leases within this area, with Guratba (Coronation Hill) a focus. In the early 1990s, during Bob Hawke's governance, the area was added to the already existing Kakadu National Park, giving relief to those concerned about the international impacts of digging up the earth. Not all positions in support of looking after country have been respected, as areas further north within Kakadu National Park were excised, allowing uranium mines to go ahead despite resistance by the Mirarr people. Following nuclear disasters in Japan, Yvonne Margarula, senior Mirarr custodian, wrote a detailed letter in 2011 to Ban Ki-moon, secretary-general of the United Nations at the time. These short excerpts show her concerns:

Dear Secretary-General,
It was with great sadness that we Mirarr People of the World Heritage listed Kakadu National Park in the Northern Territory of Australia learned of the suffering of the Japanese people due [to] the recent earthquake, tsunami and nuclear crisis. Our thoughts and prayers are with the people of Japan at this most difficult of times ...

Given the long history between Japanese nuclear companies and Australian uranium miners, it is likely that the radiation problems at Fukushima are, at least in part, fuelled by uranium derived from our traditional lands. This makes us feel very sad. Ranger [mine] has operated since 1980 and has brought much hardship to local Aboriginal people and environmental damage to our country.

Today some 12 million litres of radioactive contaminated water lies on site at the Ranger Uranium Mine, upstream of Indigenous communities and internationally recognised Ramsar listed wetlands.

If you read Yvonne Margarula's eloquent letter you will gain some understanding of her commitment and connection to her country, her community's participation in the international movement against the nuclear industry, and her concerns for the disproportionate impact on the world's Indigenous minority groups whose

Idyllic pools at Leliyn (also known as Edith Falls), one of many significant sites of the region.

homelands provide seventy per cent of the world's uranium used in nuclear reactors. You may be struck by her concluding words, which reflect the same beliefs of power held within country as expressed by Jawoyn people:

> We believe and have always believed that when this Djang is disturbed a great and dangerous power is unleashed upon the entire world. My father warned the Australian Government about this in the 1970s, but no one in positions of power listened to him. We hope that people such as yourself will listen, and act, today.

Much closer to Katherine is Nitmiluk, a complex system of gorges just thirty kilometres from town. The Jawoyn people tell of the name being given by Nabilil, a crocodile or dragon-like being from the early days of earth's formation. He had travelled from the coastal area west of here, carrying water and firesticks in a dilly bag. In dry country, animals were thirsty and seeking water. His interactions with Lumbuk the pigeon, Garrkayn the brown goshawk, Wakwak the crow and Walarrk the cave bat, among others, gave life to the country here and its waters. Nabilil also travelled through Garrakla, an area you will traverse just north of Katherine. This impressive limestone formation is an important place to be respected, despite now being physically divided by the Stuart Highway. Nabilil also moved through Wurliwurliyn-jang, Mosquito Dreaming place, which is near the central business district and now overlayed with footpaths, roads and buildings.

As you move about Katherine, you might see the name Wurli Wurlinjang Health Service. This is a community-controlled Aboriginal medical service, which was originally situated at Wurliwurliyn-jang site. Their logo is an acknowledgement of this, as well as the important billygoat plum. The walls of the meeting room are richly animated with figures from old stories, painted by Paddy Fordham Wainburranga. There are hundreds of sites within the town of Katherine that have been significantly altered in the last 150 years, the details of which are mostly withheld from public knowledge. This is often considered to be the most effective way to provide greatest protection from potential damage. As we all deepen our understanding of country, cultural protocols and each other, alternative approaches will emerge.

During his journey, Nabilil rested at the gorge, where he heard 'Nit! Nit! Nitnit!', the song of Nitmi the cicada. The richly layered story continues with his travels and describes how Walarrk speared Nabilil a long way from the mouth of the gorge. The stone-tipped spear caused Nabilil's death and released the life-giving water he was carrying, now flowing through the country.

Among the rise and drop of the plateau are innumerable ancient paintings and those tools holding human stories from long ago. In descriptions of the region during the early 1900s, English anthropologist Baldwin Spencer wrote:

> Up on the hill sides, among the rocks, wherever there is an overhanging shelter where the native can screen himself from the sun and rain, these drawings are certain to be found in the country of the Kakadu.

Near the headwaters of rivers including the Katherine, Nawarla Gabarnmang exists as a breathtaking example of human creativity, adaptation and belief. Specific conditions of powerful geological forces and the interplay of water and wind over millions of years shaped this site of stepped escarpments and striking pillars.

A very old path used by Jawoyn people begins at Nitmiluk Gorge and follows the edge of the Arnhem Land escarpment through diverse country. The trail is named after Peter Jatbula, a highly respected Jawoyn man whose commitment to caring for country was key in securing land rights.

The space between pillars is intriguing. This is an ancient gallery, a celebration, a living area that has been modified with sensitivity and refinement. Surfaces are vibrant with hundreds of dynamic figures, various animals and tools painted with distinct local traits.

Most of us will only see photographs or read words that will always fall short. Gleaning joy from our absence and delighting in its presence gives Nawarla Gabarnmang the protection it needs. Extensive scientific papers bring its remarkable history to our attention – at least 47,000 years since first occupation, 26,000 years of painting tradition and 35,000 years of crafting stone axes with ground edges for specific purposes. That's the oldest of such tools found worldwide – significant in the context of human movement and cognitive development plus transfer of knowledge. The space raises countless questions, and we may endlessly ponder the reasoning of those old people and the experiments they conducted when shaping and removing pillars that provided more room and alternative uses. The layers and connections here are infinite and abundant with human spirit.

Among the rocks that have been chipped, removed, shaped, piled and placed are pillows. That's right, pillows. Some Jawoyn people speak of them today in much the same way others living in distant places with different views of this vast island, speaking distinct languages and eating their local foods, also speak of stones being used as pillows. Someone's head was held here while they rested, perhaps after throwing that last bone from their meal onto the fire or before grinding pigment in preparation for a concentrated time of painting.

What would be the feelings of the very first painters whose images carry layers of others if they saw the structure today? When did they first harvest sugarbag, valuing it for the energy provided and wax applied in creation of images? Today's stories of tracking native bees in this country describe fluffy surrounds of pamjon (yellow kapok) or jej (red flowered kapok) being placed onto the little creatures, making them easy to follow. What would they think of your interest in their story and this land, and commitment to its care?

Madjedbebe, in Mirarr country, is another site of extensive research offering clues to the global human puzzle. Thousands of tools lie within the ground, with the oldest being in use 53,000 to 65,000 years ago. These include grinding stones for processing several types of plant foods – including fruits, seeds and tubers. Among the tools are

Nitmiluk Gorge's quiet majesty.

copious quantities of ochre and fine sparkling layers of mica, enhancing paintings on the rock walls. Perhaps here too, as in other parts of the land, people applied it onto their bodies, the firelight glinting dramatic shapes of dance and ancient story.

Each curve of a particular edge, angle of a point, and image honoured on a wall brought to life with the most meticulous of strokes offers insights into the minds and capacities of the first colonisers of this land. These riches invite our contemplation, a journey to another time when the country's sounds and smells would be somewhat familiar to us today. How would we solve the vast array of challenges in sourcing foods that provide adequate nourishment, and what decisions would we make in establishing and maintaining cohesion within and among groups while venturing into unknown territory and constructing comfortable homes?

Dramatic changes in climate and geology, seasonal variation and fluctuations in the prevalence of flora and fauna on which each human relies demanded innovation for survival. The propensity of life to respond to an opportunity, to fill an apparent gap, is relentless. Inventive people could more easily travel long distances, equipped with knowledge from lands already inhabited. As humans colonised this island and established priorities through testing ideas and refining processes, impacts on other lifeforms were likely observed and actions adjusted as deemed appropriate. Some innovations were pursued while others were put aside, shaping the country with every decision. These ongoing processes with waves of refinement and occupation

This page and opposite: Some plants of the region, many at the Banatjarl Garden, including (clockwise from top) kirringkirring (jungle beads), mangal (cocky apple), djirr (lemongrass), pangaynpangayn (bush tomato) and jarrmarn (red-flowered kurrajong).

across our planet are evident in tools of various forms and here they were handed to the people by the great ancestors who remain in the country today. These tools vary dramatically – largely shaped by location and energy efficiency – from barely manipulated and utilised as hammers, to constructions with multiple parts and materials, or beautifully refined like the T-shaped 'Ooyurka' from the north-east tropics. Researchers describe tools that have lasted three million years of being bedded down, upheaved and exposed, though what kind of individual or group made them and left them in what is now a riverbed in Kenya is unknown. The country here holds clues to significant questions.

If you walk the steep slopes of Nitmiluk or have the opportunity to admire the glowing rock and brilliant water from a riverboat, you'll be immersed in the economy of the early humans of this island – evident in the images on rock walls, in biodiversity, in knowledge shared today. Every decision led to what exists here, and the Jawoyn people are passionate about sharing their culture with you. The old people warned against certain transgressions. Today we are faced with similar decisions, leading to equally reflective outcomes. The Mirarr people know this too well.

The White Paper on Developing Northern Australia describes the government's aspiration for Australia to be 'Asia's energy supplier of choice from a balance of sources – natural gas, uranium, coal and next generation biofuels'. Its overview document does not mention climate change despite the Defence White Paper identifying climate change as a 'contributing factor to a number of security

Above (left): The Banatjarl garden with prominent pandanus and grove of native fruit trees.
Above (right): Healing balms made by the women, with pandanus baskets coloured using plant dyes.

issues, such as state fragility and the undermining of economic development in our immediate region'. While the words 'Indigenous' and 'Native Title' appear, surprisingly you will not find words such as responsibility, flora, fauna, plants, animals, sustainability, biodiversity and nature.

Banatjarl Strongbala Wimun Grup is an Indigenous enterprise achieving strong outcomes for women, their families and the broader community of the Katherine region. This collective, guided by a Council of Elders and connected to the Jawoyn Association, has developed an effective presence since forming in 2003 and is an important resource generated, and turned to, by women and their families who carry Jawoyn language and those of surrounding areas including Dalabon, Rembarrnga, Mayali and Gunwinggu. Their activities and documents emphasise cultural well-being and traditional healing, nurturing and sharing knowledge. Ensuring young ones are supported in strengthening their connection to country while learning with Elders is critical. Promoting and enabling time on country, where growing, harvesting and processing plants whose properties have been highly regarded for millennia, is a key focus and opportunity for cultivating rich understandings.

The women gather and care for the garden established on culturally important land, and tend to the various plants including djirr (native lemongrass), jampurl/

kayawal (long yam), mangal/pamkujji (cocky apple) and yiwung/murrungkurn (black currant). These provide many functions within and beyond their ecosystems, as seeds, tubers, bark, fruits and leaves are seasonally harvested and eaten; woven; made into string or rope; chewed; used for dying fibre, repelling insects, flavouring and wrapping food, and ceremonial purposes; or are prepared as medicines for the community and for sale to the public. Having sustained thousands of generations of people, we know these are tested and proven ingredients and processes. It is a wonderful thing to contemplate whether one of the marntappurru (milky plum), pirt (canarium/white beech) or other plants currently growing in the Banatjarl garden is a descendant of the one whose residue was left behind after processing and eating and now found and dated to tens of thousands of years.

As you travel through any part of Australia and contemplate the depth of story that resides here and the ongoing care in relation *with* country, what value do you see in the land, its waters and all they hold? What kind of a map would you draw, and how could you show the potential of our nation? What emphasis would you choose and what plans would you propose for the future?

Inclusions or exclusions on a map indicate priorities, as we can readily notice while travelling. As part of their Developing Northern Australia Plan, industry and government produced a detailed map. How it would compare to one prepared by Jawoyn, Mirarr and other Elders raises interesting questions.

Sharing Our Country is the Jawoyn Association's 'tagline', and these words are carried through their work. It recognises the sentiment Elders carried even through the turmoil of the late 1970s when a claim was lodged for the Jawoyn to be recognised as traditional custodians. People of the Jawoyn Association are still bolstered and guided by the Elders' welcoming philosophy instilled in many from a young age. They explain that we are all invited to share in their vision for the future. In striving to 'improve the cultural, social and economic well-being of the Jawoyn people, while always caring for country', the Jawoyn Association has prepared a Healthy Country Plan in consultation with the community. Their vision of healthy country is 'a place where our cultural sites, plants and animals and water places are thriving and cared for'.

Their plan identifies key values including language, knowledge, law, art sites, burial and ceremonial grounds, 'wark' (water places), regenerative fire, appropriate community connection and employment with care for country. They have also identified key threats including weeds and feral animals such as buffalo, cats, cane toads and pigs, destructive fire practices, climate change, unauthorised land use, unhealthy lifestyles and the pressure of development including groundwater extraction and damming, pastoralism, agriculture, land clearing and mining.

These complexities are evident as we move through this country if we take the time and care to see. If we embrace the invitation extended to us by the Jawoyn people, what could be our best contribution, knowing what is at stake?

Wugularr (Beswick) community offers opportunities to delve deeply, respectfully, in an incredible space for quiet contemplation. Gunwinjgu, or the Company of People, is a rich embodiment of the lives of people here, of all that has come to be. In 1996, senior Mayali speakers Djoli Laiwonga, David Blanasi, Paddy Fordham Wainburranga and Tom Kelly decided to create a collection of artwork as one of the many ways to share, establish and maintain cultural connection for their young ones, for visitors, for others in distant cities. After years of patience, determination, tragedies and activity, the paintings were housed in a renovated building, at home, within the Wugularr community. This building is a temple of sorts – a distinctly sacred feeling rests within. Terrific life force and wisdom reside here. The paintings are of this country – not just in what they depict. Layers embedded within each image will be unknown to most of us, but, because we are all human, we will understand a lot and, the more loving our eye, the richer our perception. We could talk for hours about each painting and never stop carrying them in our being; the deftness of hands that drew the lines, the cross-hatching in precisely the way it needs to be arranged depending on who the painter is and which part of the extraordinary web of community they fit, the dynamic yet subtle movement of creatures with their country, plants, waterways, their interactions, and complex spirits who shape stories of all life. These are ways of being in the world, of cultivating a particular ethos that yields the outcomes you perceive in escarpments, between rocks, along riverbeds, in bush gardens. One of the paintings shows animals of freshwater – food provided by healthy country. A young man who used to watch his grandfather paint each day explains that the composition speaks of a different story from another one nearby that could appear to be similar in imagery. It would be reasonable to say that these paintings show country and food sources including the long-neck turtle, crab, crayfish and other creatures. Another reading tells us that these paintings speak

Left: Boab.

Below: The power of fire on country.

for the care of country and neighbours, for respecting their place and following protocols should we wish to enter. It is a painting for honouring relationships and health, for ensuring vitality in country whose abundance is not just there for taking.

It is said that within this island the conditions were just what were needed for songbirds of the world to develop their evolutionary path. The scents and sounds, colours, textures, fruits, flowers, nectar, tubers, rocks, cicada songs, pigments, animals' feet, nests, pouches and mammalian eggs of this land continue to be part of these incredible stories. Such immense wealth. The old people observed carefully, and recognised cause and effect. They read and interpreted impacts on life in innumerable forms and refined all they could accordingly. Did they ever have to consider the silence that falls upon a place when it loses capacity to provide for life? What may have been their response? As we travel this country, whether in thought or movement, what can we activate to ease threats and cultivate values? If we consider the legacy of those old people and what we cherish today, how can we honour the invitation of the Jawoyn people and ensure the scent of this country, and all that it holds, remains strong?

Katherine

Indigenous cultural experiences, tours and relevant organisations

Nitmiluk National Park, Visitor Centre and Tours

The Nitmiluk National Park Visitor Centre is an award-winning enterprise offering all you could wish for when you visit Nitmiluk Gorge. You can book tours on the river by canoe or boat, informative walks, and various options for accommodation from camping to special private rooms at Cicada Lodge.

People who work here can share their knowledge of the walking trails through the national park. Be aware that many walks can be gruelling in the heat of the day, especially in rocky country. There is also a cafe and shop with terrific publications for sale. Being wholly Jawoyn owned, proceeds fund important services and programs and support employment and training in tourism and land management. Explore their website for more.

30km north-east of Katherine, along Gorge Rd
08 8972 1253 or 1300 146 743
nitmiluktours.com.au

Leliyn (Edith Falls)

If you are well prepared and fit enough to walk the 60km Jatbula Trail, you will travel through diverse country including monsoon forest, woodland and riverine systems. The trail begins at Nitmiluk and ends at Leliyn – a spectacular place, full of ancient stories, that transforms dramatically with the seasons.

60km north of Katherine, along Stuart Hwy (park entry is 20km further along Edith Falls Rd)
08 8975 4852

Mimi Aboriginal Art & Craft

Representing artists from freshwater and saltwater country, from the desert to the Kimberley and Arnhem Land. Mimi exhibits and sells paintings, pottery, textiles, prints, carvings and more. Check the website for details of workshops.

6 Pearce St
08 8971 0036
mimiarts.com

Merrepen Arts

You could enjoy many hours in this wonderful arts centre with paintings, ceramics, prints, weavings and textiles made by artists of the Nauiyu (Daly River) area. They also sell some interesting publications. Cultural tours can be arranged.

Lot 37 Nauiyu Community, Nauiyu (263km from Katherine)
08 8978 2533
merrepenarts.com.au

Djilpin Arts

As described on their informative website, Djilpin Arts is a community-owned, not-for-profit organisation based in the remote Indigenous community of Beswick/Wugularr. Revel in the Blanasi Collection, the colourful retail store, and find out about accommodation options, tours and if the Walking with Spirits Festival is on at the time of your visit.

Ghunmarn Culture Centre, 2 Cameron Rd, Beswick (106km from Katherine)
0488 961 511
djilpinarts.org.au

Barunga Festival

Held in June each year – three days of dancing, live music (traditional and contemporary) art shows, cultural workshops and lots of sport. Learn about the history of the festival and how it was established, connections to the Barunga Statement and Yothu Yindi's song *Treaty*.

70km south-east of Katherine, along Central Arnhem Rd
barungafestival.com.au

Other things to see and do

Katherine Visitor Information Centre

Cnr Lindsay St & Katherine Tce
08 8972 2650 or 1800 653 142
visitkatherine.com.au

Godinymayin Yijard Rivers Arts & Cultural Centre

Regional art centre with changing exhibitions as well as performances.

Lot 3238 Stuart Hwy,
Katherine East
08 8972 3751
gyracc.org.au

Katherine Bird Festival

This festival for bird lovers has a focus on conservation with many events focused on the vulnerable Gouldian finch, Check the festival's Facebook page or contact the Katherine Visitor Information Centre for information. Look out for the Northern Territory Birding Trails map.

Further reading and listening

MalakMalak and Matngala Plants and Animals: Aboriginal Flora and Fauna Knowledge from the Daly River Area, Northern Australia is a wonderful resource embodying the knowledge of many people. This book provides information for more than 400 plants and animals, and gives interesting details regarding language.

The Jawoyn Association, in partnership with other organisations, has a similar publication relevant to Jawoyn country and language. Look for *Jawoyn Plants and Animals: Aboriginal Flora and Fauna Knowledge from Nitmiluk National Park and the Katherine Area, Northern Australia*.

Also search the CSIRO website for Indigenous calendars offering a view into the seasons of the region and other areas.

csiro.au/en/Research/Environment/Land-management/Indigenous/Indigenous-calendars

The Arnhem, Northern and Kimberley Artists Aboriginal Corporation (ANKA) provides a terrific overview of arts centres and organisations.

anka.org.au

Listen to *Nitmiluk*, a song by Blekbala Mujik, which celebrates the strength of cultural identity through connection to country and so much more.

BROO

Bruce Pascoe

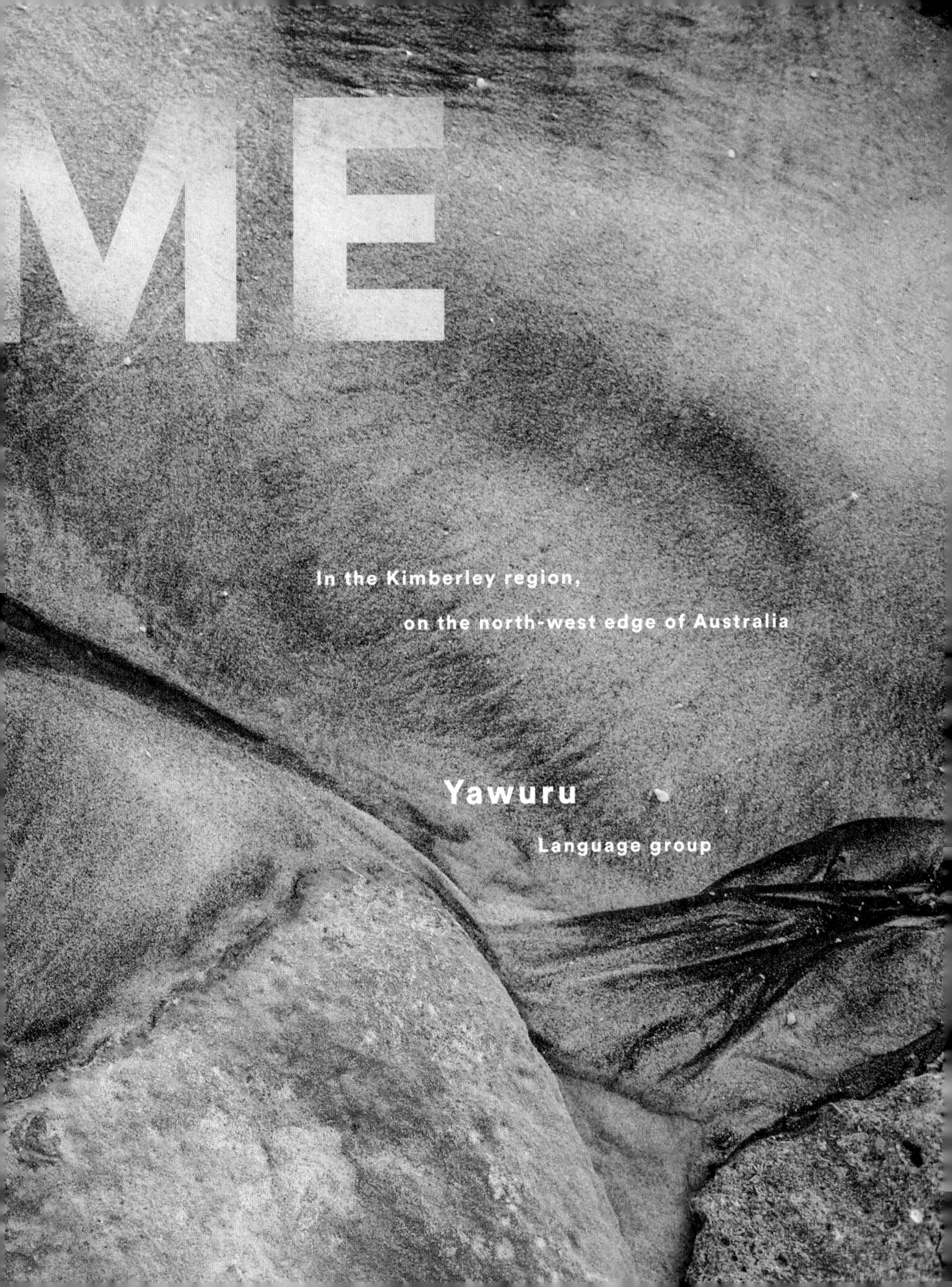

ME

In the Kimberley region,

on the north-west edge of Australia

Yawuru

Language group

The four-wheel drives often look like
military vehicles. Shovels, jacks, ramps,
enough equipment to enter a war.
And some tourists, like their forefathers,
see themselves at war with the country;
they are going to attack the Gibb River
Road, defeat the perils of the road to
Cape Leveque, overcome all opposition
on the Tanami Track.

The journey is not in sympathy with
the land but against it. Dominion:
I went there, I conquered it! There's a
hint that the invasion is not yet over.

But we beg you to forget the dust, the glory of digging yourself out of sand and bog, and instead come with us to the mangrove. Mangroves are not the sexiest tourism lure but for our people they are a larder, a kitchen, a playground.

You can literally walk out of the centre of Broome with a hat and water bottle and be deep in the mangroves in twenty minutes. Sit down, listen. Have a drink of water, quieten your soul.

What is that clicking? Click, click, click, shuffle. Whose was that wing, the sudden explosion of voice? The crab and the bird and that other noise – you almost missed it. That subtle creeping muffled sibilance. The tide is coming in, whispering its lore. Listen to the crab and worm holes breathe and sigh as they are engulfed by the incoming tide. This is what the crab was beckoning, this is what the bird was telling you, the great pulse of the mangroves is stealing towards your feet, unseen until there it is, sloughing at the base of the mangroves, truckling around their knotted roots, obedient as ever to the unseen moon.

And if you are lucky enough to be with one of the Aboriginal guides, you might even see the sacred lagoon deep in the mangrove heart. Most who come to Broome see the Staircase to the Moon over Roebuck Bay, visit the dinosaur footprints at Gantheaume Point and are moved by the touching story of Anastasia's Pool. And why not? They are fabulous experiences. But who has seen the secret lagoon? Who has listened to the quiet whisper of that secret, seen the discreet display of its feathered and fishy life?

Discovering the lagoon is part of your tidal immersion in Broome because the town has an extraordinary history of blended cultures thanks to the colonial pearling industry. People from Malaya, Japan, Indonesia and China came to the area to dive and trade in pearls. The diving skills of the local Aboriginal people meant that they participated in the industry too.

Many Broome families are blended as a result of this cosmopolitan mix. These times were exciting, as life often is in fishing villages, but they were also very dangerous, another ingredient that boats, fishing and diving regularly supply.

Walk around Broome, have a beer or wine in the pubs the locals go to and absorb the story of this town, not just what the brochures tell you. This great blend of nationalities created a special culture of food, music and art and the town is still influenced by it today. Matso's Broome Brewery is steeped in this flavour and regional history; the Broome Bird Observatory has it too.

The ground at the observatory has many artefacts of Aboriginal occupation and several trees have been marked by the old people in the process of preparing foods, medicines and tools. Please respect this history of the area because the custodians are, more than likely, fishing on the beach below the campground. The culture is not dead, just shared.

Left: Roebuck Plains after heavy rain.

Opposite: Network of mangroves and other coastal details of the area.

The observatory is peopled by twitchers with binoculars dangling, sensible hats and serious shoes. They are here for a variety of birds but mostly the waders, which appear in spring and leave in autumn. The mud flats of the shore are crowded with whimbrels, turnstones, godwits, dotterels and curlews – a crowd of fossicking birds and nervous crabs.

The battleground of the mud flats is replicated by the district's history. The discovery of Broome's valuable pearls was similar to the gold rushes elsewhere. Colonists, frenetic with greedy energy, descended on the area and fought with the local people for access to the land and waters, and labour.

Below: Vibrant colours of coastal country.

Right: Pathways of sea creatures.

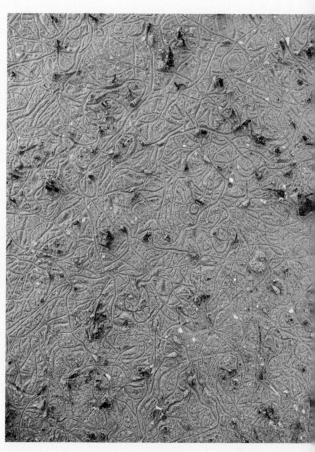

The colonial period first began when nations from Europe could build big ships to cross the open seas. The first dispossession of Indigenous people started when their lands were invaded and the killings began, but the second stage of colonial practice was when the 'natives' were used as labour to establish European wealth.

Minerals, cotton, corn, coffee and tobacco – all used Indigenous labour up until a machine could be invented to dispense with the need for labour or until the resource was destroyed or exhausted. These inventions gradually left whole communities destitute. The land was lost, the culture shredded, but now the First Peoples were on the bottom of the economic ladder as well as the social one.

In the case of pearls, both dispossessions happened. Once the European weapons had won the contact war, and the Chinese, Japanese and Malays had joined the industry, the local Yawuru people were overwhelmed and had little choice but to scrape a living from diving for the pearlers. It was a crude and brutal industry. The danger of diving fell to the most impoverished. The old brass helmets and hose systems were chancy at the best of times and many accidents occurred. Meanwhile the owners of luggers counted their money, leaving the injured diver to look after himself.

Better, safer diving equipment meant that white men started to dive for pearls themselves and the subsequent plunder decimated the pearl beds. At that point dispossession was total. The ramifications of that period of history are still being felt today. When Aboriginal labour was no longer required, the necessity to keep the population fed disappeared. Medicine was no longer supplied and the education provided through the Missions evaporated.

The cemetery at Broome reflects these perils and the preponderance of Asian and Aboriginal divers killed. All in the pursuit of other people's fortunes.

The pearl retailers are housed today in swish outlets in various parts of Broome. The business of retail emphasises the romance of the industry and the sexiness of the pearl without recognition that the industry began as a massive dispossession of the Yawuru people. The people have survived but not without enormous trauma.

The Pigram Brothers, a seven-piece Indigenous band, have been enormously successful with their music, which reflects the entire history of the region; their contribution to the play *Bran Nue Dae* was a transformative moment in Australian culture. The songs encompass the rich tropical beauty of this area but also the trauma of loss. That music is the perfect accompaniment to your visit.

Country around Wunaamin Miliwundi Ranges, approximately 350 kilometres east of Broome; known as King Leopold Ranges from 1879 until mid-2020, the ranges were renamed in acknowledgement of Indigenous groups' connection to country and in response to King Leopold II's reputation as a tyrant under whose rule millions of Congolese men, women and children were massacred and severely tortured. Wunaamin Miliwundi are words connected to the Ngarinyin and Bunuba languages, though many other groups have connection to the 500-kilometre span of the ranges.

Broome is lauded as the multicultural capital of Australia but, as with the rest of Australia's history, there is a lot to be learned, returned and repaired.

The massive footprints of dinosaurs were a feature of tourism until someone sawed a number of the prints into blocks and sold them to someone rich enough to have them on display in their private house. The pearls of Broome have incredible beauty but a sad history; much of the distinctive tropical Asian–Aboriginal art is morphing into a bland kitsch representation.

Visit the Saturday market to eat, to listen, to buy – it is a wonderful experience but try to make sure that anything that looks like it might be Aboriginal art is actually the work of an Aboriginal artist. Sorry to foist responsibility on to you on your holiday but our human responsibilities never cease.

You can see each phase of the colonial benchmarks of dispossession and exploitation in Broome and anywhere else you care to travel in Australia. Yet still Aboriginal and Torres Strait Islander people are willing to share some of the secrets accumulated by their culture over 120,000 years.

It is a gift this book hopes to make available to you. There is no price for this generosity but your knowledge, thought and care.

Indigenous cultural experiences, tours and relevant organisations

Narlijia Tours

Broome-based tours with Yawuru man Bart Pigram that cover the bay area, mangroves and mudflats.

08 9195 0232
toursbroome.com.au

Nyamba Buru Yawuru

An organisation committed to the prosperity of the Yawuru people. They often arrange cultural performances for events such as NAIDOC Week, have a language centre and offer services such as welcomes to country, smoking ceremonies and cultural immersion training, among other projects. Public art is on display at the Liyan-ngan Nyirrwa Cultural Wellbeing Centre.

55 Reid Rd, Cable Beach
08 9192 9600
yawuru.org.au

Jetty to Jetty

Download the app developed by the Yawuru and follow the trail along the foreshore of Roebuck Bay for first person stories of the pearling days. During the Shinju Matsuri Festival in late August to early September, there are live performances at various points along the way.

yawuru.org.au/culture/the-jetty-to-jetty

Magabala Books

Australia's only independent not-for-profit Indigenous publishing house, with a bookstore in town.

1 Bagot St
08 9192 1991
magabala.com

Dampier Peninsula

There are several community campgrounds and eco-retreats on the Dampier Peninsula, north of Broome, including Kooljaman at Cape Leveque, Lombadina and Natures Hideaway at Middle Lagoon.

kooljaman.com.au
lombadina.com
waitoc.com/culture-experiences/tours-experiences/directory/natures-hideaway-middle-lagoon

Other things to see and do

Broome Visitor Centre

Start here to find out about a range of available Indigenous tours.

1 Hamersley St (first round-about as you enter town)
08 9195 2200
visitbroome.com.au

WAITOC

The peak not-for-profit organisation representing Aboriginal tourism in Western Australia. The free touring map showing details of Indigenous tours and community-run campgrounds is a great travelling tool.

waitoc.com

Sacred Heart Church, Beagle Bay

Possibly Australia's most beautiful church, definitely it's most lustrous. The interior of this church is almost completely covered in mother of pearl and other shells, including a pearl shell altar. Designed by community artists during WWI, it combines Indigenous totems with Christian symbols and Aboriginal figures in the 'holy story' panels.

100km north of Broome

Uunguu Visitor Pass

If you're planning on visiting Wunambal Gaambera country, which includes Ngauwudu (Mitchell Plateau), this pass grants permission to visit approved locations including Punamii-Uunpuu (Mitchell Falls). Rock-art tours are available at Munurru (King Edward River) Campground.

wunambalgaambera.org.au

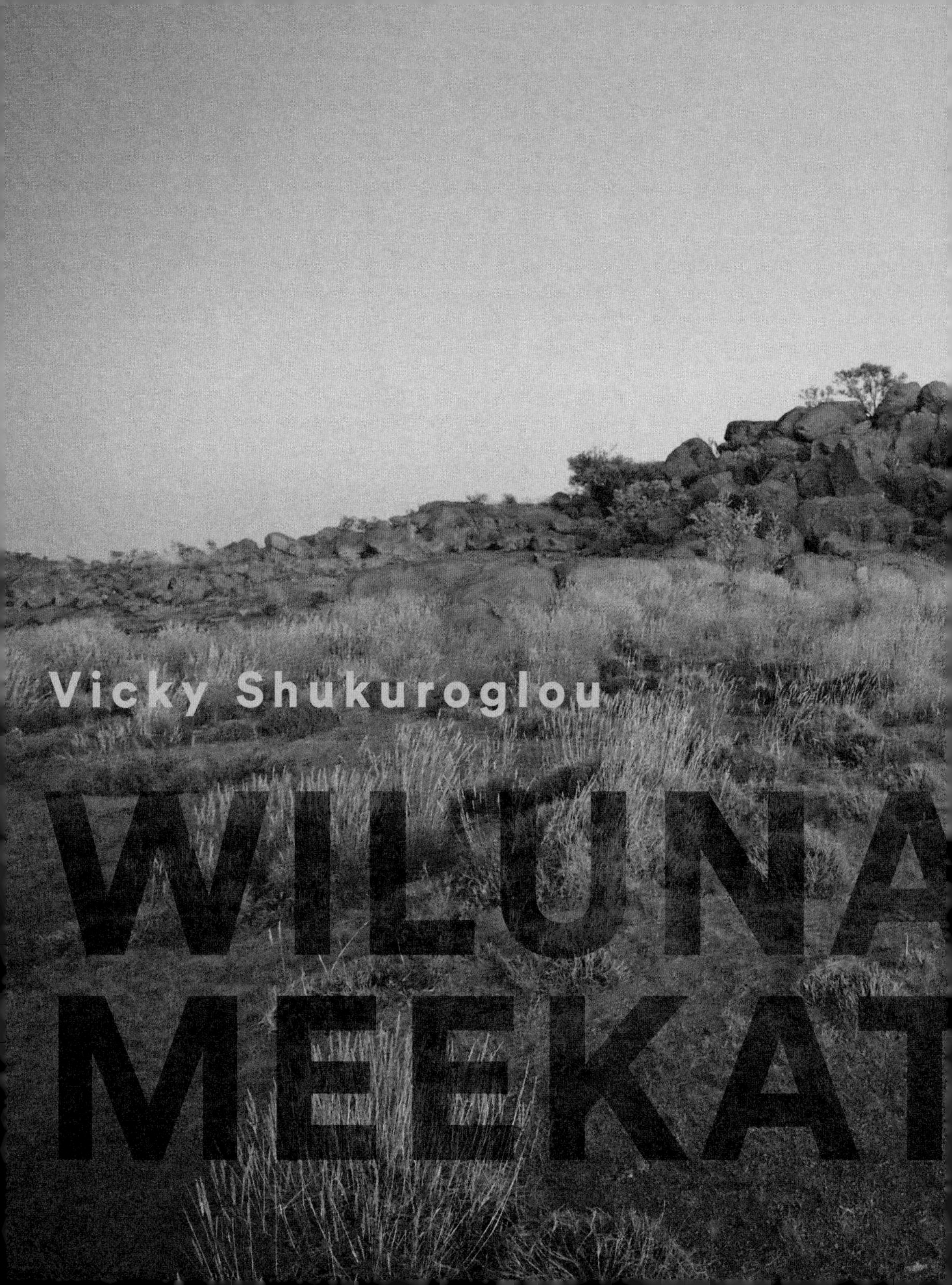

Vicky Shukuroglou

WILUNA
MEEKAT

In the central west of Australia, at the edge of
the Western Desert and towards the rangelands

Martu, Wajarri Yamatji

Language groups

& HARRA

REGION

You know that feeling when you see wise, long-lived eyes that you've come to know become creased and half-closed from the spread and gleam of a cheeky giggle? There's nothing quite like it.

Darling Road in Wiluna gets things going. Here, at the edge of the Western Desert, much has changed in recent decades and the Martu ladies who sit together and reminisce are excellent storytellers because they've lived these changes and love good yarns. Friends joke and lament how quiet Darling Road is these days, teasing each other about heading out, milk crate in hand, waiting for a stroke of luck along the old track. It's one of the places where romance blossomed in the desert. Stockmen working in the north would come into town and, in one way or another, news would get around. That was in the days well before we embraced mobile phones and the internet. The ladies tell of walking with the handsome men, so fit in their trim-cut shirts, coloured neckerchiefs and broad-brimmed hats. Some developed lifelong bonds, lived and worked together, started their own families.

It is impossible to know the full story of a path, of expressive glances and shared words, of lives that have intersected. Many venture deep into the desert, travelling through spectacular and diverse country including salt lakes, sandhills, sandstone ranges, soaks, gibber plains and claypans. You'll often notice dramatic shifts, at times with great stands of trees. Some, such as mulga, desert kurrajong, sandalwood and desert oak, are easy to identify and have been used as indicators for thousands of years. If we know their language, they tell us about the presence of water and the likelihood of particular animals living in the area, while their stages of reproduction suggest it's time to look for various kinds of eggs and prepare for certain ceremonies. Colours illuminated by the sun are intense and soak into our spirit: distinct reds and oranges of sandy soils, golden-yellow to soft blue-green of expanding spinifex rings,

sparkling stretches of salt, vivid new growth of kurrajong leaves, metallic reflections of gibber plains. Stars revealed by the sun's absence are incredibly dense. Here you'll see more glowing than dark space between them, and nights of looking skyward will give you another perspective on the ground beneath your body.

This great expanse of country receives an average of less than 250 millimetres of rain a year – with seasonal and locational variation – and has been broadly defined as Little Sandy Desert, Gibson Desert and Great Victoria Desert. Today the *Encyclopaedia Britannica* describes the Great Sandy Desert as an 'arid wasteland'. Written much closer to home is the government's own Gibson Desert bioregion information sheet where, under the heading of Socioeconomic Characteristics, we read: 'Land use and value: None of the Gibson Desert bioregion is used for commercial livestock grazing.' Nothing more than that. It doesn't take much to appreciate what's here and, if you develop your love, you will be stunned by incredible abundance, from the smallest creatures to the furthest reaches of our galaxy, and all the stories that lie within.

One of these speaks of Warri and Yatungka, memories of whom are tenderly carried by the older people living in Wiluna and surrounding communities. The ladies who talk of Darling Road with a glint in their eye bring a grieving tone to this tale for all that it embodies reaches deep into their country. They say with softness in

Opposite: Nardoo, one of the aquatic ferns. Below: Storm about to quench country.

their voices that this is one of the greatest love stories and it comes from the desert. Warri and Yatungka had developed intense affection for each other, forbidden by tribal laws explicitly delineating relationship protocols. Their options were limited if they were to be together, so they decided to run away despite the severity of consequences. Their families were distressed at the breaking of strict rules and the couple's struggles ahead. Before long, Manyjilyjarra Elders sent Mudjon to find Warri and Yatungka. He and Warri were close friends and knew each other well, could identify footprints and contemplate likely movements, especially in seeking water, food and shelter. When Mudjon found the couple in Putijarra country he realised they had the protection of the people and, despite commitment to his Elders and personal desire for his friend to return, Mudjon had to leave and venture home without them. His journey would have been difficult.

Warri and Yatungka continued to live together, but missed their home country, family and everything that is connected. After years, they decided to return with their children, for their yearning was too strong. They found Manyjilyjarra country was not as they had left it; most people were now in settlements, and those who remained were unable to continue in ways they had known. As a result, Warri and Yatungka did not receive the punishment they were expecting. Slowly, everyone else left for towns such as Wiluna, and so Warri and Yatungka were alone again. They wanted to remain with their country.

A documentary focusing on what happens from this point on has been created with original footage and re-enactments. If you visit Wiluna and make your way to Tjukurba Art Gallery within the Canning-Gunbarrel Discovery Centre, check if they are showing *The Last of the Nomads*. If so, you might have the great fortune of being surrounded by people who were born in that country, and people whose parents knew this iconic couple, who understand what it means to remain and what it means to leave. Their commentary in Martu language may mingle with the sound from the film, and whether you understand the words or not you will grasp layers of meaning and significance. People's emotions flow empathetically and it's no surprise most responses are similar in timing and sentiment, because this is a human story.

Warri and Yatungka loved their country. They made their own Darling Road. The Martu ladies speak thoughtfully for matters of the heart while also expressing greatest respect for their old people, knowledge shared and protocols followed in the

Lena Long and Rita
Cutter revisit old camps,
pointing out leaning
remnants of a shelter,
and make the most of
their time on country.

structures of a society. These are ancient challenges faced by human beings, from the very earliest days of our movement across unknown parts of the earth.

In the mid-1970s a period of drought made life extremely difficult. Manyjilyjarra Elders suspected Warri and Yatungka were still alive, having seen smoke in the area months prior. They were worried for their two people living without support typically present in a community while also knowing what the country could and could not provide – many waterholes would have dried and access to plants and animals for food would be severely diminished by extreme conditions. Manyjilyjarra Elders, including Mudjon, gathered with a plan. They decided to reach out and seek help from William Peasley, a man Mudjon had previously met and trusted. Apart from his personality, he had a suitable vehicle and experience to travel through remote country. Once again, Mudjon's commitment and skills were vital.

After much preparation, a small team set out, this time with the speed and ease brought by vehicles. They relied on Mudjon's knowledge of his country and ability to detect and read the most subtle traces left by movements of humans, their companion dogs and other animals. He suspected which waterholes would be dry, and so they proceeded from one to another, knowing they would soon arrive at the last most reliable source before a distance between it and the next made it impossible for people to proceed on foot. In attempts to communicate, Mudjon lit signalling fires and looked to the horizon for a response. The silence alarmed the group but they kept moving via waterholes, motivated by signs of life as they went. Peasley describes the complexity of what he had been asked to do; the gravity of this action did not escape his thinking. The details of the story that we have the privilege of learning are, of course, full of insight.

When Warri and Yatungka were found they had the option of remaining where they were. Both were extremely thin, Warri had difficulties walking and needed medical attention that Yatungka could not provide, and, while they were both emaciated, Yatungka could still collect water from the deep well and gather food – particularly walku (quandong) – though it was barely sufficient. There was no option but to come to a substantial decision, and the depth of their conversation, the complexity of their concerns and deliberations, can only be imagined. They were certainly frail, but survived together, on their country. Leaving also meant abandoning their companion dingoes, as the animals would be considered vermin and destroyed on return to town. On a previous occasion, this had deterred them. But they wanted to see their sons and Mudjon had assured them their community was worried for them and no punishment would be delivered.

The country of Ngarrinarri waterhole held their plans for time ahead. If rain fell and transformed life, their options may have changed, but they were grappling with stark realities unable to be altered. Their lives had now taken an unexpected turn, and the decision these two determined people had to make was surely informed by their longer conversations focused on their survival. They knew their country and each other, they knew their capacities and their values. The world beyond was unfamiliar – from the car in which they were to travel, to the groups of people they were to meet and the buildings they were to enter.

This love story, as told by the ladies and others, may open your view if you visit Wiluna and sit in the shade of a tree, feel the refreshment of water, walk the streets and contemplate the expanse beyond. It is here that Warri and Yatungka arrived, where their people first set eyes on their lean frames that roused grief and relief, their lives a mystery to so many. They remained for a time before being relocated to Meekatharra for medical attention, staying at each other's side. Within two years Warri, Yatungka and Mudjon passed away. Many say that when Warri departed, Yatungka's will to live went with him.

Mudjon Street runs along one side of Wiluna Remote Community School and the Training Centre next door, across the Goldfields Highway from the memorial dedicated to this story. It is here too that information for the renowned Canning Stock Route and Gunbarrel Highway are available for travellers. Over its length of around 1800 kilometres, the Canning Stock Route traverses innumerable stories from the earliest days of earth's formation. These connect distant reaches of this land and are indicative of cultural wealth and sophistication essential for people to flourish in particular environments over thousands of years. Stories of great ancestral powers and movement across country were essential for Warri and Yatungka's survival and were fundamental to their love of their country. Those stories still inform people today, transforming with time and events as culture flows within each person and is passed on to another.

Established in the early 1900s, the purpose of the Canning Stock Route was droving cattle from the Kimberley region in the north to Wiluna, which had become a busy mining town following the 'discovery' of gold in the late 1800s, with the population reaching nine thousand. Use of the Canning Stock Route declined with the advent of other infrastructure and technology, its effective function ceasing after the 1950s. Today it satisfies the adventurous desires of many. The people whose ancestors lived through its construction, and who themselves witnessed or were involved in events that followed, tell stories similar to others across the nation. In his preparations for the job of establishing the route, Alfred Canning investigated prior expeditions into the region including that of David Carnegie, seeker of gold and pastoral opportunity.

Vital to any perceived success was finding water – not only for the hundreds of sheep and cattle that were to be brought in, but for their own survival at the time. Tactics employed by the men were recorded in their own words, realities of the time and attitudes that prevailed plain for all to consider. Carnegie describes how they encountered the tracks of a young man, at the time labelled a buck, and knew he could lead them to water. The interaction described in Carnegie's documents is typical of many of the period, especially those involving desires for resources such as essential water. Potential for good relations, caution and coercion, ropes, chains and deprivation are all part of the truth. Carnegie's writing paints a vivid scene, describing how they 'plied our new friend with salt beef, both to cement our friendship, and promote thirst, in order that for his own sake he should not play us false'. He continues to tell of hours of walking, following the man to what they believed would be a waterhole. On arrival, they were dismayed to see it was dry and had been for months.

The man likely led them there because he knew his country. He was the group's greatest chance at finding water and so was tied up overnight. Attempts to escape failed, for 'Never were jailers more vigilant, for that black-fellow meant our lives.' Carnegie knew the salted beef had worked, as the man indicated thirst. With this, they were surely led to water. With the presence of mind often seen in such documents, Carnegie commented that, 'we could hardly blame him for leading us away from his own supply, which he rightly judged we and our camels would exhaust'.

Canning's research had him well prepared. Such tactics, along with dynamite and rifles, enabled his group to establish the Canning Stock Route. Waterholes were often severely disrupted. These are not mere holes in a hard surface able to hold water. These are homes or resting places of important ancestral beings – such as the snake often referred to as Jila or Kalpurtu, which also describes permanent springs,

Life-giving waterholes in arid country.

living water – and are marks left from travels of transformative beings. They moved through country creating songs, stories and dances for water and where it gathers, for the coming of rain and how places are all connected. These embodied protocols of respectful approaches by men, women and children, for appropriate use and careful maintenance. Some waterholes were significantly enlarged by blasting, therefore changing their function, often leading to contamination. We can wonder what the group of men perceived in those days, and whether they realised the importance of a branch left on a lean to help an animal should it fall in, and whether they considered the impacts of cows and sheep on country where they now lived. In those times of walking or resting, laying in a swag and hearing the night, what details and synchronicities did they notice, and did these affect their love?

An inquiry was conducted to investigate their treatment of the Indigenous people of the area and, while authorities claimed no charge was to be laid, diaries and related documents can inform and influence us today. Around the world, humans have caused immense suffering to one another, and how we remedy harm to people and country, how we can better respect and apply old knowledge in our contemporary society, presents one of Australia's greatest challenges and potentially richest learnings. As so many of the old people describe, healing the country goes hand in hand with healing every human spirit, and we are all involved.

Elders can be integral to revitalisation of ecosystems, and partnerships with various organisations, including Indigenous ranger groups, are exploring ways to apply skills

Above: Flowering and fruiting bush tomato. Opposite: Abandoned Nannine Mine affecting Lake Anneen.

refined over generations. Warri and Yatungka, Mudjon and his family, their ancestors and their neighbours, all chose to nurture these capacities over thousands of years. Their influence can make systems more effective today, leading to better health outcomes in the short- and long-term for people and country. Their expertise is instrumental in tracking and better protecting animals such as bilbies and mulgara, conducting burns at the right times in the right places, locating feral cats and camels, identifying waterholes and maintaining their function, and so much more.

In Wiluna, Meekatharra and surrounding areas, Elders gather with family members and others in the community and express their concerns and desires for appropriate care of country, and anxiety at the passing of time and opportunities. They worry as they observe limited action being taken to ease relentless pressures posed by introduced animals such as cats and camels, clearing of land for cropping and grazing, absence of proper use of fire, extraction of water and alterations of flow, and mining for gold, uranium, iron ore and other 'resources'. In their equation, they weigh up jobs and income flow into a community, and their priority remains with health of country, for they know it is bound with health of communities. Juukan Gorge, 400 kilometres north of this area and teeming with tangible and intangible significance, is one site that received media attention after it suffered devastating impacts by mining activity despite opposition by locals. This is not an uncommon process, as the mining company was legally permitted to destroy these ancient sites under a Section 18 Notice, and rarely does an ethical approach take precedence. Innumerable documents provide evidence of the need for stronger protections; much is ignored, with ramifications that largely go unnoticed. Legislation is weak and works in favour of a different kind of progress.

Brockman mine site, near the town of Tom Price, cuts through the country of Juukan Gorge whose spectacular formations boldly tell of weathering and time. From above, shapes of curved and steep rises drop into valleys and gorges with turns of waterways, offering a breathtaking perspective of our earth. Here we have an expanse that stretches our imagination, with complexity on a finer scale that is precious yet teetering. Ancestors of Puutu Kunti Kurrama and Pinikura people would have also developed highly sophisticated systems of navigation through this country and protocols for its care, with stories that shape and guide, connecting to distant lands. Today an area spanning 80,000 square kilometres bears the massive scars of the Brockman 4 mine site, with countless pits, tracks, exploration gouges, dumping and refinement areas and so on, some of which flattened the country of Juukan Gorge.

As massive trucks drive off with loads of earth, no doubt carrying history of people and their activities, the incomparable floral seed bank and unfathomable numbers of homes of extraordinary animals such as marsupial moles, we must all

ask ourselves at what point do we pause and turn a blind eye or turn another way, facing towards the Elders.

Lake Wells is an ephemeral body of water east of Wiluna and is another area under threat for the extraction of potash, as is an area thirty kilometres south of Wiluna described by the mining company as Centipede, Millipede, Lake Maitland and Lake Way uranium deposits. There is much more here than uranium. Thuwarri Thaa, commonly known as Wilgie Mia, lies west of Meekatharra and is one of this country's greatest ochre mines. The Department of Agriculture, Water and the Environment states that the mine demonstrates:

the importance of ochre in Aboriginal society and is the largest and deepest underground Aboriginal ochre mine in Australia. Ochre from Wilgie Mia was traded over a large area and was the most extensive pre-contact ochre network recorded in Australia.

Its physical footprint bears no resemblance to other mines in the area that have functioned for much less time. Associated stories are rich and dynamic, connecting to countless others many days' walk away. Every aspect is integral to the 'mapping' structures of this land, yet year after year the Wajarri Yamatji Elders feel the potential encroachment of mining companies and flow-on effects. The significance of this site is immense – its presence a rare treasure for all humanity – and, as with any such place, is irreplaceable.

Some Elders openly speak of pain caused by working on their country in roles that deplete rather than nurture. They have skills and knowledge to share and seek ways for them to be valued more fully, for the sake of the country and younger generations. They believe country yearns for the presence of people, but it must be the right way. Such transitions demand patience and change from everyone, willingness to develop alternatives, leave some things behind, and honour what the land has long held. We can pose questions to the past, of what may have taken place if individuals like Alfred Canning asked themselves whether each action is the best we can do for this land and all people, or if another way to proceed here could yield different outcomes. These are useful queries if we relate them to today, if we invite them to shape our choices and ways, wherever we may be.

Top: Nallan Lake, south of Meekatharra. Bottom: Country near the 'Camel Soak'.

In Meekatharra, yarns with Elders reveal the town's greater history through interconnected family stories brought to life by countless siblings and cousins, many growing up along the creek and making use of the area now called the Camel Soak because of its recent history. Long-used by the people of this country and known to them as Bumba, this important and subtle place is flanked by the creek that runs through town and hosts countless foods and medicines including the aquatic fern nardoo, various emu bushes and yams, flax lily and woody pear, to name just a few. Women recall sharing time with their mothers and aunties, learning their country and finding ways to adjust to life that involved missions, school, prejudice and slow change with new opportunities. Many do not have such memories for they were taken by authorities at the time, often to towns hundreds of kilometres away, and at times without their siblings. These are remarkably common stories of the distressing recent past, and each one brings another perspective.

The hills surrounding town all hold ancient stories, some connected to the great emu, the centipede, the kangaroo, sisters and brothers. You can visit these places, but rarely will you see a sign alerting you to any significance, and you are asked to show your greatest respect regardless of graffiti you might see, tyre tracks that roam and

Distinctively shaped nardoo growing in waterways of Meekatharra.

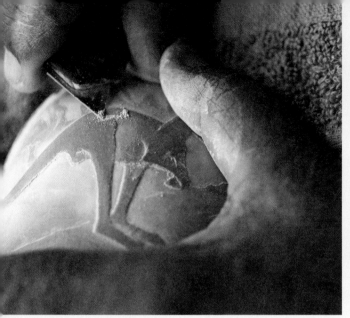
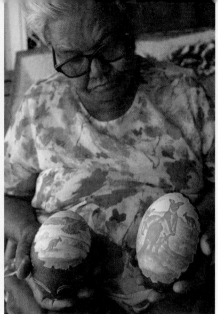

Beryl Walsh and her emu eggs.

churn, and rubbish dumped. If you are unsure of what resides there, caution should be your companion. Peace Gorge, just a few kilometres from the centre of town, is a powerful place where visitors are invited to spend time, but venturing deeper into the expansive tumble of rocks is not encouraged as important sites rest here.

Around town you may drive across old camps, remnants of a time when people of this country were not allowed to mingle with recent arrivals and were forbidden to own a car or enjoy basic freedoms. You can connect with this history by meeting locals, sharing yarns or visiting a festival. Exquisitely carved emu eggs embody terrific layers of understanding of the animal in its country, its habits and qualities of its eggs. These crafted objects are still made by hands that have had decades of practice, guided by eyes that watched parents and grandparents from a very young age.

Buttah Windee is a tiny community just five kilometres west of Meekatharra where life has taken on another dimension. Here young community members have been instrumental in the installation of water purification systems. This was deemed necessary to address high concentrations of uranium and other elements. Clean and safe water is a basic need and can make a place liveable, opening doors to other opportunities. Now, Buttah Windee is renowned for the small-scale barramundi farm housed in a shed and impressively run with increasing attention to sustainable practices. Ventures such as this provide new possibilities for the community to explore and, with their knowledge of local plants and animals, many things are possible with the right support. Yamaji Language Centre published a book some years ago titled *Wajarri Wisdom: Food and Medicine Plants of the Mullewa/Murchison District of Western Australia as Used by the Wajarri People.* This book of nearly 200 pages represents incredible wisdom and care over generations. It's the kind of knowledge implicit in the minds of Warri and Yatungka, allowing them to move through their country, ensuring their survival through extreme conditions. Each plant in this book has stories that are connected to place, that in turn connect to ways of respectful travel.

For most people in Australia, finely tuned skills of navigation are an inspiring mystery. Ways of valuing perception and analysis have changed, and without use, much is lost. Stories float around Wiluna detailing how people have reconnected with distant country via helicopters, revealing an awareness so rich that from high above and at a fast-moving pace individual waterholes are found, paths are identified and their route known, and paintings and grinding stones located in a hideaway. Layers of understanding, ways of seeing and capacity for retention of information

The amazing tenacity and beauty of country, where plants rely on their diverse relationships with insects, fungi and bacteria.

tell us much about the human being. Where the horizon often barely changes and feels endlessly outstretched, people developed specific methods to find their way. These all sustained an impressive diversity of life, and the intention of doing so was interwoven within their system.

Similar brilliance and refinement of human potential is evident across the world, and in spectacularly varied locations. The Marshall Islands are another fine example. Who Marshall was and how he is linked to Australia would be worthy of investigation. Nuclear testing and ramifications on land, sea and all life, the displacement of people now heightened due to climate change and sea level rise, are similarly worthy of our attention and contemplation. The beauty of their rebbelib (navigational charts) and all they contain give relief from such horrors, indicate our human bond and perhaps reshape the flow of our thinking. Sea and desert, some would say, have little in common. What could be revealed if seniors from each community sat together and shared their way? Vast expanses were navigated through nuanced senses and knowledge transmitted across generations. Commonly made from slivers of coconut frond and shells, the rebbelib may appear simple to unknowing eyes. Precisely placed and bound together in straight or curved forms, parallel or perpendicular to each other with variation in between, these collections of lines represent all or part of the atolls that make up the Marshall Islands and the swells and currents of the sea. These 'maps' convey many details including the effects on the movement of water created by the sea floor and distant lands. Sailors were perceptive to intersecting swell, the rocking of their canoe indicating their location in relation to land out of view.

The sailors explain that every journey nurtures connections and, the more they invest their attention, the more they sense and understand. Who else could notice the slightest change in angle or height of water, the frequency of intersections, and calculate the most discreet interplay of wind? These sailors are wholly entwined with their country, which includes the sea. These are also the ways of Warri, Yatungka, Mudjon and the Elders in the helicopter. Is it any wonder then that we are all asked to progress with care, no matter who we are, no matter where we come from? These are intimate relationships and none exist in isolation.

The semi-parasitic
mistletoe is an important
plant in ecosystems and
often displays complex
flower structures.

Important information

Permits are required for Indigenous Protected Areas (IPAs) and other regions – please ask local councils or information services before you set out to travel. Be sure you allow adequate time for arrangements.

As always, carry ample water and necessary supplies. If you are going off main roads, be sure you know what you are doing – for your own safety and that of others. Always check and respect road condition reports available at various locations including shire offices, online and police stations. Conditions can change very quickly. Be aware that mining vehicles are common features on many roads here, and some require both lanes. Be prepared to move off the road to allow oncoming vehicles to pass.

Indigenous cultural experiences, tours and relevant organisations

Tjukurba Art Gallery

Housed in the former Wiluna District Hospital, this art centre and gallery is a wonderful place to visit, learn local stories, perhaps meet artists and purchase their work.

28 Scotia St, Wiluna
08 9981 8000
tjukurbagallery.com.au

Meekatharra Museum

Located in the library of the Shire Building, at this museum you'll see and read about a diversity of objects and photographs offering insights into the local history. Take the opportunity to browse through the library, which holds some interesting publications specific to the region, and is where you might find a friendly local ready for a chat.

Main St, Meekatharra
meekashire.wa.gov.au/
museum.aspx

Meeka Rangelands Discovery Trail

This trail provides informative signage featuring diverse sites connected to Meekatharra's Indigenous and settlement history.

meekashire.wa.gov.
au/meeka-rangelands-
discovery-trail.aspx

Buttah Windee

Seek permission before heading out to Buttah Windee Community – ask for details at the Meekatharra Shire Council. A worthwhile stop for a yarn and a visit to the barramundi farm and art gallery, with a studio belonging to local artist, Andrew Binsiar. If you are there at the time of the Barramundi Festival you are in for a treat.

Landor-Carnarvon Rd,
Meekatharra

Wirnda Barna Art Centre – Mount Magnet

One of the many art centres of the region, Wirnda Barna shows the work of artists of Mount Magnet, Yalgoo, Meekatharra, Yulga Jinna, Cue and Sandstone areas. Badimaya, Wajarri and surrounding country shape the artists' work, who, as described on the website, draw inspiration from the rich landscape, spectacular spring wildflower season and important cultural sites

of the region including the Granites, Wilgie Mia Aboriginal Ochre Mine and Walga Rock, Western Australia's largest gallery of Aboriginal rock paintings (also worth a visit).

79 Hepburn St, Mount Magnet (almost 200km south of Meekatharra along the Great Northern Highway) 0438 757 274 wirndabarna.com.au

Other things to see and do

Canning-Gunbarrel Discovery Centre

Located in the same building as the Tjukurba Art Gallery, this display offers a diverse view of the region and has numerous publications for sale in the shop. The building itself is a fine example of change over time. As described by the Heritage Council of Western Australia, 'Wiluna District Hospital Group (fmr) illustrates changing hospital and medical practices, and institutionalised racism through the provision of a separate ward for "Natives".'

28 Scotia St, Wiluna

Wiluna Wire

Read the community newsletter, 'Wiluna Wire', for some interesting stories of the area and its people, including artists and rangers. Available on the Shire of Wiluna website documents page.

wiluna.wa.gov.au

Emu eggs

Look in the Meekatharra pub or local shops for emu eggs carved by artist Beryl Walsh.

Wildflowers

Find out about wildflowers of the region, maps, self-drive trails and more.

australiasgoldenoutback. com/page/outback-wildflowers

Further reading

Jordan Crugnale (ed.), *Footprints Across Our Land: Short Stories by Senior Western Desert Women*, Magabala Books, Broome, 1995.

WJ Peasley, *The Last of the Nomads*, Fremantle Press, North Fremantle, 2009.

Yiwarra Kuju: The Canning Stock Route, National Museum of Australia, Canberra, 2010.

Wiluna & Meekatharra Region

MARO
RIVER

Bruce Pascoe

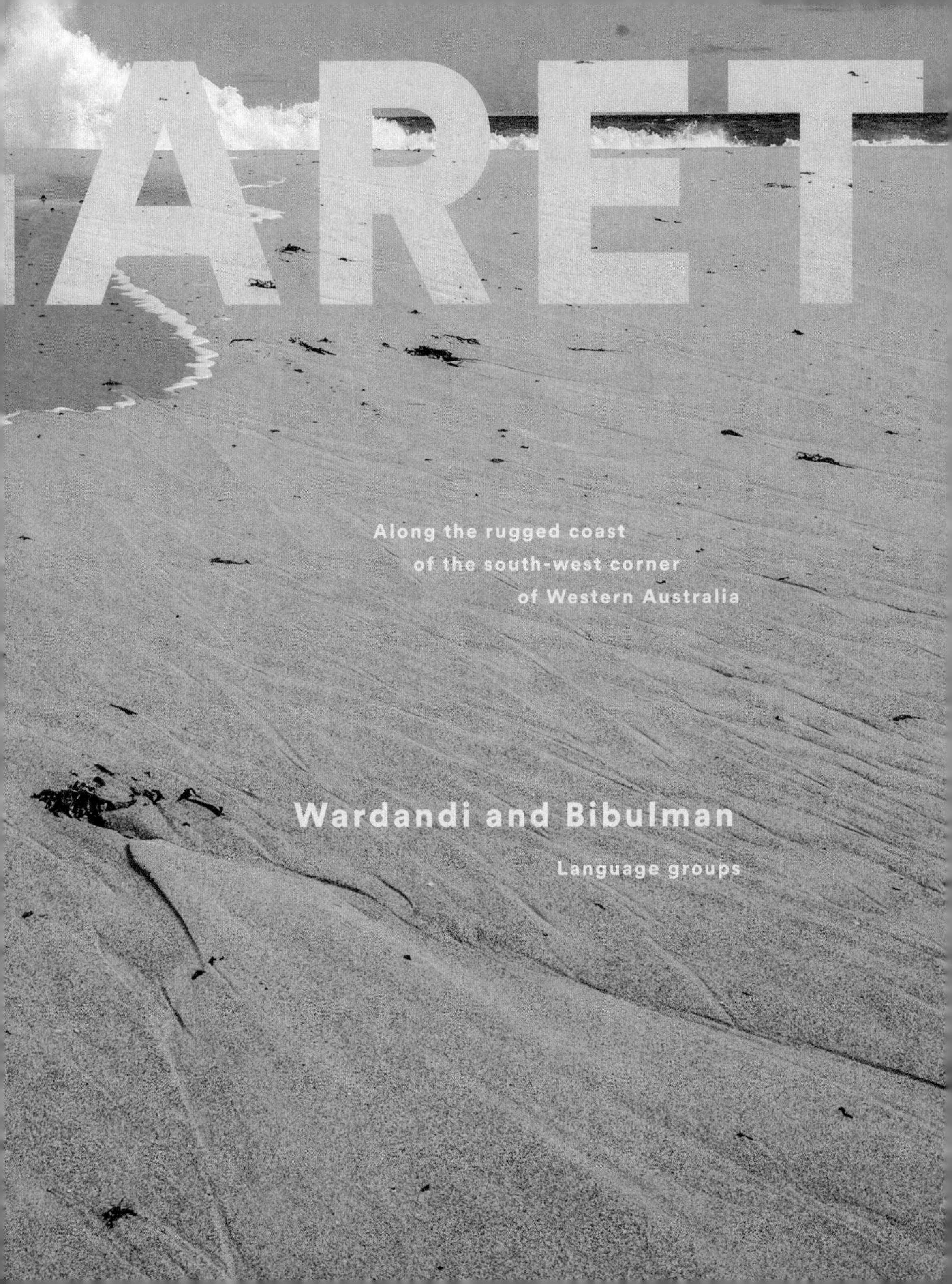

ARET

Along the rugged coast
of the south-west corner
of Western Australia

Wardandi and Bibulman

Language groups

They like a good festival in Margaret River, preferably with a cheese platter and a glass of red. The climate and soils favour food production – it's an incredibly rich agricultural area – and if you combine that with the beaches and surf then it's understandable that the region boasts comfort and ease. The Vasse Felix winery was one of the first in Margaret River and is worth a visit but so too is Leeuwin Estate. Mammoth Cave and Lake Cave in Leeuwin–Naturaliste National Park, fifteen minutes from town, are quite remarkable. And if that isn't enough you can watch the sun set over the Indian Ocean at Surfers Point or visit the famous Margaret River Farmers' Markets. The region produces an abundance of high-quality food.

But it always did. The local Noongar people had substantial crops of tubers and grains and seasonal fruits. The beaches were used for the same things then as today: fishing, swimming, dandling baby nieces in the shallows, sand castles ... no, forget the sand castles because, while the old people were cautious of the entry of unknown people into their territory, they built neither moat nor fortress.

Instead they built a lore so strong, so egalitarian, so insistent, that fighting over land was prohibited and, as a consequence of that philosophical attitude, the castle, the moat, the drawbridge, the boiling oil, the rack and the pike were never invented. Not through inability, because a people who created massive fish traps and log houses could be expected to conceive of erecting a fortress if they could conceive of a people so unruly that they would invade another's land. But they didn't. It was inconceivable.

The first European entries into Western Australia remarked on the substantial villages, the croplands stretching to the horizon, the wells, the roads and the dams, but they did not see embattlements. Although capable of the human characteristics of bad humour, spite and violence, the Aboriginal people had their lore, which meant that they would never have to prepare to defend the land they belonged to from imperialists and carpetbaggers.

Until, that is, Europeans arrived with their god-sanctioned invasion.

Lieutenant George Grey wasn't a very good explorer – he sank his boats, lost his horses and spoiled his supplies – but those mistakes meant he had to walk and during that walk he reported the houses, villages, wells, roads, crops and harvests.

Margaret River sea and river scapes with fish making their way back to water.

These things are not part of a noble savage myth, they are evidence of an economy as witnessed by Australian explorers.

Grey was in Western Australia but similar examples are found everywhere in our country. Most Australian 'explorers' wrote about them. Grey is a particularly useful source because he wrote so expansively about these huge fields of agriculture. The native path is, he wrote in his *Journals of Two Expeditions of Discovery in North-West and Western Australia* from 1841:

quite wide, well beaten and differing altogether by its permanent character, from any I had seen in the southern part of the continent ... And as we wound along the native path my wonder augmented; the path increased in breadth and its beaten appearance, whilst along the side we found frequent wells, some of which were ten and twelve feet [three to four metres] deep, and were altogether executed in a superior manner. We now crossed the dry bed of a stream, and from that emerged upon a tract of light fertile soil quite overrun with warran plants [the yam plant *Dioscorea hastifolia*], the root of which is a favourite article of food with the natives. This was the first time we had seen this plant on our journey and now for three and a half consecutive miles [over five kilometres] traversed a piece of land, literally perforated with holes the natives made to dig this root; indeed we could with difficulty walk across it on that account whilst the tract extended east and west as far as we could see ... more had been done to secure provision from the ground by hard manual labour than I could believe it in the power of uncivilised man to accomplish.

He went on to talk further about roads, wells and houses – a strikingly different picture of our country than most history books allow. In what is now the Perth region, the first European arrivals found huge market gardens; the truth of their existence was demonstrated by the gardens' inclusion in the early survey maps from that era.

Margaret River had similar examples of horticulture but very little of that information was included in the early histories. I visited the region recently for its annual literary festival. I swam, I drank, I ate, thoroughly enjoying the pleasures and easefulness of the region but then an old man approached me.

'I drove through the night to speak to you,' he said.

Not an Ancient Mariner experience, because he was neither mad nor regretful, but wanted instead to tell me a story and sing me a song.

This Noongar man wanted to show me his country. As I got out of the car above the estuary of the Margaret River I had the uncanny feeling that I knew what he was going to sing. He danced and sang the song of the whale and some of the words and most of the story were similar to a story told on my Yuin land in south-east Australia.

It was an incredible experience and I rang my Elders and brothers the next day and urged them to come over and see for themselves how the whale story had been carried across the continent.

David Mowaljarlai, in his book *Yorro Yorro: Everything Standing Up Alive*, drew a picture of the culture tracks that meshed across the continent and its islands, and here at Margaret River I found evidence of how they operated to bring story and dance across the vast distances.

As we have travelled around the land seeking out the whale story, our journey and the mesh of stories we have been told takes on a very similar appearance to Mowaljarlai's map. A web, a net of songlines encompassing the entire continent and its islands (see map, Following the whale, page 300).

On this occasion the old man's story told how the whale began life as an ancient land mammal but was harassed during the day by a dog and when it changed its eating habits to forage at night it was attacked by a cat. The people say cat and dog but they are referring to thylacine and marsupial lion because the story is so ancient.

Flowers of the forest: (left) swamp bottlebrush, also known as gravel bottlebrush; and (above) candle cranberry.

The interference from these animals was too much for the cumbersome creature so it decided to live its life in the sea. Its human friends were concerned for its welfare, but the creature reassured them that there were grasses in the sea that it could eat and, anyway, it would return to the land at the end of its life.

On the south-east coast of the continent we say the whale took its lore into the ocean to guard the sea and its creatures and returns to land to regurgitate its lore, which may be a reference to the whale's periodic purge of ambergris.

The elements of the story are not just consistent from east to west but from north to south to centre as well. Everybody has a whale story and it binds the country together in story and lore. That's what the old man wanted to tell me and I was able to bring my uncle back to meet him so that we could assure him that we followed the same lore and destiny.

Forestscapes including green flower-spikes of *Kingia australis*, which superficially appears similar to *Xanthorrhoea* species. Their dark sap was often used as a binding agent when making implements.

It's a long story and covers aeons of time just like the Iliad, the Inuit song cycles, the Norse legends and the Mahabharata. Except that it is older, much older. Aboriginal people recognised that the whale had once belonged on land; that knowledge may have been the result of investigations of the pelvises of beached whales, although western science didn't know this until about fifty years ago. We know the whale story is at least 12,000 years old because many clans have stories of the whale saving people during sea level rises.

The fascinating thing about this story is that it doesn't mention *which* sea level rise. Aboriginal Australia is ancient and our people have said that we have always been on this land. That, of course, was considered as mere metaphor by Europeans, who were certain that anything of any cultural value had to come from the northern hemisphere.

Some of our peoples also say that the whale taught them to speak. The people of Margaret River communicated with the whales as they migrated north for the birthing season. A large rock was pivoted above a cave and when it was rocked back and forth its booming resonance was transmitted out to sea and the whales would come close to shore to investigate. The *boomp boomp* of the cave echo was produced to the beat of the human heart because we and the whale share that rhythm also.

The entrance of Margaret River holds deep and powerful stories and is also the site where whales beach themselves frequently, or, as we say, return their lore to the land.

The whale story is an incredible link between land and sea, humans and animals – it's a mammalian story of unity and peace.

A sad aspect of this story was clear to me when I was invited to speak at a school deep in the forests to the east of Margaret River. While waiting for the class to arrive I browsed in the library, as I always do, wondering what one of the Aboriginal students, who made up sixty per cent of the school population, could find there.

Nothing. An earnest student wanting to write about her people's culture would find nothing, absolutely nothing, in the Australian history section of that school library.

Imagine what goes through that girl's mind as she realises her school and country care nothing for her story.

But *you* can. Take an Aboriginal tour around Margaret River. There aren't many because tourism here seems most interested in food and wine, but they do exist – try Cape Cultural Tours and Koomal Dreaming Cultural Experiences – and they tell a story older than any other story in the world. Why wouldn't we want to listen?

The books of Noel Nannup, Kim Scott, Sally Morgan and other Western Australian Indigenous writers tell stories of those old days and old ways. Worth reading as you explore this fabulous coast.

The karri and jarrah forests are a feature of this magnificent region but you will also see marri, Darling Range ghost gums and any number of banksias and heath plants. Sea birds abound but in the forests look out for western rosellas, red-capped parrots, western golden whistlers, white-breasted robins, crested shrike-tits, red-tailed black cockatoos and the rare Baudin's cockatoo.

Modern English convention requires that real nouns are capitalised so that Baudin and Darling Range receive the distinction of capitals but the birds do not. Aboriginal Australia does not treat birds and people separately as we are one and share common ancestors.

This is a cultural difference but it need not be a division, rather an enrichment.

Indigenous cultural experiences, tours and relevant organisations

Koomal Dreaming Cultural Experiences

This Indigenous-owned business offers a range of fascinating tours, including one to Ngilgi Cave and an Aboriginal Food Cave and Didge tour.

Yallingup Caves Rd, Yallingup
0412 415 355
koomaldreaming.com.au

Cape Cultural Tours

This is the sister company to Koomal Dreaming. You can explore the Margaret River region from an Indigenous perspective on a range of tours including a fishing experience.

1267 Cape Naturaliste Rd, Leeuwin–Naturaliste National Park
0412 415 355
capeculturaltours.com.au

Other things to see and do

Margaret River Visitor Centre

100 Bussell Hwy
08 9780 5911
margaretriver.com

Caves Road

This is a 110km scenic drive from Cape Naturaliste in the north to Cape Leeuwin in the south, via a string of beaches and forests of karri.

Cape to Cape Track

This is a 123km walking trail between the two capes. You can do this walk in sections if you wish, as there are plenty of places along the way where you can access the track and walk for hours. If you visit around August to November you'll enjoy greater numbers of wildflowers in bloom, and between June to December you're more likely to spot a whale.

trailswa.com.au/trails/cape-to-cape-track

Caves

There are four main caves in the Margaret River region that are open to the public. Jewel is the largest and has one of the longest straw stalactites in the country. Lake Cave has beautiful reflections. Mammoth has megafauna fossils. Ngili is best for those that like tight spaces and lots of steps.

margaretriver.com/attractions/caves

Margaret River Farmers' Markets

Just food, produce and flowers, and only local. Every Saturday morning.

Margaret River Education Campus, Lot 272 Bussell Hwy
margaretriverfarmersmarket.com.au

Bruce Pascoe

ALBA

On the south coast of Western Australia,
just under five hours' drive from Perth

Minang Noohgar

Language group

There's a caravan park at Albany where you can pull your tinpot van up to the fence and have a perfect view of the harbour. We must keep that opportunity in Australia, perfect holidays for the poor. My van was as collapsible as a deckchair and subsequently handy for travel, but she was likely to collapse at inconvenient times. It's a sound that stays with me to this day: a chaotic spiralling of rods and springs and a gentle decline into flatness, not a little house anymore but a pile of unsaleable hardware.

Anyway, my van's collapse didn't happen in Albany, perhaps part of the reason this city remains as the second-most wonderful place in my memory. After the three salt rivers of Mallacoota, of course. Sorry to everywhere else.

The harbour of Albany is surrounded by giant granite tors like a whole family of women gone suddenly sleepy by the shore. I looked at those old torsos and thought fish and darkness.

So, later that night I got the rod and a small bag of pilchardy things I caught at the beach, and wound my way down to the somnolent and dusk-dreaming women and reclined on a particular rock and caught herring, literally while laying prone on stone.

Soon I had enough for two meals and I stopped casting onto the water, which I had watched change from jade to deepest dark emerald. I think it was September but the night was so warm I stretched out on the rock and stared out to the bay, easing myself against the body warmth of some old matron who did not disallow my stolen comfort.

There, there, lad. Get yourself comfy but make sure your spirit is good, because this is all about privilege, the ancient Australian privilege. Enjoy yourself but remember the tax; each privilege might seem like it's free of charge but the real price is responsibility. You might think you've avoided paying tax, a tradition that Australians laud, but it is not so. You caught fish, didn't you? Paid nothing, didn't you? Rested among a family of women, didn't you? What is the price for that? Care. Just care. But care is taxing because it asks you to care for the water, the fish within it, and for the old women who guard it. No such thing as a free lunch. Learn to love your debt, embrace your indebtedness.

I slept there all night, the warmth of the family sustaining me, the sound of the ocean's breath rocking me to sleep inside the embrace of limbs and bellies of stone.

Never ever has that night left my mind and I am still paying for it, such beautiful, loving bankruptcy.

But this harbour hasn't always been like this. It has been the place of atrocity, an unimaginable lust for blood. The Minang people who lived here at the beginning of the colonial period had been lulled and strengthened by the wonderful ease and plenitude of their country, but also indebted to its spirit and its claim for care, the responsibility to protect.

And then came the European whalers. Men from Belgium, England, America, Russia. Where there is money to be made the Europeans were quick to arrive. And there was money in whales – their bone, their oil, their ambergris – but the people already there had a profound association with the whale, a long conversation, a duty of care.

That duty did not prohibit eating the flesh of the whale and using all of its body for food and health, but it was discreet and bound by a lore so old we are still guessing at how old. The people say that 'we have always been here' and some on this coast say that it was the whale who taught them to speak, an unimaginably long period of human history.

Around Whaling Cove.

Above: Jimmy Newell's Inlet.

Right: The isthmus from Quaranup/Point Possession trail, rock that often meets the sea, and The Gap.

Left: Coastal habitat, looking out towards hills and islands holding important stories.

Opposite (left to right): Sundews entangled in foxtails, extraordinarily robust yet dainty redcoats, and coastal samphire.

But despite those aeons of care, the bay was soon awash with blood and the howls of rage and torment. Try to imagine the pain of such sudden bedlam, try to have empathy for how long such pain must last, how much damage it can do to the psyche. And if you can't imagine it, read Kim Scott's Miles Franklin Award–winning novel *That Deadman Dance*, but be careful when reading: there is a tax to be paid for that knowledge. Care, respect, empathy, all of them capable of causing hurt and exhaustion as they require dedication and energy. This is what it takes to be Australian.

The carnage of the whaling industry almost destroyed the great families of whales around the globe. The whalers and sealers of Europe, having destroyed the pods in the northern hemisphere, descended on the south with the barbarity of their lifestyle. Men and slaughter do not lend themselves to civilisation: the irony being that the whalebone they hunted made the corsets for gentle women, the ambergris became the perfume for their pale necks and the sperm oil lit lamps so that they might read Victorian novels in the evening. No tax? Yes, we are paying for it still.

The deep wound to Minang life cannot be closed in a mere couple of centuries. Be patient, be empathetic. Keep your sympathy to yourself but spend your empathy

Fish traps of Miyaritj
(Oyster Harbour) and
the nearby creek. For
thousands of years,
relationships within and
among local groups
ensured the ongoing
care and vitality of such
structures and ecosystems
across Australia.

generously. Call it rent or tax if you like, or better still call it respect for the whole human family, call it justice. You're up to it, Australia, I know you are. It might become your joy to pay it, not in coins, but in care and love.

Visit Albany. The family of rockin' women is still there, the warmth of the evenings still sublime, the whales and dolphins have returned thanks to the ragtag mob of protesters who insisted on our responsibility to care for the leviathan. But where is the street march for the Minang and Noongar? There is still much to do.

But the Aboriginal people have not caved in to despair. Some suffer the horrible memory-dream of Albany slaughter but many, many others have risen above it like a whale surging from the darkest depth and breaching superbly into sunlight.

Recently agriculturalists, permaculturalists, botanists and a whole mob of other 'ists' were invited to share knowledge with the local people in a bid to regenerate degraded farmland. Australians have been spending the agricultural capital built by Aboriginal land care and that capital is all but gone, as if a wayward child had surrendered the family fortune to gambling and decadence.

But local farmers flocked to the event because they were aware that the old inheritance was running out, that the time for change had come. This is a conversation we need to have in this country and it will require tact, patience, care and love. Don't expect it to be a re-run of *The Sound of Music* or *Happy Feet*; this is tax time, and it will be gruelling and painful. We will bruise each other during this debate and we must endure that discomfort.

Sorry to dwell on this, but it seems most Australians realise that the time has come to care for the planet and its history.

If you need to ease your mind from the demands of these questions, visit Two Peoples Bay Nature Reserve. Apart from the question this presents of how you punctuate the word 'peoples' and how that alters its meaning, this is a superb piece of the nation's geography. Dolphins and whales disport themselves in water that sways gently over white, white sand and the colour of its jade does something to your heart. Looking over the bay gives you one of those moments of sublime peace you will never forget.

There is a superb visitor centre at Two Peoples Bay, but don't forget to go to Kurrah Mia in town, a Minang Noongar business with tours and an art gallery. The tours are a revelatory experience and the art is superb. One young artist made me a pair of

Dramatic rocks of Toolbrunup with evidence of recent fires in the background.

boomerangs from the raspberry jam tree (*Acacia acuminata*) and I treasure them. The bicoloured wood is highly decorative but also produces an amazing sound.

The Vancouver Arts Centre at the historic old hospital site is full of interesting local art and craft, displayed against rarely preserved architecture from the colonial period.

You won't forget Albany easily; it's the only place where I linger in front of real-estate windows. The town is built for ease and comfort, and the extraordinary coastal scenery is exceptional. But, as you know, all this beauty and soul satisfaction has a price!

Indigenous cultural experiences, tours and relevant organisations

Kurrah Mia – Culturally Noongar

Walking tours on Corndarup (Mt Clarence) in the Albany Heritage Park and other locations.

364 Middleton Loop
0419 320 533
kurrahmia.com.au

Other things to see and do

Albany Visitor Centre

Book whale-watching tours here and get insider tips of the best beaches and places to see wildflowers (and wineries).

221 York St
08 6820 3700

Vancouver Arts Centre

85 Vancouver St
08 6820 3740

Clockwise (from top left):
Brilliance of young leaves;
banksia cone having released
seeds after fire; rock formed by
lava flow; and detail of lichen
and paperbark in swamp.

National ANZAC Centre

Ask at the information desk and you'll be pointed in the direction of several exhibitions that focus on the involvement of Indigenous soldiers, including Gordon Naley, who fought at Gallipoli and France in WWI.

67 Forts Rd
08 6820 3500
nationalanzaccentre.com.au

Two Peoples Bay Nature Reserve

A stunning nature reserve, this is an ideal spot for whale-watching, bushwalking and spotting the endangered noisy scrub bird and the critically endangered Gilbert's potoroo.

35km east of Albany
08 9842 4500
parks.dpaw.wa.gov.au/park/two-peoples-bay

Granite Sky Walk

Suspended lookout platform offering fabulous coastal views from Castle Rock in Porongurup National Park.

47km north of Albany
parks.dpaw.wa.gov.au/site/granite-skywalk

Further reading and listening

Go to the Wirlomin Noongar Language & Stories Project website to watch videos of stories being told or purchase books in Noongar language.

wirlomin.com.au

Bruce Pascoe

KANG

ISLAN

AROO

A 20-kilometre ferry ride off

the coast of South Australia

Islands and islanders hold a special place in the imaginations of many people. Lighthouses, shipwrecks, hardy fishermen, lonely beaches, wildlife and good food are common to the Bass Strait islands. Kangaroo Island is no different, it has them all and to a very refined degree.

It also has an Aboriginal past but, unlike the wine, sheep, cheese, marron and bread, it does nothing to advertise the fact. On the contrary, it hides from that history.

Kangaroo Island's devastating fires of 2019–2020 destroyed buildings but it also scorched souls. The island will take a long time to revive physically and psychologically. So much tourist infrastructure was destroyed that the island's economy received a massive hit. Recovery will be slow and painful.

It is easy to celebrate and promote great food, idyllic beaches and the island wildlife but it will take a while for tourists to return. Don't be detered from visiting the island, it really is an exceptional part of the country and a few years back probably produced one of the most beguiling tourism advertising campaigns ever seen. It deserves the return of visitors.

And hopefully this is an opportunity to broaden the tourist appeal through the untold story of its Aboriginal history.

Overseas tourists regularly list Aboriginal culture as among the top three on their wish list of Australian experiences. They rarely have it granted. There is an opportunity here for entrepreneurs and history sleuths, but hang on just a minute – shouldn't Aboriginal people supply that opportunity. Australia likes to Intervene and fail, we try to Close the Gap and fail, but what is really needed is respect for the culture and a determination by government and public that Aboriginal people will deliver this story.

This is a way for the island to respect the past and profit from the future – Aboriginal and non-Aboriginal people together. I invite you to explore this past with me now, which first takes us to Australia's sealing industry and its largest island, Tasmania.

The sealing industry of colonial Australia is a perfect example of why western industrial capitalism is wrecking the world. Unsustainable exploitation with no thought for the environment. Plunder for profit, move on and leave the damage in your wake. Abuse of Mother Earth.

And abuse of any people who happen to be in the way. In this case, Aboriginal people. Aboriginal women.

Tasmanian Aboriginal people had a division of labour where women were largely responsible for collection of resources from the sea. Aboriginal lore required that that extraction be undertaken under spiritual rules because the economy could not be separated from the spiritual life.

Mannalargenna was an important man in Tasmanian Aboriginal politics. After the war in Tasmania had drastically reduced the Aboriginal population, he tried to find ways of negotiating with the invaders in order to secure a future for his people. He worked with the missionary George Augustus Robinson, whose plan it was to round up the remnant clans and transport them to the offshore islands.

Robinson's scheme appealed to the colonial administration as a way of ridding themselves of the nuisance of the guerrilla attacks of Aboriginal people on outlying farm communities. The missionary sold the plan to the Aboriginal people as a temporary removal 'while things settled down' on mainland Tasmania, after which they would be brought back to their homelands.

The reality was that the translocated people were never returned to their clan lands and in unhealthy conditions on Flinders Island most gradually died, always looking south to the land that was stolen from them. Robinson moved on to a better career opportunity, leaving those he had 'saved' from the wilderness to their holes in the cemetery.

Mannalargenna was aware of Robinson's ruse and led him on wild goose chases all over mainland Tasmania in an attempt to delay removal and give his people a chance to escape, but in the end his efforts were unable to outmatch the combined colonial forces. When he himself was removed to Green Island on a ship under the orders of Robinson, he waited until the bow of the ship ground into the beach and there he cut off his dreadlocks and threw them into the sea. His hope and authority were gone. This is one of the great acts of Indigenous despair, a profound repudiation of the invaders' tactics and immorality.

Mannalargenna's daughter Woretemoeteyenner was then captured or traded by a Bass Strait sealer, George Briggs. He sold Woretemoeteyenner to another sealer, John

Opposite: Imprint left by the outgoing tide.

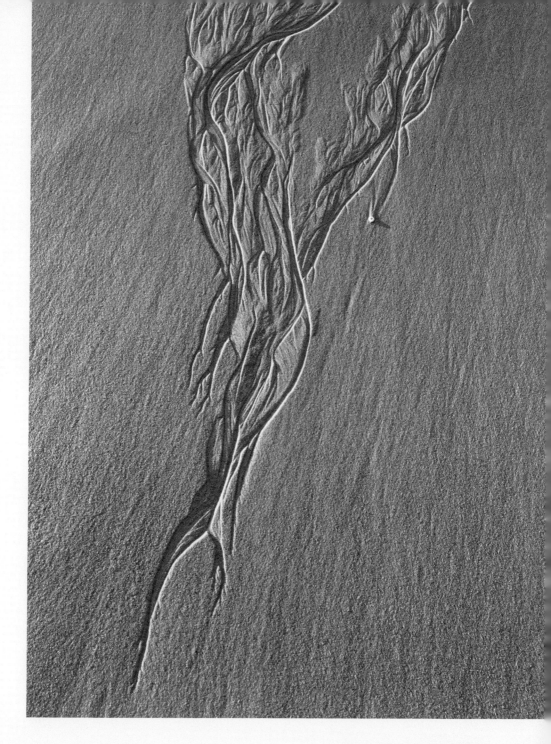

Waratah anemones
responding to water.

Thomas, and then went on to capture other Aboriginal women, profiting from their industry and sex.

Thomas, like most of the sealers, thought it reasonable to purchase a woman for these purposes and, while church and government tut-tutted about the practice, it was an important plank of the colony's success.

Typical of many sealers, Thomas roved the islands of Tasmania but when the seals became scarce he set his sails, with Woretemoeteyenner and other women on board, for new shores to plunder. He went to Western Australia but then headed across the Indian Ocean for Mauritius in the hunt for more seals.

He claimed to be running out of food so dumped the Aboriginal women on Rodrigues Island and left them. It took Woretemoeteyenner three years to get back to Australia and in this she was helped by the governor of Mauritius.

Many other Aboriginal women ended up in Mauritius and, unlike Woretemoeteyenner, never returned home. Sealers routinely dropped off women on isolated islands when they were pregnant or no longer able to work. Quite a few were left at Kangaroo Island off the South Australian coast.

Today Kangaroo Island appears not to remember this history. You will search in vain in the tourist information for reference to the Aboriginal women. If you ask about Aboriginal history in the outlets where you might expect to find such things, you might receive a belligerent stare, as I did. Fortunately an art shop was more forthcoming and I was given the phone number of an Aboriginal family who gave me a more complete history.

Australia's bellicose resistance to the nation's history is an unedifying reflection of our national character, but Rebe Taylor's brilliant history of Kangaroo Island, *Unearthed: The Aboriginal Tasmanians of Kangaroo Island*, is the exception. Seek out a copy to read before you visit the island.

Taylor reflected on the absence of Aboriginal history in the island's museums and, visiting a couple of years after the book's release, I found it to be no different. The history is fascinating and full of enthralling stories but not enthralling enough to some Australians who seem to find the very presence of Aborigines a threat to their ideas of legitimacy and identity.

It's such a shame because adopting the true history of the country, despite the pain it must cause, is the only way to finding an Australian identity. The country doesn't have to be in constant genuflection to that pain but must acknowledge it if any intelligent discussion of our nationhood is to take place. Surely it is within our capability to understand the past while celebrating and looking forward to our future.

You will have a wonderful island holiday here. To wash away the bitter taste of the reception I was given on my request for information on Aboriginal history, I dived for abalone at the remote and beautiful Snelling Beach. Kangaroo Island is beautiful and it is common to have an entire beach to yourself. This is an experience our crowded world craves.

While strolling along the sand, reflect on the Australian bounty. Accepting a truer national history does not mean having to forgo our beach culture. There will be times of discomfort on both sides but the conversation between us can deepen and mature. Australia is capable of this transition. The national identity is not tossed out but enriched, built on substance and fact.

The national parks across the island and the lighthouses at Cape Borda and Cape du Couedic are wonderful places to visit even after the devastating fires of 2019–2020. The fires on the island that summer were catastrophic. A long period of drought was followed by hot, dry winds. Climate change has been contributing to the warming of the planet because of our reliance on fossil fuels and the consequent release of carbon into the atmosphere. But we contribute in other ways too. Cattle and sheep release methane into the atmosphere at greater rates than our native animals.

One of our contributions is rarely mentioned. Growing trees is considered to be environmentally friendly but it is more about how we grow them. Aboriginal burning and cultivation meant that in most parts of eastern Australia there were rarely more than twelve to fifteen trees to the hectare.

Television footage from the 2019–2020 fires shows a firefighter walking through a burnt plantation of forest timber where the trees are no more than three metres apart. With a fire in a forest like that, there is no way of stopping a crown fire occurring. It is a recipe for wildfire.

In December 2019 we knew we were in for a horrific fire season. Knowing what was coming, I measured the number of trees in an acre of silvertop ash plantation; there were over 300 trees to the acre and all the leftovers from the previous crop. This was going to go up like a bomb. Driving through that plantation on 1 January 2020 I have never seen the results of a hotter fire.

Above: Frog spawn of
pobblebonk frogs, as seen
mating on pages 258–9.

Right: Glowing remnants
and feather after rain.

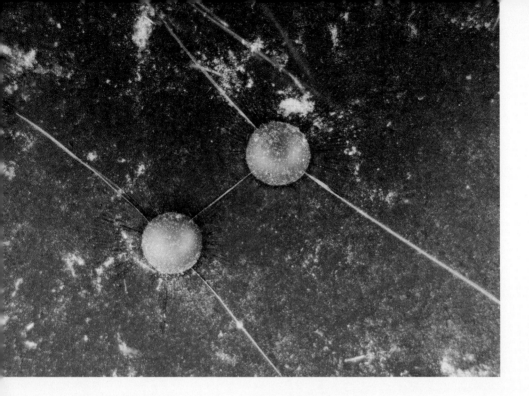

Extraordinary interactions of wind, water, pollen and more.

The process of forestry designed to provide wood pulp for overseas paper manufacture is destroying our forests. We need to source our fibre from other plants. Hemp provides an enormously long, smooth fibre and makes a vastly superior paper.

Clear felling forests exposes our landscape to fire. We need to change our forestry science to one that values every stick of timber and doesn't hate big trees. Big trees are not our problem; it is the millions of small plantation trees that are fuel for danger – that and our failure to cool burn our parks in carefully planned and timed mosaics.

After the Gippsland fires, contractors targeted the biggest trees and cut a swathe through magnificent forests. A small number of those trees may have been at risk of falling across roads but the majority were cut down needlessly, including at least fifty trees that were important in local Aboriginal culture.

Anyway, let's get back to nature on the island. Watching the seals bask and play at Cape du Couedic is an eerie experience given their centrality to the story of the Aboriginal women that the island finds it so difficult to acknowledge.

But discovering a male Cape Barren goose harassing a female at the national park centre was disconcerting. A fascinating close-up view of these extraordinarily rare and beautiful birds disturbed by the brutish impositions of the male. An unnerving reminder of the island's history. The goose is another bird that almost disappeared as a result of overhunting. They are more common on the islands off Australia's southern coast but the conservancy at Tower Hill near Warrnambool in Victoria has had a lot to do with the species' preservation.

The eastern end of Kangaroo Island is a truly remarkable coast, and as a saltwater man I know some remarkable coasts, but it was a peculiar feeling watching seals disporting themselves in the water and on the sandstone slabs around the giant arches and caves. So close to extinction yet so oblivious of their fate. The story of the seals and the women with whom they are associated seems so compelling, but Australian tourism at times wears a blindfold to history and ties its hands behind its back. Perhaps that attitude is reflected in the fact that, whereas Aboriginal names represent as much as 70 per cent of all placenames in many parts of Australia, on this island and its sister in Bass Strait, King Island, they are almost entirely absent.

There are a few myths floating about these islands that Aboriginal people didn't eat scale fish and knew nothing about the making of fire. Both are nonsense but their persistence is part and parcel of an amnesiac history and some islanders might tell you that there were never any Aborigines on the island anyway.

Presumably then the artefacts on the southern coast were imported! Many of the artefacts found are for the preparation of fish and animals prior to cooking. A cursory familiarity with world history and Aboriginal story will tell you that in periods of lower sea levels these islands were close enough to the mainland to be easily accessible. And, like the offshore island Lady Julia Percy near Portland in Victoria, they may always have been accessible to Aboriginal sailors.

If there were Aboriginal people on the island at contact they were either soon murdered or joined the ragtag parade of shipwrecked sailors or disenchanted sealers and their Aboriginal women from Tasmania.

A history of Bass Strait is full of gruesome and unlikely stories made possible by the eclectic mix of the mad, the eccentric and the dispossessed. One story that has never left me tells of a sealer dumping a pregnant Aboriginal woman on a deserted Bass Strait island. Her fate was never told, nobody bothering to go back and find out what became of her. How that woman and her child fared still troubles me. I retold the story as fiction in 'Australians Awl', from the collection *Nightjar*, but the true histories need no embellishment. Most Tasmanian Aboriginal people are descended from the survivors of this vicious era.

This knowledge may temper the delight in your holiday but it can be the opportunity to gain a perspective of the previous civilisation. Crayfish and yabbies are features of the Kangaroo Island cuisine now, but they always were. Oysters and mussels feature too, but then they always did. Aboriginal people were not living from hand to mouth but living off the fat of the land.

The island still caters for those rich ocean flavours. The fisher is prominent on Kangaroo Island today, but then she always was.

Islands tend to cherish the eccentric and so it is an odd delight to watch the unfamiliar activity of sheep being milked for the island's famous cheese. You can walk right into the dairy and be among the animals who seem habituated to the procedure. Buy some of the delicious cheese and take it down to one of the hundreds of beaches and eat it with crusty bread from the island's bakery at Parndana, the second-best bakery in the world, a genuine island experience.

The marron farm is the place to lunch. The succulent yabbies are farmed there and, given that the catch of wild rock lobster has long been unsustainable, the ability to farm marron is an important culinary pursuit. The texture and flavour are the equal of lobster in my opinion, and the outside tables in the sun are the place to enjoy them. A local white wine is the perfect accompaniment; allow the wine to soothe, the sun to bless and the lobster to nourish.

Penneshaw receives the ferry from Cape Jervis on the mainland and there's that air of transience about the place, the mood of a transit point. You can get pizza and beer but the feeling is that you then move on. It's a shame because a walk around the shoreline is a wonderful experience.

Hire a bike or a car and enjoy the island at your leisure. If you hear prejudicial and uninformed conversation on the nature of Aborigines while crossing on the ferry, put that down as an Australian tourist experience too, but one that we hope will soon be replaced by discussions informed by the distinction of Aboriginal placenames and the entree they provide to a more real and complete Australian history.

Other things to see and do

Kangaroo Island Gateway Visitor Centre

Howard Dr, Penneshaw
tourkangarooisland.com.au

Kangaroo Island Gallery

1 Murray St, Kingscote
08 8553 2868

Fine Art Kangaroo Island

91 Dauncey St, Kingscote
08 8553 0448
fineartkangarooisland.com.au

Parndana Bakery and Cafe

32 Cook St, Parndana
0429 671 728

The Oyster Farm Shop

Try some delicious wild marron or native oysters and abalone at this working oyster farm that also sells sustainable seafood produce from across the island.

44 Tangara Dr,
American River
08 8553 7122
oysterfarmshop.com.au

Cliffords Honey Farm

Kangaroo Island is a bee sanctuary and home to a population of Ligurian bees (introduced from Italy). You can buy honey and various related products here, but the real reason to visit is for the honey ice-cream.

1157 Elsegood Rd
08 8553 8295
cliffordshoney.com.au

Seal Bay

Join a guided tour and walk along a beach filled with snoozing sea lions. Self-guided tours to a boardwalk and observation platform are also available, but you won't get as close to the wildlife.

sealbay.sa.gov.au

Flinders Chase National Park

You'll still see scars of the 2019–2020 bushfires, but highlights of this vast park include the colony of seals at Admirals Arch, Cape du Couedic lighthouse and the much-photographed Remarkable Rocks.

parks.sa.gov.au/find-a-park/Browse_by_region/kangaroo-island/flinders-chase-national-park

Further reading

For more on the fascinating Aboriginal history of Kangaroo Island, read Rebe Taylor's *Unearthed: The Aboriginal Tasmanians of Kangaroo Island*, Wakefield Press, Adelaide, 2002.

Kangaroo Island

Bruce Pascoe

GARI

Western plains of Victoria

Djab Wurrung, Jardwadjali
Language groups

VERD
(GRAMPIANS NATIONAL PARK)

Sir Thomas Mitchell hauled his wagons across the plain to the foot of the mountains he would call the Grampians after his native Scotland. The wheels of the carts sank easily into the soft soils.

Those ruts were still visible a decade later.

This is not just a fascinating little yarn like the Dig Tree of Cooper's Creek fame or the beaching of the *Endeavour* at Cooktown. This small detail holds the secret to our economic survival.

The Aboriginal people of the area were cultivating tubers and herbs across the length and breadth of most of Victoria. 'Explorers' like Mitchell and 'settlers' like George Lloyd and Edward Curr wrote extensively about this phenomenon.

Curr, in Bangerang country south of Echuca, was one of the first Europeans in the area and wrote that as his carts ploughed through the soft soil, each turn of the wheel turned up bushels of murrnong tubers (*Microseris lanceolata*). He is describing a massive agricultural enterprise.

Lloyd, at Colac, describes a very similar scene to the one Mitchell describes in the Gariwerd (Grampians National Park) lands. For Mitchell, it was a place of such verdant delight that he named it Australia Felix and said that it was as if God had created it just for his arrival. In volume two of his *Three Expeditions into the Interior of Eastern Australia* from 1839, he said: 'Certainly a land more favourable for colonisation could not be found.'

As Lloyd explained in great detail, however, this cornucopia had been created by Aboriginal people tending and tilling crops of murrnong. The local people had been observed harvesting the tubers by lifting the plants with their agricultural tools and taking some of the plants' tubers before then pressing the parent plant back into the soil.

When settlers around Melbourne saw Aboriginal people harvesting colonial potatoes in this manner, they accused the people of deception and sly robbery but, in fact, the people were repeating their own agricultural practice.

Lloyd and others noticed that across the fields there was no monoculture but at least three different tubers: murrnong, bulbine lily and moth orchid. Tellingly, the tubers were growing in a bed of moss. Sometimes kangaroo grass was growing among the tubers.

As Heather Le Griffon mentions in her book *Campfires at the Cross*, Lloyd said that the ground was so soft that you could barely ride or walk across it and the dews were so intense that it was impossible to walk without your socks becoming saturated.

Later he recounts that with the arrival of sheep the moss was trampled to elimination, the soil became hard and the dews ended. Australian farmers reading that passage should look out across their paddocks with wonder and alarm. What happened to that wonderful soil?

There is a lesson in this for all of us about agricultural management. A system of land management, created after many thousands of years of knowledge of the country, was so carelessly cast aside by the Europeans to institute their own system devised in a different hemisphere and a catastrophically different climate.

In this age of devastating fires, massive soil loss and shocking fish kills, it is time we listened to the old ways adapted specifically for this old, eroded and dry continent.

In the annals of Australian culture we have created classics like *Picnic at Hanging Rock* where the country is an active malignant force, but Curr, Mitchell and Lloyd were describing a land of gentle and bucolic verdancy.

When you tour around the great vineyards of this district and the charming towns of Cherrypool, Ararat and Stawell, remember that this is Aboriginal land and for all its agricultural production today it is a shadow of the managed verdancy of pre-colonial times.

There are not many better places to camp than in this wonderful region. The rock art within Gariwerd is extraordinary, the scenery just as phenomenal as Mitchell described, but make sure you don't accept this without searching for contemporary Aboriginal culture.

The Brambuk Cultural Centre at Halls Gap is simply extraordinary. Apart from being an architectural wonder, it is the start of several exciting Aboriginal-led tours

Dynamic river red gum.

of the region. It will be a highlight of your year. Here you will also find a map of the rock-art sites that you are permitted to visit. While Gariwerd has hundreds of sites, only a handful are open to visitors.

I remember driving through this region in my childhood with my father in his Standard Vanguard and being shocked by the amount of graffiti on the amazing granite rock outcrops. There were declarations of love for Shirley and Monica and abundant misspelt support for the Collingwood Football Club. (The latter could be a trick of childhood memory or an understandable prejudice.)

It showed Australia's crass attitude to the country because this region is home to some of the world's oldest art.

One day while climbing the path to Manja, the Cave of Hands rock-art site, I had my way crossed by a brown snake and, cautioned by this, I trod on carefully, but then a wallaby exploded out of a bush beside the path and that was that, enough cautions

Red gum branches manipulated by Aboriginal people leave a dramatic window.

from the old spirits. It is a country to treat with respect. I returned to my car and waited to visit on another day.

The flowers and heaths are sufficient reason to walk that path but the art is an unnerving reminder of an ancient culture. It is a shame that we now have to view this art through cyclone wire but the graffitists thought it wonderful sport to defile this art. The steel and wire protection became a necessity.

There is a wonderful depiction of Bunjil, the great creator spirit, in a cave close by but when I visited in the 1980s someone called Anna wrote her name across the image of Bunjil's three dogs. There are very few images of Bunjil so the defacement of this one was a cruel blow to the local Aboriginal people. The painting has since been restored but, once again, viewing it now has to be done through wire.

Travelling through this region is a joy. The wine, the food, the art, the culture, the scenery, the flora, the bushwalking – and if they all fail to excite, there's always the Pomborneit antique market. Whatever you choose to do, though, take time to seek out the Indigenous history and culture of this ancient place.

Indigenous cultural experiences, tours and relevant organisations

Brambuk – The National Park and Cultural Centre

Excellent displays as well as an on-site cafe that offers dishes with kangaroo, emu and crocodile (also some vegetarian options). Two different tours are available – the Bunjil Creation Tour and a rock-art tour throughout the park.

277 Grampians Tourist Rd
(2.5km south of Halls Gap shops)
03 5361 4000
brambuk.com.au

Other things to see and do

Halls Gap Visitor Centre

117 Grampians Rd
1800 065 599
visitgrampians.com.au

Grampians National Park

13 1963
parks.vic.gov.au/places-to-see/parks/grampians-national-park

MacKenzie Falls

Widely considered to be Victoria's largest waterfall. Best seen from below, either climb down the 260 steps (and up again) or take the easy way on the three-hour walk from Zumsteins picnic area.

parks.vic.gov.au/places-to-see/parks/grampians-national-park

Grampians Peaks Trail

Eventually this trail will be a 13-day hike across the mountains, but for now it's a three-day 36km loop walk from Halls Gap that includes the Grand Canyon and Pinnacle lookouts. Register before you walk at Brambuk, where you can also pick up a map.

Boroka Lookout and the Balconies

Two spectacular lookouts in the national park. Boroka is 15km from Halls Gap on the Mt Difficult Rd, the Balconies are off the Mt Victory Rd in the centre of the park.

Drive the Grampians Road

The 65km-long road from Dunkeld to Halls Gap is wonderfully scenic.

Further reading

For more information about life in this area in the 1800s, read Heather Le Griffon's *Campfires at the Cross: an Account of the Bunting Dale Aboriginal Mission 1839–1951 at Birregurra, near Colac, Victoria,* Australian Scholarly Publishing, Melbourne, 2006.

Bruce Pascoe

MOYJ

Point Ritchie, Warrnambool, Victoria

Gunditjmara

Language group

IL

(POINT RITCHIE)

Warrnambool is a large rural city on the ocean at the edge of the Western District volcanic plains. Europeans arrived here early in the colony's history because the Henty brothers were operating a whaling station and township at Portland just to the west. The 'settlement' was illegal because the colonial government was trying to limit expansion to the areas around Sydney and Hobart for administrative efficiency.

The white-shoe brigade of money men, however, was quick to pounce on the information they were garnering from sealers along the southern coast of Australia. Sealers, when replenishing food and water supplies, would sometimes call in to the Bass Strait ports but favoured Hobart as the most established. Their stories of lands they had seen in western Victoria galvanised the land grabbers of the Tasmanian colony. It had become common practice for men close to government circles to buy up cheap land and then sell it at extortionate prices to free settlers as they arrived in Australia. People like John Batman, John Fawkner and Joseph Tice Gellibrand had made fortunes by trading Tasmanian lands, and soon there was discussion about replicating the scheme across the Strait in Victoria. The Port Phillip Association was formed to exploit the greenfield estate. The Henty brothers jumped the gun and established their whaling station at Portland and began stealing land there in 1834. The battles with the Gunditjmara began soon afterwards but the more deadly English weapons took a huge toll on the Indigenous population.

Naturally, the arrival of Europeans created a contest for resources. Aboriginal people tried to defend their land and their families and violent battles broke out. If you drive around either Portland or Warrnambool today, you will find very little evidence of this history but plenty for the winners of the war. Monuments aplenty for the Hentys.

At Warrnambool the famous Flagstaff Hill Maritime Museum tells the early colonial history of the area's shipping. There are plenty of boats, telescopes and crinoline on display. It's a good museum but blind to the ancient and highly successful occupation of the area by the Gunditjmara. Whales are a feature but the fact that they were a major part of the Gunditjmara economy is not.

Whales have become a major tourist attraction in the area. Whaling almost destroyed the whale populations but the call for their protection by activists saved them from extinction. Millions of dollars are made by tour companies today but there is little mention of how their enterprise was made possible by the activists who received such sustained vilification from some sections of the press and public. Forests and whales have been saved by the commitment of dedicated environmentalists and it is thanks to the spin doctors that such benefit for entrepreneurs has been acquired without recognition of those who campaigned against the destruction of natural resources.

Similarly the early colonists flourished on the back of Indigenous agriculture. The Aboriginal crops of murnong (yam daisy), bulbine lily, orchids and a host of others had created verdant plains. The Port Phillip Association soon had sheep grazing on these rich gardens that stretched right across the vast volcanic plain. Sheep prospered to such a degree that they often lambed twice a year. Men who envisioned becoming very wealthy were suddenly twice as rich as they had expected.

The provision of such excellent pasture was only due to the continuous work of the clans of western Victoria. Constant harvesting and weeding had cultivated the land into an idyllic state that many 'settlers' referred to as an English gentleman's estate.

But the agricultural practice of the clans is even less likely to be recognised than the pre-colonial occupation. The method of farming had brought the soil to such a wonderful tilth that you could run your fingers through it. Farmers like Isaac Batey, Edward Curr and George Lloyd refer to this incredible fertility and how it had been created. As Heather Le Griffon mentioned in her book *Campfires at the Cross*, Lloyd recalled that 'the ground had been so protected by mosses and lichens so thick that it was difficult to ride across the country at any pace exceeding the "farmers" jog trot'. But he noticed things change after the arrival of stock: 'With the onslaught of the sharp little hooves and teeth of herbivore sheep, goats, pigs and cattle driven in by the settlers, the ground covers were destroyed and the dews ceased.'

It had been a triumph of conservative land management but, apart from these few farmers, most new arrivals never mentioned the prior agricultural activity and

A few birds of the district, including black swan; white-faced heron; and laughing kookaburra.

simply plundered the fertility. It was as if the nation tried to erase from its mind the occupation of the continent by Aboriginal Australians. Terra nullius, empty land.

The Gunditjmara people, however, knew of a site on the Hopkins River that they believed was very, very old and had tried to interest archaeologists in examining it for at least thirty years before, around 2007, it finally attracted a full-scale dig. There were archaeologists interested in Aboriginal sites and culture but they were few on the ground and it took an emerging public interest in Indigenous history for research institutions to accept that there was value in Australian Aboriginal cultural sites.

Research grants had concentrated on European sites, the examination of convict barracks and demolished buildings in Melbourne's city centre, a direct reflection of cultural priorities. Even as recently as the last decade, one archaeologist and university lecturer complained that her best students were still finding more career opportunities in the pyramids of Egypt than the ancient sites of Australia. But persistence and an awakening interest in the pre-colonial history of the country gradually turned the ship of Australian archaeology about. New technologies helped the cause too.

The findings of new searches in the last few decades have been astounding. A grinding dish at Cuddie Springs in central northern New South Wales was found to have been used to grind grain 36,000 years ago. Soon after, one found at Madjedbebe, Arnhem Land, was dated at 65,000 years. On the other side of the continent, the constructed yam garden terraces in Western Australia changed forever what we knew about the Aboriginal agricultural economy.

And then came Moyjil, an ancient site precious to the Gunditjmara. A rocky headland where the Hopkins River meets the sea, Moyjil showed signs of ancient fire use with its hearth-like features and blackened stones, as well as shell middens. Geologist Jim Bowler, who had worked on the Mungo Man and Mungo Lady archaeology at Lake Mungo, undertook the work in conjunction with Ian McNiven, whose work at Lake Condah has been pivotal. Other archaeologists and many local Aboriginal people took part in the research.

The results yielded an initial age of occupation of 80,000 years, an incredible age in terms of human history, but a subsequent survey came up with 120,000 years, far older than any other site in Australia. The release of that date was treated with caution by some experts simply because it was so much older than anything that has previously been published. Parts of Moyjil are fenced off to protect the fragile heritage site, but if you visit you will see the wild ocean and windswept cliffs of Victoria's south-western coast and imagine the lives lived here possibly more than 100,000 years ago.

Old dates from Arnhem Land, Tasmania and Western Australia are supporting further investigation across Australia using the most advanced analysis methods. As a point of comparison, the Out of Africa theory says that modern people left southern Africa around 75,000 years ago. Either humans left Africa a lot earlier than previously thought or there were parallel human developments around the globe. Recent archaeology is suggesting modern humans were in Israel around 190,000 years ago, but that date and the other parts of the study are under question.

Whatever happened, it makes Australian Aboriginal society much older than was thought possible, a subject that should fascinate Australians and the world. It also causes us to reflect on a culture that managed human society without resorting to territorial war. The age of Australian languages and their ancient links to specific regions indicates an enormous stability. This prolonged peace, unmatched by any other continent, may have its genesis in the reciprocal nature of skin and family structures.

Marrying outside the clan under strict organisational rules meant that neighbouring clans had members of each other's clan embedded within their structure. To go to war meant you would have to fight members of your own family.

This reciprocity did not preclude enmities and violence from flaring up but full-scale war could not be maintained, especially as the lore insisted that each clan had been given orders by Baiame and other authority figures to keep to their own lands and to care for them. Land war was forbidden and seen as the act of lawless barbarians.

This is the system that operated in the Warrnambool region long before Europeans arrived. The lore also required guests to be included in the skin system, brought within the lore. Aboriginal groups all over Australia tried to maintain this system of reciprocity until it became obvious that the Europeans had no intention of entering the harmony of the lore.

Once this situation became apparent, Aboriginal people defied the invasion of the Henty family in the west and later incursions from the east in a resistance that became known in its later years as the Eumeralla Wars.

This region is a cornucopia of food, some of the best growing country on the continent. Its largesse guaranteed conflict. The Hentys wanted whales, the pastoralists wanted to run their sheep, the local Gunditjmara wanted to hold the land of their ancestors. They were brutal days and Australian history pays scant regard to either the wars or the economy of the people. Seek out the modern opera, written by Deborah Cheetham, which mourns this period of our history.

There are fish traps and houses from Warrnambool to Winchelsea and beyond; it is a trove of incredible human interest. These rich volcanic plains also have a kind growing climate so concentrations of people have been higher here than in less favourable zones.

An examination of the Moyjil middens reflects this luxuriance. Conversations with Uncle Banjo Clarke in the 1990s emphasised this abundance. He talked of tubers and vegetables aplenty, but the range of seafood was astounding. Crayfish, abalone, scutus, urchins, mussels, whiting, trumpeter, sweep, flathead, salmon, snapper – he had a story for all of them.

Uncle Banjo's people also killed seals and whales when the opportunity arose. The fishing process for each was highly ritualised and the capture of such large animals usually meant an invitation to surrounding clans to attend the feast.

James Dawson wrote extensively about the life of the Gunditjmara. He was a Scottish colonist who had a much more kindly relationship with the people than the vast majority of his fellow invaders. He despised the Irish but was interested in the culture of the local Aboriginal people and wrote many letters to newspapers urging his townsfolk to show more restraint and kindness.

The treatment of Aboriginal people by colonists was incredibly cruel, violent and prejudiced. Dawson involved himself in the lore of the Gunditjmara and kept a journal of language and cultural stories. He was helped in this by his daughter, Isabella, who knew enough language to communicate with the people, a very rare case of respect.

Together they collected the language and defended the people where they could. Isabella's role is an important one. Most of the commentators in this period are men and the attitude towards the people is skewed by this imbalance. Isabella's attitude was much more humane and respectful but, despite the Dawsons' more enlightened views, it has to be acknowledged that they were still taking up and benefitting from the land of the Gunditjmara.

Nevertheless the writings of James and Isabella provide the most complete recollection of the people from a European point of view. Passages like this, from James Dawson's book, published in 1881, are illuminating when compared to the vicious bias of most other commentators:

Habitations – wuurns – are of various kinds, and are constructed to suit the seasons. The principal one is the permanent family dwelling, which is made of strong limbs of trees stuck up in dome shape, high enough to allow a tall man to stand upright underneath them. Small limbs fill up the intermediate spaces, and these are covered with sheets of bark, thatch, sods, and earth till the roof and sides are proof against wind and rain. The doorway is low, and generally faces the morning sun or a sheltering rock. The family wuurn is sufficiently large to accommodate a dozen or more persons; and when the family is grown up the wuurn is partitioned off into apartments, each facing the fire in the centre. One of these is appropriated to the parents and children, one to the young unmarried women and widows,

Above: Moonlit seascape.

Right: Treasures of sea and forest, including fungus; seaweed; and fallen mudnest made by choughs. Fungi, seaweeds and nests are remarkably variable, as can be seen when we compare, for example, the fungus to the right with the spectacular group on pages 280–1.

and one to the bachelors and widowers. While travelling or occupying temporary habitations, each one of these parties must erect separate wuurns. When several families live together, each builds its wuurn facing one central fire. The fire is not much used for cooking, which is generally done outside. Thus in what appears to be one dwelling fifty or more persons can be accommodated, when, to use the words of the aborigines, they are 'like bees in a hive'.

These comfortable and healthy habitations are occupied by the owners of the land in the neighbourhood, and are situated on dry spots on the bank of a lake or stream, or healthy swamp, but never near a malarious morass, nor under large trees, which might fall or be struck by lightning. When it is necessary to abandon them for a season in search of food, or for visiting neighbouring families or tribes, the doorway is closed with sheets of bark or bushes, and, for the information of visitors, a crooked stick is placed above it pointing in the direction which the family intends to go. They then depart, with the remark, 'Muurtee bunna meen' – 'close the door and pull away'.

Unfortunately Dawson was a minority. His efforts to raise a monument for Hissing Swan, his friend and Gunditjmara Elder, were met with derision from the local press. That attitude persisted right up to the 1970s where Aboriginal people were still not allowed into the central business district of Warrnambool. (Read *The Mish* by Robert Lowe for greater insight into this area during the 1950s and 1960s.) Australia was demonstrating volubly about the apartheid Springbok rugby team on their visit to Australia, led by university activists appalled by the treatment of black South Africans, but in the students' own country blatant racism occurring beneath their noses was going unnoticed.

We have so much to learn about our country and Moyjil offers all Australians an opportunity to celebrate Aboriginal history and culture. The rest of the world is going to be astounded when it hears the news about the age of this incredible site, simply because it changes our understanding of human development around the globe. Hopefully Australian governments will embrace the opportunity and ensure that the descendants of the people at Point Ritchie are given the opportunity to tell the story and benefit from the telling.

Indigenous cultural experiences, tours and relevant organisations

Worn Gundidj Visitor Centre

Guided twilight bush and nature walks operated by Worn Gundgji Enterprises in a dormant volcano at Tower Hill, between Warrnambool and Port Fairy.

03 5561 5315 or
0448 509 522
worngundidj.org.au

Budj Bim Cultural Landscape

Inscribed on the UNESCO World Heritage list in 2019, this is one of the world's oldest and most extensive freshwater aquaculture systems and human settlement sites. Gunditjmara-led guided tours are available for groups, or you can take a self-guided tour on the 45-minute walking trail in Tyrendarra Indigenous Protected Area near Heywood.

4/48 Edgar St, Heywood
(48km north-west of
Port Fairy)
03 5527 1427
budjbim.com.au

Other things to see and do

Point Ritchie – Moyjil Aboriginal Place

Visit this website, run by the Warrnambool City Council, for a fascinating range of information about the science, culture and history of Moyjil.

Warrnambool City Council,
25 Liebeg St
1300 003 280
moyjil.com.au

Warrnambool Visitor Centre

89 Merri St
1800 637 725
visitwarrnambool.com.au

Further reading

Discover more about the research into the shell middens and hearths of Moyjil by reading John Sherwood's online paper: 'The Moyjil Site, Southwest Victoria, Australia: Prologue – of People, Birds, Shell and Fire', 130(2) 7–13, 2019, publish.csiro.au/RS/RS18003.

Also seek out Jim Bowler's article 'The Moyjil Dilemma: People at 120ka, Fact or Fiction?', *Quarternary Australasia*, 36(2) 29–36, 2019.

For more information about life in this area, read Robert Lowe & Framlingham Mission (Vic.), *The Mish*, University of Queensland Press, St Lucia, Qld, 2002, and Heather Le Griffon's *Campfires at the Cross: an Account of the Bunting Dale Aboriginal Mission 1839–1951 at Birregurra, near Colac, Victoria*, Australian Scholarly Publishing, Melbourne, 2006.

Moyjil (Point Ritchie)

BRUN
ISLAN

Bruce Pascoe

Off the south-east coast of Tasmania,
consisting of North Bruny and
South Bruny, joined by 'the Neck',
a narrow isthmus

Nuenonne

Language group

We were eating a mutton bird and yarning
about the island and fishing stories.
Rodney Dillon is a supreme fisherman and
his knowledge of the sea is second to none.
Not just the rollicking tales of ships and
mighty catches but also the environment.
Observation at such close quarters over many
decades is a sound basis for opinion and in
the last decade he has seen a plummeting
fertility in the ocean. As global warming
influences the sea temperature, he has seen
the giant kelp forests wither to five per cent
of their former state with an incredible effect
on fish stocks. And on the environment
that once supported them.

You could listen all day to Rodney's yarns about boats and dives, sharks and whales but eventually our thoughts turn to the history of Bruny. The sad history. Soon after their arrival, the English took more and more of the land and hunted the Aboriginal people into smaller and smaller refuges until one night the vigilantes descended on the terrified clan, who, by this stage of 'settlement', did not have a billy or a stick to their name and were too scared to light a fire lest it expose their hiding place. But despite that caution they were hunted down, in a small gully near the Bruny Island Neck. This last massacre would have been heard by the people on the mainland across the strait. Horrible to listen to, even more horrible for the people realising that after countless thousands of years of care for their island it was now at the mercy of barbarians.

The mutton bird was aromatic and flavourful but our thoughts were sour and painful.

Tobias Furneaux is credited as the first European to land at Adventure Bay, on the island's east coast, in 1773 but the island was named after Bruni D'Entrecasteaux, who landed there in 1792. Originally Bruni Island, it was anglicised to Bruny in 1918, perhaps as a rebuff to claims of French exploration of Australia earlier than James Cook.

Many of the early French explorations were conducted for cultural, scientific and anthropological purposes whereas most English exploration was totally imperialistic. The difference can be seen in the writings of the two voyaging nations.

Left: Rodney stands on the beach at Great Bay, North Bruny.

Opposite: The vista of Adventure Bay, South Bruny.

English mariners often derided the inhabitants as loathsome and infantile but D'Entrecasteaux's party had a different impression:

> We never noticed among them the least sign of temper or anger. They did not ever behave in a way which disappointed us and were always thoughtful of our regard. They seemed to live in great harmony with each other. We did not notice anything, either in their behaviour or in their customs, which could make us deviate from the good opinion which we had held them from the first.

A lot happened in a very few years, culminating in the final slaughter of these people so admired by D'Entrecasteaux. What was the difference between the English and the French in their perception of the people? Differential intelligences or differential intentions? Perhaps it was the determination of the English to take the land that precluded them from seeing the possessors of the soil as human.

Beginning at that point you can then trace the various English descriptions and deceptions in occupation and legislation to the legitimisation that the Australian state assumes today.

Rodney and I continued to chew the mutton bird bones and the fat of Australian history. This was late in 2019 and the next day we were due to discuss Aboriginal land care with an audience full of enthusiasm for a different relationship with the land and the First Australians. Was there a wheel turning? It seemed such a different attitude to the one under which we had grown up.

The following day proved to be climactic. Large numbers of Aboriginal Tasmanians and non-Aboriginal Tasmanians discussed these difficult issues in a climate of peace and harmony, much closer to D'Entrecasteaux than Cook.

And all the while south-eastern Australia was burning. My neighbour sent me a film of flames rising two metres above my shed at Mallacoota. The text ended with 'I don't think we can save your house'. I had no idea what to expect but then Shelly Morris sang and Patsy Cameron hugged me. That's how we survive.

As it turned out my house was left unmarked and the shed was saved with a dozen sturdy bush poles, the heaviest lifted by the son of a German baker. It's a funny world.

But a harrowing world. After a day of us talking dispossession and land degradation, Rodney's wife, Tracey, called a halt and took us down to her favourite beach. It is hard to find a place more placidly beautiful than that cove near the beautifully named Cygnet, less than an hour south of Hobart and not far from Bruny Island.

Right: Missionary Bay's natural setting. The hill in the background is where the hut stood that was once occupied by George Augustus Robinson, whom Truganini joined on his so-called 'Friendly Missions'.

Below: Rodney speaks of how '[Robinson] took a big group of our people here. It's a sad place ... our people died here in despair.'

Opposite (left): Rodney holds an ancient stone axe found on the beach.
Opposite (right): Grass trees (*Xanthorrhoea* species) 'represent our people and our landscapes, which we've lived in for more than 40,000 years', explains Rodney.

People use the word 'perfect' loosely these days, referring to anything from a pasta sauce to a kick into the forward line by Dusty Martin, but this beach has a calm that is deep and comforting. Comforting but not comfortable. The seduction of its beauty is immediate but no sooner has it begun its magic than your thoughts turn to the life of the people on this bay before the sails of Tasman, Flinders and D'Entrecasteaux.

Everywhere you look there are knapped stones, knives, scrapers, points, rasps and hammers. It is an incredible site and at the far end of the beach there is a rock just like a horse's saddle with a flat section in front that is just right for stone knapping and shellfish preparation. And the view – it is breathtaking. Imagine how minds must have dreamt of this rock during the years when they were denied access to it. Silence descended on the beach as we contemplated this loss, which is still felt today 250 years later.

This history is almost invisible on Bruny Island. The jolly ferry commentary doesn't mention it and the visitor centre is cryptic at best.

The pub at Alonnah, on the island's western coast, is lively on a Friday night, raffle night, but there's no sense of that history at the pub either. In winter the welcome is warm, the raffle tickets are many and the local lamb and fish trays much sought after. After a day in kayaks it is comforting to have your fellow humans sounding happy around you. It's warm in here, a little lonely sanctuary. The beer is cold and welcome too. But there is a gap in our knowledge of each other.

By kayak you can paddle around the tiny Satellite Island, just offshore from Bruny, where an exclusive house hides its luxury. The island has magnificent fishing but it is private and a night will cost you $2000. A snack for having your own private island.

The jetty and boathouse are straight out of Hollywood, complete with a love seat and, somewhere handy presumably, chilled champagne.

The island's website even features a quote from Lord Byron: 'And they were canopied by the blue sky, so cloudless, clear and purely beautiful.' This just goes to show that even those with a poetic sensibility can be blind to history. And some write poetry to distract us from history.

The previous occupiers didn't dream of the privileged isolation and luxury spruiked in the Satellite Island promotion; they dreamt of family and community. And the universe. At Satellite there is a story to explain one of the remarkable stone

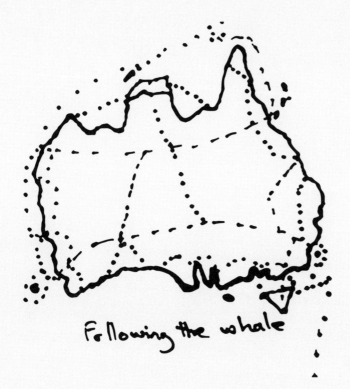

Following the whale

Bruce's hand-drawn map
showing journeys he's followed
while looking for whale
story, mostly with Uncle
Max Harrison. This map is
an indication of how these
stories carry right around
the continent.

features on the island. A shark is harassing a whale to such a degree that the leviathan leaps from the water and plunges through a rocky promontory to escape, leaving a giant hole. Just another cute story about sea creatures? No, the dynamic interaction between whales, sharks, dolphins and dugongs is told from Hervey Bay to Hobart. Versions of the same story are told at Esperance, Margaret River, Broome, Stradbroke Island and the Tanami Desert. Yes, in the desert they tell whale stories just as they do at St Helens' nearby peaks and at Mount Kosciuszko in the Australian Alps.

The songlines carry these stories right around the continent. There is enormous variability and changes in details but in most the whale leaves the land to look after the ocean and interact with other great sea creatures. They are tales about the turbulent relationship between right and wrong, betrayal and honour, good and bad. But there is also a sense that lurking behind the tale is an all-encompassing story about human development and our responsibility to the globe, Mother Earth. You sense it at Australia Peak, it is palpable at Tomahawk and Cape Portland in north-east Tasmania, but it is ever present on Bruny Island.

Each year a celebration for Mannalargenna, a great Aboriginal leader who died in 1835, is held near Cape Portland to honour his life. It can be a cold and windy coast at its worst and delightfully warm and inviting at its best, but here you will find one of the greatest whale stories of all. It's said that when the sea level rose and people were horrified to find their country disappearing the whale urged them to follow her to dry land, but she cautioned them that they would need to employ diplomacy and peace because they would be asking their cousins to share their land. It is a story the world needs to know. It may be a long way from Bruny but it offers a perspective of the indelible connection between Tasmanian Aboriginal life and the sea.

There is a charter tour that takes you around part of the Bruny coast near Lunawanna and it is highly recommended, if only for the offshore perspective of this mild coastline. Look and dream of that earlier life.

For a different view, climb the 270-odd steps to the Neck Lookout between North and South Bruny and it's here that you will most likely spot mutton birds. You will also find a monument to Aboriginal woman Truganini, a highly intelligent woman who seemed to realise that amid the incredible violence being perpetrated on her people there were few options. Her sacrifice was infinite when she agreed to join the so-called 'Friendly Missions' led by George Augustus Robinson, who, despite all his arrogance, ignorance and selfishness, was the best white man, a terrible indictment on the rest. She travelled with Robinson in an attempt to ameliorate the condition of her people. Robinson was a pompous dill but he did attempt to learn something about the culture and, unlike most other white people, did not shoot Aboriginal people at will.

Today the local Aboriginal people run Murrayfield, a 4000-hectare farm. It's not just a sheep farm on a stunningly beautiful coast but also a cultural and training centre for young Aboriginal people. Frustrated with continuous promises of employment and training, the Bruny Island Aboriginal people took matters into their own hands to deliver these things themselves. It is a highly successful venture and a model that could well be used by other communities.

If you can manage a visit to Murrayfield, it will be a revelation.

Murrayfield, the 4000-hectare coastal property that has been 'handed back' to the Aboriginal community. It is a crucial habitat to a number of endangered species including the swift parrot.

It is hard not to be astounded by the failure of Australian tourism to tell the Aboriginal story. It is as rare as hens' teeth and to have it told by Aboriginal people is even more rare. This astounds overseas tourists including those from New Zealand, where they are surrounded by Maori language and culture, and where that language and culture is acknowledged as one of the country's twin legal forms.

Aboriginal language suffuses the continent of Australia. Around sixty-five per cent of us live in or near a town or suburb with an Aboriginal name, yet precious few can explain what those names mean. In Australia we often turn our back on the blindingly obvious history of our country.

We must learn from New Zealand and value our Indigenous culture and language. Let us remember the harmonious people and life that D'Entrecasteaux wrote about. Let us tell these stories to travellers and locals alike. They are too important to forget.

Indigenous cultural experiences, tours and relevant organisations

Murrayfield Station

Before visiting, please contact the weetapoona Aboriginal Corporation via email: weetapoona@hotmail.com

Trumpeter Rd, North Bruny

Other things to see and do

Bruny D'Entrecasteaux Visitor Centre

Ferry Terminal, Kettering
03 6263 4494
brunyisland.org.au

The Neck

There are great views from the top, and a platform at the bottom of the steps where you can watch little penguins come back to their burrows at dusk.

South Bruny National Park

Coastal cliff-top bushwalking trails, historic Cape Bruny lighthouse and beach-side camping.

parks.tas.gov.au/explore-our-parks/south-bruny-national-park

Bruny Island Cruises

Three-hour cruises around the island's most spectacular stretches of coastline, with a wildlife focus.

1005 Adventure Bay Rd, Adventure Bay
03 6293 1465
brunycruises.com.au

Inala Nature Tours

Birdwatching and guided wildlife tours on a private conservation reserve.

320 Cloudy Bay Rd
03 6293 1217
inalanaturetours.com.au

Bruny Island Bird Festival

Bruny is a sanctuary for the forty-spotted pardalote and swift parrot. The bird festival is held every second year.

brunybirdfestival.org.au

Further reading

Stephanie Anderson, 'French anthropology in Australia, a prelude: the encounters between Aboriginal Tasmanians and the expedition of Bruny d'Entrecasteaux, 1793', *Aboriginal History*, vol 24, 212–23, 2000.

Index

About the authors

Bruce Pascoe is a Yuin, Bunurong and Tasmanian man born in the Melbourne suburb of Richmond. He's worked as a teacher, farmer, fisherman, barman, fencing contractor, lecturer, Aboriginal language researcher, archaeological site worker and editor. He's also written thirty other books including the short story collections *Night Animals* and *Nightjar*, and academic texts including *The Little Red Yellow Black Book* with AIATSIS. *Dark Emu* (Magabala Books) won Book of the Year and the Indigenous Writer's Prize at the NSW Premier's Literary Awards in 2016, and has now sold in excess of 200,000 copies.

Vicky Shukuroglou is a multidisciplinary artist and researcher dedicated to deepening her understanding of the Earth through careful observation and hands-on care of country. These drive her creative process, with which she hopes to rouse your heart. She has worked collaboratively with writers, musicians, scientists, Indigenous communities and young people. Remarkable projects have evolved out of her commitment to shifting perceptions and bringing young people's powerful work to the attention of 'grown-ups'. Vicky's supporters and partners have included UNESCO, Sanskriti Kendra, Instituto Sacatar, and other organisations, schools and universities.

Author acknowledgements

Bruce Pascoe

I thank the following people for the valuable contribution each has made to *Loving Country*:

Uncle Max Harrison, Lynne Thomas, Shanna Provost, Dwayne Bannon Harrison, Gurandgi, Wally Bell, Paul House, Brad Steadman, Erica Glynn, Liz Warning, Reg Dodd, Malcolm McKinnon, Don Rowlands, Jim Crombie, Jean Barr, Rachel Bin Salleh, Lloyd Pigram, Wayne Webb, Zac Webb, Noel Nannup, Archie Weller, the Murray family, Vicki Couzens, John Clarke, Joel Wright, Rod Dillon, Tracey Dillon, David Gough, Lyn Harwood, Marcia Langton, Veronica Dobson, Margaret Bowman, Alex Payne, Melissa Kayser, Hamish Freeman, Anne-Marie McWatters.

Vicky Shukuroglou

I am deeply grateful to the old people of this country who sustained care and vibrant life for so very long, and to all who carry a similar ethos today.

Each person I met along this journey has made their own contribution.

Boundless gratitude for my mama and baba, always and no matter what. Hearty thanks to family and friends – especially Peter Yates, and my perfect Queenie.

Huge thanks to all who shared yarns, laughs, tears, walks and provided comfort and challenge, without whom this book would not be the same. There's every chance I've forgotten to name a few – but not through lack of respect. Particularly (for simplicity roughly grouped by area of travel): Brad Steadman, Bradley Hardy, David Coad, Glynnis & Tom, Matt at Bourke police and the mechanic, Rhonda & Gary, Joel Wright, Uncle Max Harrison, Wally Bell, Nikki & Scott, Tania Thomas, Uncle Fred Conway, Kristine Sloman, Kel & Jens, Uncle Milton Lawton, Mel, Nathan Milhouse and Ai, Akira & Sayuki Miller, Roslyn Miller, Eden Jupurrula, Lance Sullivan, Aunty Gwen Schreiber, Eric Orcher, Bill Harrigan, Bradley Creek, Desmond Tayley, Francis Walker, Kathleen Walker & family, Lily Creek, Marie Shipton, Vanessa Kennedy, Alberta Hornsby, Graeme Chibnall, Jeff Shellberg, Davey Naylor, Phylomena Annita Naylor, Willie Gordon, Aileen Gale, Betty Bramwell, Chrissy Musgrave, Clancy Streeter, Francis Lee Cheu, Gene Ross, Jack Lowdown, Johnny Ross, Joseph Lee Cheu, Margaret Lowdown, Matt Trezise, Megan Bramwell, Mike Ross, Nancy Coleman, Robert Ross, Roseanne George, Stephen Trezise, Steve Wilson, Sue Marsh, Trevor Bramwell, Gerard, Kevin woodturner, Mark Woodchopper, Friarbird, Jim Hill, Brian & family, Dorothea Pouesi-Seumanutafa, Dorsey Hill, Ken Nelder & his tap, Kurt Caulton, Ron Croft, Sean Wade, Betty Berry, Chiyo Andrews, Dorothy Bienuwanga, Jocelyn McCartney, John Berto, Joris & Yaro, Lazarus Manbulloo, Lisa Mumbin, Majella Friel, Marileen Dullman, Mihalis Kokinos & Stewart the strong stockman, Miliwanga Wurrben, Nellie Camfoo, Pip Gordon & family, Queenie Brennan & her beloved Maggie, Shaun Johnson & family, Miriam-Rose Ungunmerr Baumann & family, Grace Mardigan, Troy Mulvien Mardigan, Angie, Augie, Jesse, Julie, Kate, Noreen, Vera, & other ladies from Wugularr and Djilpin Arts, Daryl Laiwanga & Angelica and family, Frankie Lane, Amelia, Angela Harrison, Doris Stuart Kngwarreye, Kenneth Lechleitner Pangarte, Veronica Dobson [and others in Mparntwe who shared conversations but whose names were unfortunately written in ink made soggy during cyclone in Broome], Angela Berry, Bruce Gorring, Carlie, Eliana, Aunty Di Appleby, Djingo & brave Fitzy, Gina Albert, Naomi Appleby, Thomas 'Unda' Edgar, Tesikah & family, Wayne Edgar, Wes Morris, June Oscar & family, Andrew Binsiar, Avy Curley, Ben Brown, Beryl Walsh, Chantelle Long, Colin Jones, Evelyn, Joedy, Joslyn & mum, Gary Allsaints, G Wongawol, Heather Gilbert, Jackie, Jasmen Gilbert, Kristy Kyanga, Lena Long, Mac Jensen, Margaret Anderson, Aunty Pam Mongoo & Uncle Shorty, Rita Cutter, Sharon Ashwin, Stewart Long, Vera Anderson, Yullala Boss, Aunty Roma, Charlotte Penny, Jenny, special thanks to the Smargiassi family - particularly beloved Lidia, Steve & the kangaroos, Elsie & Len Calneggia & lovely Sandi, Paul Mackett, Robbi Bishop-Taylor, The Australian National Botanic Gardens, Banatjarl Stongbala Wimun Grup, Gundjeihmi Aboriginal Corporation, Jawoyn Association & Jawoyn Rangers, Laura Indigenous Land and Sea Rangers, Murrumbung Rangers, Nyamba Buru Yawuru, Ryan Hayward and the Australian Arid Lands Botanic Gardens, the Hardie Grant team; Marg Bowman and Hamish Freeman; all libraries, cafes & pubs that provided places to work; and AnkeCheyenne the trusty house-car and all the animals who kept me company.